A TWITCH IN TIME

Jack Douglas' Life Story

60 years in show biz!

written by Sue Benwell

A TWITCH IN TIME

ISBN 1 903607 24 8

Typeset and published by:

ABLE PUBLISHING
13 Station Road, Knebworth
Hertfordshire SG3 6AP

Tel: (01438) 812320 / 814316   Fax: (01438) 815232

Website: www.ablepublishing.co.uk
email: fp@ablepublishing.co.uk

FOR MY WONDERFUL FAMILY
AND FOR THE LADY IN MY LIFE, VIVIEN

THIS BOOK IS DEDICATED TO
THE MEMORY OF MY DEAR PARENTS
WHO TAUGHT ME EVERYTHING I KNOW.
ALSO, TO THE MEMORY OF MY BROTHER BILL,
WHO WAS ALWAYS MY GUIDING LIGHT

ACKNOWLEDGEMENTS

The authors and publishers would like to thank the following:

Joe Aveline
Beardsalls of Shanklin
Blackpool Library
Frank Bonser
Morris Bright
Debbie Cartwright
Brian Clemens
Derry and Tina Derbyshire (at The Crab)
Jean Ferguson
David Graham
John Hannam
Helen and Martin at "Friends of the Animals"
Mike Holden
Chrissie & John Hurt
Terry and Theresa Hyde
Steve King
David Paramor
Pinewood Studios
Stephen Rabson
Craig Roberton
Peter Rogers
Robert Ross
Vivien Russell
Audrey Skinner
Thelma Squibb
Cyril Stansfield
Steve Thearle
Ken Thomas (Watney's Archive)
Phil Trusler
Rick Wakeman

I would also like to say a big thank you to Phil Dale and everyone at Qodos for looking after me so well.   J.D.

FOREWORD by Rick Wakeman

One of the strangest feelings in the world is that of having the opportunity to meet one of your all-time boyhood heroes. There are, however, no words in the English language to truly describe the feeling you get when they turn out to be all you had ever hoped for and more.

It happened to me in the mid 1990s during a tour where I was performing in churches around Britain and one such performance just happened to be on the Isle of Wight.

Now I was well aware that Jack Douglas, yes, my boyhood hero, lived on the island, and also that he was close friends with my tour manager, Mike Holden. It did come as a shock to me though, when Mike told me that Jack was not only coming to the concert where I would obviously get to meet him, but also that it had been arranged for us all to have dinner together the evening before.

I can't remember feeling quite so nervous about meeting somebody face to face for a long time. (I think standing outside the headmaster's study in the spring of 1967, waiting to be caned by Dr Evans just after I had driven my father's Standard Ensign through his beloved rose garden, was probably the last, but who cares about that anymore? I left school the following summer anyway).

I was going to meet Jack Douglas.

Just like every other like-minded youth of my era and many before and since, the Carry On films were an integral part of my upbringing. My mother and father laughed uproariously at them, just like all the other parents and, just like my friends, so did I.

At school we knew all the films by name, most of the scripts and all the main actors, too. A few of us could even imitate some of the characters to quite a high standard ... or so we thought! However, all of us could imitate Jack Douglas and the wonderful "Alf" in one way or another.

Now, I don't know how to spell "Wohay" properly, but I can still "voice it" pretty well to this day, along with all the appropriate actions. In fact, now I come to think of it, my last encounter with Dr Evans may not have been the driving of my father's car through the headmaster's flower bed, but actually for being "Alf" during the British Constitution lecture, along with the rest of the Upper Sixth. It's all coming back to me now.

'Wakeman! Explain the rule of law at the turn of the century.'

'The rule of law, sir ... wohay ... at the turn of the century, wohay, sir, is when the wohay wohay, government create a wohay.'

'Wakeman! Go and stand outside the headmaster's study along with the rest of the class.'

Ah, happy days.

I arrived on the Isle of Wight on the day of the dinner. I spent the afternoon wondering how best to approach the conversation that would undoubtedly ensue once the food had been ordered. I had no idea whether or not Jack was sick to death of talking about his life and career and therefore would be fending off my never-ending questions all evening. Or, if he was as wonderful as all that knew him said he was and I could ask away, then sit back and listen and learn.

Meeting boyhood heroes is not easy, you know.

Well, for all those of you who will sadly never get the chance to meet the man himself, let me tell you that he's everything you hope he is and more.

Jack never fended off one question and gave me answers so fresh it was almost as if it was the first time he had ever had to reply to questions about the likes of Des O'Connor, Joe Baker, Sid James, Peter Rogers, or Hylda Baker. Plus, topics like the theatre, film, pantomime and his theatrical family.

What I do know is that it was way past both our bedtimes by the time we went our separate ways at the end of the meal.

The following evening Jack and Viv came to see my performance and afterwards I felt as if I was meeting old friends, such is the nature of the man.

Since then, we've met up on numerous occasions, both social and professional. He has given me invaluable advice as regards performing my first pantomime role as Abanazer, supported innumerable charitable evenings that I've been a party to and we have even performed on stage together in a hilarious sketch at the Gaiety Theatre on the Isle of Man.

But, back to the first dinner. I will always remember being both exhausted and exhilarated listening to the wonderful stories that Jack told that evening about his life and career and, as we left the table I can vividly recall saying to Jack:

'Your life, career and knowledge are absolutely priceless, you know. You really should write a book.'

He replied: 'I have … and you should write the Foreword.'

And I said 'I'd love to.'

… and so I did.

… and you've just read it!

Rick Wakeman

INTRODUCTION

It was such a thrill when Jack asked me to ghost write his autobiography, especially as it's my first attempt at writing a book.

I've always loved comedy and I can remember seeing Jack with Des O'Connor in the pantomime Cinderella, back in 1964 when I was eleven years old … giving my age away now!

His twitchy 'Alf' character is the only thing I can recall about that pantomime, so he must have made a huge impression on me. Little did I realise that years later I would meet the man himself and end up writing his memoirs.

Thank you Jack, for honouring me with this delightful challenge. I hope that when people read the book they will think that I've done you justice.

The Abba song says 'Thank you for the music', but I think that we should be grateful for every form of self-expression, particularly comedy.

In my book, at least, it's simply too awful to contemplate how miserable and mundane life would be without comedians.

Sue Benwell

The street where I was born in Newcastle-upon-Tyne

PREFACE

As I write this, I find it hard to believe that I'm now seventy-five. Yet, when I look back over my full and happy life, a lot of water (some of it flood water!) has gone under the bridge.

My mother was the biggest single influence in my life and I loved her dearly. Dear Mum has always been my guiding light and that light never dimmed not even when she died in 1984.God bless you, Mum.

Dad was a theatre impresario and a businessman through and through. I was a bit in awe of him, I suppose, but I loved him very much.

My elder brother Bill was very much like Dad.

As a child, I was hopeless at school and eventually ran away to join the theatre. Since those days, I've been lucky enough to work with the best in show business. I had a double-act with the inimitable Joe Baker and I've freelanced as a straight man to the likes of Bruce Forsyth and Arthur Haynes. I've worked alongside Des O'Connor, and, of course, I appeared in eight Carry On films.

I've worked on this book with journalist Sue Benwell, with whom I have reminisced about the funny, hilarious, poignant and, sometimes, downright painful moments in my life. It's certainly been therapeutic getting it all down on paper like this, although my memory isn't what it should be I'm afraid, which is strange when you consider that I can remember pages and pages of scripts, word-perfect.

Thank you to all the people who have enriched my life beyond measure, especially my family.

Thank you to my wonderful son and daughter, Craig and Debbie, from my first marriage to Rita. Also, thank you to my adopted daughter Sarah, from my second marriage to Susan. Thanks to my grandchildren: Daniel, Joanna, Jasmin and Harvey. They all brighten my life, even though it's a great source of sadness to me that I don't hear from Sarah anymore.

Thanks to Sue Benwell for slaving away over her computer for the past months.

A big thank you to Theresa Hyde for checking the final book proof so thoroughly.

Last, but certainly not least, thanks to my wonderful partner, Vivien, for all her invaluable help and encouragement with the book and for sharing her life with me.

Finally, thank you, dear reader, for buying 'A Twitch In Time', I hope that you will enjoy reading it as much as I've enjoyed writing it.

Jack Douglas

Jack and Ted

CHAPTER ONE

I could have murdered him!

I knew I had better get out of the waiting room pretty darn quick, or risk throttling the vet with the little red dog lead that was hanging limply in my hand. I wasn't a violent child, but when the vet had kindly offered to look after my beloved wire-haired terrier while the family was away, I never dreamt that he'd betray my trust.

My first companion when I was young was a cuddly toy called Jemima Puddleduck. As I grew older, though, my mother became concerned that I was spending too much time on my own and so she bought me Peter the puppy to bring me out of myself.

I will never forget the day she put this squirming bundle of fun into my arms.

'Oh! Thanks, Mam,' I said, as Peter licked my cheek, then nipped the end of my nose with his needle-sharp baby teeth.

My mother was still worried that I didn't go out and mix with other kids of my own age, but Peter was all the company I needed.

'You've always got your head buried in a book, Jack,' she would say, in her broad Geordie accent. 'Come on now, pet, take Peter outside and get some fresh air.'

Sensible people sit on the lawn, but Peter and I would climb on top of the garden shed. You can understand why she was worried about me, can't you? What she didn't know, however, was that the cracking young sisters next door would often sunbathe in their bikinis.

'He's up their stargazing, Bill,' Mum told her puzzled brother, as they observed me from the kitchen window one morning.

'What, in daylight, Betty?' he'd answered.

She was right about one thing. I did get to see some heavenly bodies from time to time!

I would chat to Peter as if he was a human friend and he would look up at me with his trusting brown eyes, obviously thinking to himself, *'How the hell does he expect me to concentrate on what's he's saying while I'm straddled across this bloody apex?'*

Actually, I'm exaggerating a bit there, because Peter never swore.

When we arrived back from our holiday on that fateful Friday morning, I was already running down the street to the vet's surgery before the rest of the family had got out of the car. I expected Peter to dash out and greet me as he always did, with his stubby little tail wagging madly.

'Oh, you've come to collect Peter,' said the vet. 'I'm sorry, lad, but there was an air-raid warning yesterday and we put all the animals down.'

'Give me my dog back!' I demanded.

'I'm really sorry, lad.'

'I hate you!' I shouted, running out of the surgery. I stood outside and thought *'Big boys don't cry'*. Then I looked at the lead and burst into tears.

For a long time afterwards I would wake with a start in the night, convinced I'd heard Peter whimpering in his dreams.

I'd stretch out my hand fully expecting to find his little body curled up next to me on the bed.

His favourite spot always empty, yet strangely warm to the touch.

* * * * *

I've thought about that incident many times over the years.

Friends say: 'Well, maybe Peter was ill and your parents didn't have the heart to tell you.'

If this had been the case, though, surely they would have explained this to me later on. I think that the truth lies in the fact that it was wartime London. Imagine for one moment that the vet's surgery had sustained a direct hit. The city could have been awash with injured animals, all adding to the mayhem of the Blitz.

I think it happened very early on in the war, when people were jumpy and didn't quite know what to expect. My own feeling is that the poor man simply panicked when he heard the air-raid siren. Whatever the reason for his drastic action, I was devastated. I'm a Christian and I've long since forgiven the vet, but as a result, I've always felt closer to animals than to human beings.

* * * * *

To recap a bit, I was born in Newcastle-upon-Tyne on the 26th April 1927. At the very moment I came into the world, the skies darkened ominously and the local church tower was struck by a terrifying bolt of lightning. Local people gathered round the base of the tower and gazed up at the still- smouldering clock hands, which were firmly welded at twenty-past-one and destined never to move again.

Just kidding! That didn't happen really, I just thought that if I made my birth sound more dramatic, it would make you want to read on.

Oh, please yourself!

The family home at that time was in Streatham, London, but my dear mother had travelled up to Newcastle when she was eight month's pregnant so that I wouldn't be born on foreign soil. I suppose that she didn't want me to be an 'Away lad'!

Life must have been hard for people, but there was always that great sense of community. The wonderful smell of soap from Hedley's Soap Works on nearby City Road would help mask the unpleasant smells from the heavy industry that went on in the area. Mum, however, stayed with her father in his tiny miners' cottage during her confinement. My grandfather was a retired miner and he literally lived in one room with a bed in the wall. I can still see it now.

* * * * *

Show business is quite literally in my blood.

In fact, they gave a woman a transfusion of my blood the other week and afterwards she said to the doctor, 'Will I be able to play the violin?'

'I don't see why not, dear,' he told her kindly.

To which she answered, 'That's funny, I couldn't play before.'

Ha, the old ones are the best.

I can even boast that my great, great, great grandfather brought the Minstrels over from Kentucky. They didn't want to come, you understand, it was just that he could be very persuasive.

Seriously, I can trace my show business family back for several generations. My father was the theatre impresario, John Douglas Roberton, and I was by his side every Christmas while he was directing pantomimes. I knew all the scripts word-for-word by the age of seven and if someone made a mistake I could correct them. It's not that I was a know-all or anything. Oh well, all right then, I was, but show business was the only thing I was interested in.

Dear Mum and Dad on their wedding day

My father was a Winston Churchill look-a-like, even down to the cigar. He was a big man with a ruddy complexion, balding brown hair and good teeth. At home, he was gentle yet firm and I have to admit that I was rather in awe of him. I don't know what he thought of his youngest son, but I always felt that he was closer to my brother Bill than he was to me.

Dad was the manager for the late George Black and when he married my mother (I mean, my dad, not George Black!) he then became Promoter of Revues and Pantomimes, specialising in comedy shows and pantomimes.

My brother, William Douglas Roberton, was four years older than me and followed in my father's footsteps. Again, I looked up to Bill, quite literally when he became six foot tall. He was everything I wasn't. Slim, good-looking, muscular, a good athlete, and always surrounded by friends. Bill was also a bit of a ladies man and his girlfriends were all beautiful model-types … the lucky swine.

I, on the other hand, was short and very fat and certainly no athlete, apart from a bit of swimming, and, of course, always a loner. However, by the time I was fourteen I had blossomed into a James Stewart look-a-like, without the stammer, and was happiest in the company of ladies. I don't mean that in the 'wolf' sense, just that I preferred their company. Men always seemed to talk about sport or sex, whereas, ladies talked about cookery and the price of eggs.

It sounds as if I was a right ponce! I wasn't though it was just that I found the company of men intimidating, I suppose.

My mother, Isabel, had once been in a double act with her brother. In their clever dance and juggling act they were known as Betty and Billy Clark, but they split up, in the professional sense, after she married my father. My mother was extremely close to her brother and I was very much like him, so he and I became very close, too, despite the vast age difference. Mum was an open, honest, bubbly lady, with brown eyes, an olive skin and good teeth. All this talk of 'good teeth' makes us sound like a family of rottweillers! Her Geordie accent was coupled with the most marvellous sense of humour and I adored her.

Her brother, Billy, had a way of explaining things to me about show business. He also shared my mother's sense of humour and taught me how important it was to laugh and look on the funny side of life. It seems awful to admit that I felt closer to Uncle Billy than I did to my own father, but we were simply on the same wavelength.

My brother, Bill, as I said, was more like my dad, who was such an involved businessman. Dad and Bill would do seven or eight pantomimes and four or five summer shows, many of which they would direct themselves. I never had that closeness with my father, although he was a good father.

* * * * *

Like many people, I can remember my first day at school quite clearly.

I'd walked down the road in Streatham with Peter trailing along behind me. His reluctance to continue with the journey only adding to my feeling of foreboding.

'Come on, bonny lad,' said my mother. 'You'll love school once you've made friends with all the other boys.'

I peered through the railings, realising immediately that I would have nothing in common with these boisterous kids racing round the playground with their arms outstretched, pretending to be aeroplanes. Another group of older boys had a smaller lad pinned against a wall and the look on his face was one of abject terror. The school bell rang and the boys formed obedient lines, until a teacher blew the whistle and they began filing in through the doors. Mum accompanied me into the cloakroom, along with all the other new boys and their mothers.

An overwhelming odour pervaded that cloakroom, which I can only describe as disinfectant laced with rubber. Looking back, I suppose the stale rubbery smell came from the hundreds of pairs of plimsolls. I walked in, with a brown leather satchel over one shoulder and a blue PT bag over the other, which Mum had made especially for me. She had embroidered my initials on it, in neat, inch-high red letters.

Another interest from my childhood is cooking.

It stems from the time my parents took me to tea at one of their friends and she served up a salad. After unsuccessfully scanning the table for salad cream and being too shy to ask, I tasted a piece of lettuce.

I remember thinking: 'Oh, this tastes good' and then summoning up the courage to ask what was on it.

'It's french dressing,' she explained. 'Would you like me to show you how to make it?'

After watching her fascinating demonstration, salad cream went out of the window in our house. It made an awful mess on the pavement!

I mean, there's nothing worse than a limp lettuce leaf. Well, I suppose there is, but it would depend on what you were doing at the time.

Anyway, this started off a life-long interest in cookery and I became my mother's official helper in the kitchen. I even saved up my pocket money and bought a cookery book with Italian recipes. The resulting pasta meal went down very well with the family.

Over the years I've always cooked and when I went on tour with my brother and we couldn't afford hotels and digs, we bought a second-hand caravan in which we toured the whole of Britain. If Bill was with me, then I would experiment with dishes, not just the food kind, either!

I think it's terribly important for an actor or a comedian to have a hobby of some kind. It's one of the luckiest things in my life that I can come home and shut down. When you think of the sadness of someone like Tony Hancock, for example, who, with only show business in his life, would come home obsessed with worrying whether he would still be funny tomorrow.

In later years, cooking came to my rescue when I told my agent that I wanted to be a comedian and he said that I didn't look funny. I'd replied that if I couldn't be a comic, then I would quit the business.

His reply of: 'Oh, you'll never do that' was entirely the wrong thing to say to a stubborn Taurean like me.

More about that later, though.

* * * * *

The one thing I was frightened of as a child was the dark. I always had to sleep with the light on at night, until my mother came up with a brilliant plan to cure me.

She would suddenly ask: 'Would you like some chocolate?' And then send me upstairs to get it out of her bedside cabinet. I would switch on the bedroom light, but my mother had cunningly removed the bulb, knowing that the chocolate would be enough of a temptation to have me scrabbling round in the dark to find it.

She did this many times with many different things and, over a period of time, it cured my fear. Even today, I'm good at finding my way round in the dark, which is handy if there's ever a power cut.

My other fear was, and still is, heights. God, I must sound as if I'm neurotic, but I have a genuine reason for this particular phobia.

When I was about seven, I was playing by a cliff edge at Birchington-on-Sea while my parents were relaxing nearby. I think a boy pushed me over the cliff, but, by the grace of God, there was a ledge about six or seven feet below. Even so, I landed facedown onto the bare rocks with my hands outstretched and the fire service rescued me and I was rushed to hospital. I was a complete mess and my parents were distraught, but how's this for a bit of luck?

There was a plastic surgeon giving a lecture to the doctors at the hospital who must have thought that it was his lucky day, because he decided to demonstrate his skills on me. All the neat repair work to my hands and face was down to him and I've been left with the minimum of scarring, considering what I went through.

I'm afraid that I've never conquered my fear of heights and can't even climb a ladder to paint the upstairs windows or clean out the gutters. My lovely partner, Viv, has to do that for me.

The funny thing about that episode in hospital, though, was that my hands had been so badly damaged in the fall that I needed physiotherapy for a while. My parents were astonished when they visited me in hospital to find me sitting up in bed … knitting! Now, I can add knitting to my list of skills. It's an ill wind, I suppose. It certainly was once I'd eaten some hospital cabbage. Let's just say that I dropped more than the odd stitch!

* * * * *

I had another run-in with a boy at school, once. He was the school bully, simply because he was the biggest and had more muscle than anyone else and he ruled the playground with a rod of iron. Everyone was petrified of him and he was the type of kid who would steal your sweets from you.

We were out in the playground one-day when he deliberately pushed me. I just turned my head and said as casually as I could, 'Don't do that.'

He grabbed my arm in a vice-like grip, swivelled me round and shoved his face into mine. 'Why don't you shut up?' he said menacingly.

He then made the fatal mistake of pushing me again. I don't usually have a temper where people are concerned, but this boy had literally pushed me to my limit. I swung my arm back and planted such a punch on his jaw that it knocked him spark out. With that, the whole of St. Joseph's gathered round and started cheering. All the brothers came rushing out to see what the commotion was about. They knew this boy's reputation, so they didn't come down on me as much as they might have done and, from that moment on, I was the top boy at school. Never academically, you understand, but just because I'd floored the bully.

* * * * *

Still very much the loner, I made few really close friends at St. Joseph's. Then, a boy called Roddy McDowall joined the school and although he was a couple of years my junior, the pair of us just seemed to click. We were friends both in and out of school and did the normal thing of staying at each other's houses, when we would chat long into the night. We were great collectors of information, I don't mean in the train spotting sense, just general information.

'Did you know that if you soak a conker in malt vinegar for twenty-four hours it will go as hard as a bullet?' I said to Roddy one day.

'No, I didn't. That's very interesting, Jack.'

Not that old chestnut, I hear you cry!

Okay, so our fascinating conversations may not have set the world on fire, but in Roddy I'd at last found a friend I could relate to.

When our family moved to Blackpool during the war, Roddy's parents, who had discussed the war situation with my father, did the self-same thing. Everything was idyllic, apart from school. Then the government brought in a scheme for evacuees to go to America.

Roddy's mother was American. Quite understandably, she found windswept Blackpool no comparison to the balmy climate of her native country. When Roddy arrived at my house one morning looking tearful and worried, I feared the worst.

'What's the matter, mate?' I inquired.

'Dad says that me and Mum have to go to America on the next available ship, Jack,' he said sniffing and wiping his nose along his sleeve.

'Cor, you lucky devil,' I said, trying to cheer him up, yet feeling secretly devastated to be losing my best friend.

Our usual banter ran a bit dry that day, as we each tried to come to terms with the unthinkable.

Some weeks after their departure, we received our first letter from Roddy's mother.

'Just a note', she wrote at the beginning of her six-page letter. 'Would Jack like to come out and join us for the duration of the war?'

'What do you say, lad?' asked my mother excitedly.

'It'll be a wonderful opportunity for you,' my father added.

'I don't want to go to America,' I told them firmly.

My reluctance didn't stop my parents from making plans and they even went so far as to reserve a place for me on the next available ship. My suitcase was in the hall (isn't that a song?) packed and ready, but I sat at the bottom of the stairs with my elbows on my knees and my chin in my hands.

'I don't want to leave home,' I sobbed.

'Perhaps we shouldn't force the lad, John,' said my mother, putting a reassuring arm around my shoulders and kissing the top of my head.

'You're too soft with him, Betty. It was kind of the McDowall's to ask Jack and it will only be until the end of the war.'

'I'm not going!' I said, running upstairs to my bedroom and slamming the door.

'All right! All right!' Dad shouted after me. 'But you'll be sorry to have missed such a marvellous opportunity, you mark my words.'

As it happened my stubborn nature literally saved my skin, because the ship I would have sailed out on was torpedoed by the Germans.

'Oh, John,' said my mother, when the news came through of the great loss of life. 'To think our precious son could have been killed.'

She ran across the room and hugged me, while poor Dad, who was never one to show his feelings, remained ashen-faced and silent for the rest of the day.

The next time I heard from Roddy, he'd been chosen to play the lead in the film, Lassie. (I'm referring to the lead role, not the dog lead, you silly reader!)

Sad to say that our paths never crossed again, but Roddy was a lovely person and I always followed his career with enormous pride and interest. During the writing of this book I was saddened to learn that my old pal had died.

* * * * *

Since Roddy's departure, life had returned to the normal boring routine of going to school every day. I attended St. Joseph's College in Blackpool, which was the same school as in Streatham, but a different location. I was just as unhappy as I'd been in London and I knew that the time had come for me to take drastic action.

* * * * *

Beside the seaside with Mum, Dad and brother Bill

CHAPTER TWO

As I lay in bed one night after a particularly harrowing day at school, a plan began to form in my mind. I suppose it wasn't only my unhappiness at school that spurred me into action, but the fact that I'd lost both Peter the dog and my best friend Roddy in quick succession.

Early the next morning, I climbed out of bed, grabbed a few clothes from the wardrobe and thrust them into a small suitcase. Then, I crept downstairs, opened the back door and strode off down the path without a backward glance. I found an out-of-season boarding house in a rundown area of Blackpool, where a ferocious-looking landlady showed me up three flights of uncarpeted stairs to a broom cupboard.

'It'll be five shilling a week for the room, lad,' she said, eyeing me up and down suspiciously. 'Payment in advance, please. Oh, and no visitors late at night, mind, or you'll be out on your ear.'

I placed my suitcase down on the torn linoleum and paid her from some loose change in my trouser pocket. I had just enough money left for a cup of tea. Later on in the morning, a young boy not much older than myself greeted my knock at the stage door of the Feldman's Theatre.

'Yeah?' he said with a sniff.

'Got any jobs for a lime boy?' I asked him.

(For the uninitiated, a lime boy works on the spotlights. That's where the phrase 'being in the limelight' comes from.)

'Hang on a minute,' he said. 'I'll go and ask the governor'.

With that, he slammed the door shut and I was left standing in the alleyway for what seemed like ages. You have to bear in mind that the war was on and that there was a shortage of manpower. Needless to say, the stage manager didn't ask this lanky adolescent any questions and so started my apprenticeship in the theatre.

I remember I was earning £1 7s 6d a week (about £1.37p) although I would have worked for nothing. Anything would have been better than those dreaded school lessons.

What I hadn't realised at the time was that the manager had, in fact, recognised me as soon as he'd clapped eyes on me and immediately informed my father. Between them they had cooked up a deal that I would be given all the dirtiest jobs imaginable, so that I would soon go running home again. I was so besotted with show business, though, that nothing could have put me off. When you love what you are doing, there's no such thing as a dirty job.

'Come on now, lad' my father tried to insist, when his little ruse hadn't worked. 'Your mother's been worried sick about you and she wants you to come back home.'

'No, Dad,' I told him firmly. 'If you make me go back to school I'll only run away again.'

'Is that your last word on the matter, then?' he said. It may seem that he was giving up all too easily, but he knew how stubborn I could be.

'I'm staying here.'

He didn't press me anymore as he knew that it would be a total waste of time.

My thirst for knowledge was quenched by visits to Blackpool library, where I would spend hours swotting up on any subject I wanted to learn more about, like Egyptology. I also learned a lot from shining a light on Robb Wilton twice nightly. He was, for me, one of the funniest comedians I've ever seen in my life; his timing was impeccable.

I can remember him saying 'If you find a successful comedy format, Jack, hang on to it for the rest of your natural.

'Comedy is like a clock,' he would say. 'It starts at twelve and goes round all the numbers, but still comes back to twelve.'

If you think about it, we've had the entire fringe and the sex and the four-letter words, but now we're getting back to decent comedy again, thank God.

Robb Wilton gave me so much good advice and another of his little gems was: 'It's only an old joke when it doesn't get a laugh.'

It's true of course, because there are always youngsters coming up who won't have heard it before.

He also advised me never to drink before a performance and I was destined to find out the wisdom behind those words later on in my career.

* * * * *

As a lime boy I only erred but once from my duties. This was because I fancied one of the dancers in the show, who was a leggy young beauty called Jean.

There was a long period during one particular show when the light stayed on continuously, thus rendering me surplus to requirements for a while. I decided to take advantage of this and escorted the lovely Jean underneath the stage, where we could examine my stamp collection.

We were just studying the intricate detail on a line of perforations, when one of the stage crew screamed out: 'Where's that ruddy lime boy?'

A blackout had been needed between scenes and so my naughty absence had been noticed. Doesn't time fly when you're having fun?

From a lime boy I graduated to a property master, making all the stage props. Then I was a flyman, pulling up the scenery. After that, I became a scenic artist and then a stage carpenter. A 'Jack of all trades' in other words.

* * * * *

As a family, we were very lucky during the war because we never lost anyone. Granted, I didn't see much of the war, although I did join the Home Guard in Blackpool. It was strange to see all these people who were either too old or too young to be called up, dressed in uniform and learning drill.

Living back at home again, I trained four or five nights a week and I can remember one particular time when we first got our rifles and the sergeant yelled: 'Fix bayonets!' I was growing fast, but with the war and rationing I was a little undernourished. Anyway, when the sergeant shouted: 'Squad attention!' I promptly fainted. I suppose that's what they mean by a passing-out parade!

Unfortunately, as I gracefully sank to the ground, my chin caught the tip of the bayonet and I was sent home swathed in bandages and covered in blood.

'Ee, bonny lad,' my mother said when she saw the state of me. 'You look like you've been fighting the Germans single-handed.'

Something that kept up most people's morale during the war was going to the 'flicks'. For younger people who don't know, this is what us oldies used to call the cinema in those days, on account of the flickering films. War films made us feel particularly patriotic and I really fancied myself as a brave sea captain at the helm of a destroyer, so I put my name down to join the Navy.

Sadly, I didn't achieve my lofty ambition, because at that time Ernest Bevin, who was the Minister of Labour, brought out a system called the Bevin Boys. This meant that a percentage of the young boys who put their names down for the services were picked out to work down the mines. To literally 'keep the home fires burning', and all that. I ended up at Beighton Colliery just outside Chesterfield and one day, during my six-month stint, the instructor was telling us new boys what to do in the event of a roof fall.

'Now listen, lads,' he said, gathering us closer to him. 'If you ever see dust hurtling towards you round a corner, it means that there's been a fall.'

'What do we 'ave to do, then?' asked one boy.

'Bloody run for it, of course,' answered another and everyone laughed.

'Quiet!' snapped the instructor, obviously rattled by the flippancy of his new recruits. 'You will all have to look out for one another down here and treat your environment with the utmost respect.

'Now, as I was saying, if you see a cloud of dust … '

'Please, sir,' I shouted, but the instructor was determined to finish his lesson and would not be interrupted.

'Sir, sir!' I shouted again, frantically waving my hands above the heads of the gathered throng, who by now were turning round to see what all the fuss was about.

'What's the matter, boy?' asked the instructor crossly.

'Do you mean like that, sir?' I said, pointing to a telltale cloud of dust that was slowly drifting round the corner towards us.

'Oh, my God,' said the instructor. 'This way, lads,' he shouted.

Although our instinct was to run in the opposite direction, we followed him along the passageway into the choking cloud of dust.

We found a roof fall all right and I felt physically sick when I saw all these limbs sticking out from under the rubble. We clawed away at the coal with our bare hands, afraid that our picks and shovels might inflict even worse injuries on the trapped men. One abiding memory for me is of seeing the whites of a young boy's eyes glinting with terror in the lamplight as we pulled him clear. Thankfully, there were no fatalities, but the thick dust in the air wasn't the only thing to choke me down there. My old fear of the dark came back to haunt me that day and I couldn't breathe. The thought of being buried alive beneath tons of rubble half-a-mile underground filled me with dread and I never went back.

The closest call I ever had during the bombing in London was when I was with my father. We were driving through Streatham towards the High Road when the air-raid siren sounded.

'What shall we do, Dad?' I asked him fearfully.

'We'll keep going, son,'

Suddenly, there was a loud explosion and a block of flats disappeared in front of our eyes. My father stopped the car and we spent five-and-a-half hours helping the emergency services to pull people out of the rubble.

We even had a brush with near disaster after we'd moved to Blackpool. I remember one night when we were en route to Liverpool to see a show Dad had there. He stopped the car on a hill just outside and we watched in horror as Liverpool was bombed. We saw buildings disappear beneath terrifying sheets of flame that lit up the night sky for miles around and if we'd arrived at our destination earlier than planned, we would have been in the middle of all the mayhem. There was nothing we could have done, so, without a word, Dad turned the car round and headed back to Blackpool.

All through the war, there were fourteen theatres in Blackpool all doing live summer shows and we had three of those shows. I studied lighting under Jack Taylor, who was one of the leading directors in those days.

One day, my father said that he was taking me to Manchester to see a show, which was Irving Berlin's all male review called 'This Is The Army'. They were all service men, and men played even the girls' parts. Dad thought that it was an excellent idea and when we returned to Blackpool he put a big advert in The Stage asking for female impersonators. I thought that he was mad, but he wouldn't have it.

When we held the auditions at one of the hotels in Blackpool, the police had to control the crowds. I should think every female impersonator in Britain came to Blackpool that day and guess who had to audition them? As a young lad, I didn't know anything about blokes wearing girls' costumes (apart from in pantomimes, of course!) and it was quite incredible. The show was called 'We Were In The Forces' and I helped my father to direct it. The show played to packed houses in the first week and ran for five years, so that demonstrates how much I know. Eventually, my father had to put out a number two company and it played to capacity audiences everywhere. If I tell you that there was a young guy in the chorus called Danny La Rue and that this was one of his first jobs, then you'll realise how big a deal it was.

* * * * *

I was stage managing a show for my father at the Winter Gardens in Morecambe. For the end of the first half a set designer called Jimmy Curry had invented a wonderful scene known as 'The Waterfalls of Scotland'. As the curtains opened, some of the cast had to walk across the top of this Scottish glen, wearing kilts and singing. (I think it was a bit draughty round the Trossacks!)

The full company then joined them on the top rostrum, which was about fifteen feet high, to sing the main song. As they reached the highest mountain 'peak', the two fronts of the scene came down stage and opened up to face the audience. It's rather difficult to explain, but a tray also came down to the front of the stage to join these two rostrums. This was followed by some impressive-looking waterfalls that cascaded down from the top of the 'hills' and into the 'glens', where the water was collected in the tray and re-circulated. The whole effect was really quite stunning and always resulted in an appreciative 'ripple' of applause from the audience.

One night, I pressed the button from my usual spot in the wings and the aprons descended then the tray came out. Suddenly, however, I noticed that the left-hand apron, on what is known as the 'prompt' side of the stage, had broken away from its moorings at the back. It was heading in my direction at a rate of knots and seeing that this thing weighed well over a ton, I thought it would be sensible to get the hell out of there. The trouble was, I was trapped in my corner with no chance of escape. Thank God I was fit in those days, because I leapt up and managed to pull myself onto the electrician's rostrum above my head just in time. The runaway set crashed into the corner where I'd been standing only moments before, smashing everything in its path to smithereens. A guy called Curry may have designed the set, but I was the one who nearly had me 'chips'!

* * * * *

At that time I didn't really go in for long meaningful relationships. There were plenty of girls floating around on the horizon, but none of them near enough for me to grab hold of. Well, not often.

'How do you fancy a round of golf up at the North Shore Golf Club, Jack?' my father's friend George asked me one day.

'I've never played golf before,' I told him.

'Doesn't matter. I can soon teach you.'

'I haven't got any clubs, either.'

'You can borrow mine.'

He obviously wasn't going to take no for an answer and before long we were heading for the first tee. A keen north-westerly wind was strong enough to make our trouser legs flap noisily and a small white flag flutter tantalisingly on the distant green.

'It's four-hundred-and-twenty yards, Jack,' said George, removing a driver from his golf bag.

'This should be good,' I muttered under my breath. 'I'll manage about four-hundred-and-twenty inches in this wind.'

I watched him place the ball on top of the tee, grip the club and wiggle his hips into a comfortable position. George hit the ball with surprising force, which then whistled impressively down the centre of the fairway.

'Good shot,' I said admiringly. In truth, however, I hadn't got a clue whether it was a good shot or not and it might have ended up in the sea for all I knew.

'Not bad,' said George, shading his eyes and gazing off into the distance.

'You have a try now, Jack. Here, let me show you how to hold the club correctly and how to stand.'

Despite feeling a bit agitated when a group of players appeared behind us waiting their turn, I was determined to give it my best shot.

'Please God, don't let me remove a huge divot from this manicured grass,' I thought desperately.

Being a comedian, I suddenly saw the funny side of it and, convincing myself that everyone must make a hash of their first shot, I began to relax. I looked at the flag fluttering in the distance, then at the ball, then at the flag, then at the ball. It was now or never.

'Thwack!' The ball sailed off, thankfully, in the right direction.

'That was a brilliant shot, Jack,' said George, patting me on the back. 'Are you sure you haven't played before?'

'You're obviously a natural,' said the club professional when he read my score card after the game. 'You should join the club.'

'I wish I could afford it,' I said wistfully.

'If you come and work here in the golf shop part-time, I could teach you for free.'

So, three or four times a week I went to the North Shore Golf Club and kept the shop ticking over when the pro' wasn't there. I got heavily into golf and, with my knowledge of carpentry I was even able to repair golf clubs.

You may be wondering what all this had to do with the lack of girlfriends I mentioned earlier. Well, there was this very pretty girl called Cynthia. She lived nearby and I had been trying, unsuccessfully, to date her for some time … along with the rest of the young men in Blackpool. She finally consented and I took her to the casino in Blackpool and, being the perfect gentleman I was (and still am), I walked her home afterwards.

'I've really enjoyed this evening, Cynthia,' I said as we reached her house. 'Can I see you again tomorrow, please?'

'No,' she answered simply.

'Oh, are you busy?'

'No.'

'What about the next night, then?'

'No.'

'Are you busy all week?'

'No.'

'You might let me get a word in edgeways,' I quipped, but she didn't appreciate the joke.

'Well, don't you want to see me again?' I asked, putting my head on one side and making my eyes as doleful-looking as I could.

'No,' said Cynthia totally unmoved.

'Why?'

'Because I've never been so bored in my life!'

'Oh,' I answered feebly, completely taken aback by the obvious vehemence in her tone.

'You've talked about nothing but golf all evening and I've been bored stiff,' she snapped, turning on her two-inch heels and limping away up the garden path.

'And thanks for the blisters!' she shouted, before slamming the front door.

'I'm a golf bore,' I thought miserably as I walked home.

From that moment on, I decided to give up golf and concentrate on the more important things in life.

'These will include show business, music, cooking … and birdies,' I thought to myself smugly. *'But not the kind of birdies you get on a gold course.'* **Tee** Hee!'

* * * * *

Many years later, the T.V. Times magazine invited me to play in the Pro-Celebrity Golf Tournament in Marbella, Spain, all expenses paid. My game was a bit rusty by this time, so the singer, Toni Dalli, gave me a few lessons to help me get back in the swing of things, so to speak. He suggested that we play a round (Gerroff!) every morning for a week and I have to admit that I didn't play very well at all, because I was trying too hard. Anyway, I flew to Marbella and checked into this beautiful hotel, which was all white marble and trailing plants. A car picked me up in the morning and took me to the golf course situated just outside Marbella. In the magnificent clubhouse I mingled with the other celebrities who were playing in the four-day tournament, like Sean Connery and Jimmy Tarbuck. I was reading through the list of players when I heard a familiar voice behind me.

'Hello, my darlin'!'

I turned round but there was no-one there and I was just beginning to think that I must have been imagining things, when I felt a tug on my sleeve.

'I'm down here, Mr Bugless.'

Me and Charlie Drake – "Ooh my gawd!"

I looked down and there was Charlie Drake smiling up at me.

'Looks as if you and me are going to be partners for the day, Mr Bugless,' he said, blinking his eyes nineteen to the dozen.

'Charlie! How lovely to see you,' I said, shaking his hand warmly.

'Lovely to see the top of my head, you mean,' he said.

'Good gracious,' he chuckled. 'Talk about the long and the short and the tall. I'm short and I long to be tall.'

'What's the wevver like up there, Mr Bugless?'

With me at six-foot-four and the diminutive Charlie at four-foot-ten, I could see that this was going to be an entertaining game.

A coin was flipped and guess who had to play first?

'At least he will be able to see how everyone else on the course is getting on,' said Charlie to the crowd, as we headed for the first tee. 'I'd need a pair of scopes for that.'

'It's periscope, Charlie,' I corrected him.

'Where?' he said, looking round. 'I haven't seen him in years.'

The spectators laughed as Charlie skipped along beside me, making the most of the comic situation as he desperately tried to keep up with my giant strides. The sight of the first tee, with its television cameras, radio broadcasters and thousand-strong crowd of spectators all pushing and shoving each other for a better view, soon stopped Charlie in his tracks.

'Ooh, my gawd,' he said, clutching my arm as he realised what was so interesting about this first hole. 'Please Mr Custard, I don't wanna go.'

The crowd roared with laughter as the pair of us edged towards the front of the tee and peered gingerly down into a two-hundred foot ravine, which gaped menacingly between us and the green.

'I could lose my balls down there,' said Charlie.

'I think I've already lost mine,' I quipped back at him.

'You can go first,' said Charlie. 'I'm going to let Mr Bugless go first,' he added, addressing the spectators.

'Th … thanks, Charlie,' I said, turning to my caddy for advice. I removed a driver for my golf bag, raising the club as if I intended to whack Charlie with it and then demurely preparing for the shot, instead.

I just knew that the ball would fly briefly off the edge of the tee and disappear without trace into the ravine, never to be seen again.

'I wonder how many ducks have been knocked unconscious by stray golf balls in that stream down there?' I whispered to Charlie.

'That's why they're always on the menu in the clubhouse,' he replied and we both broke down in a fit of giggles, thereby defusing the tense situation.

'You haven't got a hope in hell, Bugless, I mean, Douglas,' I thought to myself. *'It's a beautiful day so you might as well relax and enjoy yourself.'*

I hit the ball and watched as it sailed effortlessly over the ravine and plop down onto the green, miraculously coming to rest a mere three feet from the pin. The crowd of onlookers erupted, but I just stood there rooted to the spot with my mouth open and my eyes fixed on that tiny white speck on the distant green.

'You did it, Mr Bugless!' shouted Charlie, jumping up and down with glee.

'I had no idea you could play as good as that, Jack,' he added. 'Well done.'

'Thanks, Charlie. It must have been a lucky shot.'

'Lucky shot! Listen, a professional golfer would have been proud of that one.'

I turned to the crowd and acknowledged their rapturous applause. I was right about it being a lucky shot, though, because I played like a complete idiot after that. You see my theory of playing a successful round of golf is simply to relax and enjoy the game, because as soon as you start trying too hard it'll beat you.

* * * * *

Do you recognise anyone in this photo?

The ones we've identified are:

1. Jack Taylor	8. Vic Crastonian
2. Me!	9. Jo Crastonian
3. J D Roberton (Dad)	10. Georgie Wood
4. Gypsy Petrolengo	11.
5. Bill Roberton (brother)	12. } *'The Three Shades'* (dance act)
6. Billy Scott Coomber	13.
7. Norman Evans	

'Was it something I said?'

Tommy laughed nervously: 'I've got a problem, mate,' he said, pulling up a chair.

'Oh, sorry to hear that. Anything I can help with?'

'It's that fifty quid you lent me,' he said, unable to look me in the eyes.

'What about it?'

'Look, I'm sorry, Jack, but I can't pay you back.'

'Oh, I see.'

'The only thing I've got of any value is my drum kit.'

'Drum kit?'

'Yeah. You can sell it on, Jack. It's worth a lot more than fifty quid and I can hardly take it with me to Australia, can I?'

'I suppose not,' I said with a sigh. 'Okay, that's fine by me.'

I think that's what they call 'drumming up some business'!

Funnily enough, though, I'd always fancied myself as a bit of a drummer, so I took my newly acquired Premier Drum Kit home to Newton Drive.

The set consisted of a bass drum; a snare drum; three tom-toms, four Ziljan cymbals, which were the best in the business, and a hi-hat. For those who don't know, a hi-hat is the name of the two cymbals you bash together by means of a foot pedal. I was always good at technical descriptions.

'That's worth more than fifty pounds, Jack,' my mother commented, running her hand around the rim of the bass drum. 'You got a bargain, there.'

'There's only one problem.'

'Aye, where are you going to set it all up?' she said reading my mind.

'I was just wondering, Mam,' I said, putting an arm around her. 'Could I set the drum kit up in the attic, please?'

'Oh, I'm sure your father will love listening to you banging away up there (no rude comments!) after a hard day at the office,' she said, removing my arm from her shoulder.

'There'd be no worries on that score,' I assured her.

'And how do you work that one out, bonny lad?'

'Ear muffs!'

'What! Get away with you, lad. I'll not have … '

'I'm only teasing you, Mam,' I laughed. 'Listen, I've been thinking … '

'Yeeeesss,' she said, folding her arms and tapping her foot.

'With my knowledge of carpentry I could redesign the attic and make it into a sound-proof studio.'

Eat your heart out, Laurence Llewelyn-Bowen!

Mum poked her head up through the newly enlarged loft hole one morning and looked around in wonder.

'Eee, you've done a grand job up here,' she said.

'It's great except for one thing,' I said with a sigh.

'What's that?'

'I don't know how to put a drum kit together.'

'Do you know, I've been in show business all these years and I wouldn't have a clue either, Jack.' She joined me in the attic and we both puzzled over the conun'drum'!

'Perhaps the bass drum goes there and the snare drum, just there,' she suggested. 'Or would the snare drum go there and the bass, there?'

After a morning spent scratching our heads, I suddenly remembered the manager at the Odeon Cinema in Blackpool. If anyone would know, he would.

'Here, this should help,' he said as he handed me a photo of the famous American drummer, Buddy Rich, who was sitting at his drum kit.

So, I set my kit up exactly as per the photograph, and, with the help of a gramophone and some headphones, I taught myself to play over a period of about six months.

I then met up with some semi-professional musicians and we formed a little quartet. There weren't many bands around because of the war, so I secured the contract to play at the American bases in Burtonwood and Warrington, with an occasional gig in Blackpool itself. The Americans paid well and they fed us, which was quite something, bearing in mind all the wartime food shortages.

I was at a dance at the Spanish Hall in Blackpool one evening, when the drummer invited me to sit in with the band.

'Oh, you're left-handed,' I remarked, as I sat down behind his kit.

'What do you mean?' he asked.

'Well, your drum kit is set up the wrong way round.'

'No it isn't.'

'Yes it is.'

'Oh, no it isn't,' he said indignantly and I realised that our conversation was beginning to sound like something out of a pantomime.

'You must be left-handed, Jack,' he added.

'No I'm not.'

'Well, you must have been taught by a left-handed drummer, then.'

I was just about to say 'No I wasn't' when the penny suddenly dropped.

After a bit of research I discovered that the photograph of Buddy Rich had been printed the wrong way round, from right to left, to match the other pictures in the frame. This meant, of course, that despite being right-handed, I'd set up the kit for a left-handed player. Trying to 'jam' with the group had proved to be an impossibly 'sticky' situation! Anyway, after a while, the boys in The Jack Douglas Quartet were virtually professionals, so they got various jobs and went their separate ways. We did have one extra-special reunion at the end of the war, though. I remember I was listening to my radio late at night when the programme was interrupted.

'War is over!' crackled the announcer's voice. I rushed into my parents' room to tell them the wonderful news.

We were just celebrating with a cup of tea, which is, of course, England's answer to everything, when the phone rang.

'Get your drum kit together, Jack,' said Ken the double-bass player. 'And meet me on the Town Hall steps.'

I will never forget the sight of the thousands of people who danced and sang along with our impromptu outdoor concert that night. Every pub had been opened and all the lights were on in the town – it looked just like fairyland, but that's another story!

Emotions were running high and everyone was laughing with joy one minute, then crying with happiness the next. Some poor souls were weeping for their loved ones who would never come back, of course, and we knew that their sacrifice had made our exuberant celebration possible. I had been lucky enough not to lose anyone, so, for me, it was one of the most magical times of my life and I can still remember it as if it happened yesterday.

* * * * *

I must admit that I didn't really enjoy working in Dad's office, simply because I hated being cooped up all day. My business acumen never quite matched that of my father or my brother, Bill, because they both had such excellent business brains. The turning point for me, though, came when Dad had ten pantomimes on the go at once.

'What's up, Dad?' I asked him, when I saw him pawing over his accounts, his forehead puckered with a worried frown.

'I'm stretched to the limit, cash-wise,' he told me. 'And I need some money to build the scenery for Dick Whittington at the Kingston Empire, but I've no idea where I'm going to get it from.

'Perhaps you can give it some thought, Jack.'

'Okay, Dad,' I said enthusiastically.

I glanced out of the office window and spotted the eye-catching advertisement hoarding for Watney's Red Barrel beer across the road. I had a cunning plan, as Baldrick would say, so I phoned the brewery and made an appointment to see the Publicity Manager.

'In pantomimes we have a Front Cloth,' I explained. 'This is brought in when we need to change the scenery behind this cloth and this cloth can be painted with a scene of some sort.'

'I see,' he said, leaning forward on his desk with obvious interest.

'I was thinking that we could use the Watney's advert'. The one on all the billboards with the brick wall and 'Wot We Want Is Watney's' written on it.'

'Well, yes, that would be a marvellous idea, but how much would it cost?'

'If you paid for the scenery to be built and painted, then that would be the total cost.'

'Done!' he said, shaking my hand. 'We'll draw up a contract right away.'

I raced back to the office and thrust the contract on my father's desk.

'What's this?' he said, picking it up and putting his glasses on, in order to read the small print.

'You don't have to worry about the scenery at Kingston anymore, Dad,' I told him proudly. 'Because I've done a deal with Watney's.'

Dad was overjoyed and, from that moment, I was put in charge of all the publicity and sponsorship for his shows and pantomimes.

* * * * *

I'd had a very busy and productive time in my father's office.

'You've been working hard and you're looking a bit peeky, son,' Dad commented one day. 'When did you last have a holiday?'

'It must have been about two years ago,' I told him.

'I think you've earned a break, don't you?'

'Oh, thanks Dad.'

'How do you fancy six weeks in the Welsh valleys, lad?'

'Cor! That would be lovely,' I said, thinking that somebody must have offered him the use of a caravan in Porthcawl or something.

'Let's see,' he said, flicking through his diary. 'Next week do you?'

'That'll be smashing, Dad. Thanks.'

In my mind I'd already packed my case with a beach towel and bathing trunks. I was even anticipating the feel of warm sand between my toes. What my father had neglected to tell me, however, was that he'd got a show on the road at that moment, called 'Ice Carnival'. The portable ice rink needed for this production had to be piggybacked around the country by means of a Queen Mary lorry. These lorries had been used extensively throughout the war for transporting aeroplanes. They were, in fact, half a lorry (well, there was rationing!) with towing tackle on the back and a forty or fifty foot trailer.

The ice rink itself had to be in place on the stage the day before it was required and filled with water. This was then frozen by a clever zigzag arrangement of cooling pipes. My father explained that they were without a driver for the six-week tour of Wales. So, with my newly acquired driving skill, I was literally going to have a baptism of fire, or rather, of ice, at any rate.

My 'holiday' actually involved manoeuvring this huge beast around the principality's precarious hairpin bends and up its steep mountain roads. After a week or two I had mastered this new skill and was thoroughly enjoying the experience. As an added bonus, I even managed to get a bit of a tan. Well, I did on my right elbow, which was sticking out of the open lorry window.

Some of the beautiful Welsh girls that I met on my travels were extremely impressed by my prowess behind the wheel.

I suppose it's 'ice' work if you can get it!

* * * * *

CHAPTER FOUR

When my brother Bill had come of age, he put his name down to join the RAF. He spent the war in Canada training to be a navigator. Bill said it was fantastic, because the Canadians were so pleased to see British troops that if you were in uniform they wouldn't let you pay for anything. When he came back he very kindly allowed me to pay for things!

In about 1944/45 my brother and I thought that we would put a show together and run it ourselves. We called the show 'Hi There!' and we toured it with Danny O'Dea, Peter Webster, Johnny Mac, Bill and myself. Not to mention, a bevy of female dancers and even a trio of girl singers. Bill and I did a double act and I don't think Morecambe and Wise would have had anything to worry about.

We bought an ex-army surplus Jeep, which we toured around in. Then, when we were playing at York's Theatre Royal, we met a caravan builder. He agreed to build us a caravan to our own specifications, as Bill and I were both over six-feet tall. Two months later we returned to York to collect our custom-built caravan. We hooked it up to the Jeep and set off. We were driving down a steep hill when I said to Bill, 'This is fantastic! I can't even feel the caravan on the back.'

Bill turned in his seat and I saw the colour drain from his face.

'That's because it isn't on the back,' he shouted. 'It's about to overtake us!'

A glance in my wing mirror confirmed Bill was right, so in the nick of time, I swerved the Jeep out into the path of the runaway and then I attempted to 'bump' the caravan to a halt with the Jeep.

It was a heart-stopping and highly dangerous manoeuvre worthy of James Bond himself. Luckily, the spare tyre positioned on the rear door of the Jeep acted as an ideal bumper, cushioning each impact until I finally managed to bring the Jeep and caravan to a standstill. All I can say is thank God that there wasn't a lot of traffic around in those days. Bill and I climbed out to inspect the damage, but our knees had turned to jelly and we could hardly stand up. There was a bit of a dent in the caravan, so, with a sigh of relief, we reconnected it the tow-bar and continued on our way … very, very slowly.

We eventually arrived at the caravan site in Hull hours later than planned, where we were shown to our plot. We were so exhausted that sleep was the only thing on our minds. I pulled my bed down, climbed in and went spark out like the proverbial light within minutes. When I woke up the following morning, feeling refreshed after a good night's sleep, I saw Bill lying on the floor.

'What are you doing down there, Bill?' I asked him sleepily.

'Playing tiddlywinks,' he answered crossly, rubbing a knot of cramp in his calf.

Apparently, the front of the caravan had been buckled by the impact and Bill's bed was jammed in the wall. He'd spent a cold and uncomfortable night with just a mac and a cushion for company, which meant that it was going to be back to the old routine of booking into digs for us.

The Douglas Brothers - Jack and Bill

The following morning at six we drove all the way back up to York and left the caravan for repairs. Then it was all the way back to Hull again. Oh, the glamorous showbiz life! We eventually got the caravan back and it was certainly very pleasant, with me at the stove and Bill doing the cleaning. What more could we have wanted? Well, I won't go into that side of things.

Suffice to say that we had a lot more freedom to entertain members of the opposite sex without a landlady breathing down our necks. Sometimes, we would park on farmland right out in the middle of nowhere and, invariably, the farmer's wife would take pity on us. We would be showered with milk (not literally), new-laid eggs, bacon, homemade bread and delicious pies.

When the war ended, Bill and I were invited to take 'Hi There' overseas for the Combined Services Entertainment's Unit, which was similar to ENSA only better. Our happy entourage went to Italy, Austria and Germany entertaining the troops and, when the tour finished, Bill and I stayed on to produce other shows. I remember that one of the shows we did was in the small village of Minden in Germany, which wasn't far from the notorious Belsen concentration camp.

My brother and I decided to pay this horrible place a visit and I can remember the guide saying: 'Can you hear the birds singing?'

We were a couple of miles away from the camp at that time, right in the middle of some beautiful woodland and the air was full of birdsong.

'Isn't that wonderful, Bill?' I said.

The guide assured us that when we entered Belsen we wouldn't hear a bird singing. I just thought that it was a fanciful guide's story, but he was right. The sense of evil hanging over that terrible place was just like a menacing black cloud and as soon as we entered the compound I could feel that awful choking sensation in my throat again. I had to get out of there.

* * * * *

While I was in Germany, a friend of mine called Major Newman took me to see this camp. It was a huge forbidding compound where the Germans had bred about one thousand German Shepherd dogs. Then, the Germans would dress themselves up in British uniforms and beat these dogs. This meant, of course, that as soon as the dogs saw someone wearing a British uniform they would rip them to shreds and so they were used to guard aerodromes and beaches. At the end of the war, no-one knew what to do with these poor, confused animals and Major Newman was put in charge of the compound.

I was instructed to keep away from the cages for obvious reasons, but the dogs allowed Major Newman to enter the compound and they would even wag their tails and make a fuss of him. The other guys thought that I was completely mad when I followed him in there, but like Major Newman I had no fear of animals. A large black-and-tan bitch bounded over to us with her head held low in a submissive kind of greeting. She had a huge ruff of fur round her neck and, despite resembling a moth-eaten wolf, merely licked the hand I offered her. She must have been the Alpha female, or 'top dog', because the rest of the pack seemed to take their cue from her and all these wagging tails soon surrounded us.

I felt momentarily elated and proud, but then I began to wonder what would become of these poor brainwashed creatures. As we were the only two men in the whole of the British army who could walk amongst the dogs without being ripped to pieces, their sorry fate seemed sealed. We humans have got a lot to answer for.

* * * * *

It was while I was in Germany that I met Joe Baker. I had to go to a meeting in Berlin, but at that time the Russians were very unruly and drunk and they were shooting up convoys, including ours. I asked for an armed officer and an escorting sergeant to take me through to Berlin and in the whole of the British army, who turned up but Lieutenant Roger Moore and Sergeant Joe Baker.

As soon as I set eyes on the dark-haired, rotund bundle of fun called Joe I knew we would be friends. We arrived at a checkpoint where we were greeted by a very drunken Russian sentry, who asked us for our papers. At least, I presumed that's what he was saying because I couldn't understand a word. He 'schnapped' his fingers impatiently, so I gave him the papers and he eyed them myopically … upside down! He began to babble at me in Russian, but I merely shrugged my shoulders in reply and it looked as if we were going to be in for a very long and perishing cold night.

My sergeant, who was also in our unit, suddenly tapped me on the shoulder. Sergeant George Truzzie was his name and he explained that he had an Italian mother and a Russian father … and, he spoke both languages fluently. I refrained from hugging and kissing him in gratitude, or that might have required further explanation. I handed the situation over to George and as soon as he spoke in Russian to the guard his face lit up and we were all invited into his sentry box. Many vodka's later, we wended our merry little way to Berlin.

Joe Baker and I got on like the proverbial house on fire and as we chatted in the back of the truck he told me that he was coming up for demob' the following January.

'If I can get you an early demob', would you like to be in a pantomime that I'm directing at the Kingston Empire?' I asked him.

'Sure thing.' said Joe.

Joe played Mate in Dick Whittington and when the Captain, who was Joe's counterpart, took ill on dress rehearsal, I was the only one who knew the part. So, Joe and I rehearsed like mad for a couple of hours and the show opened to capacity business the very next day. We went on to do our bit and after the show a very famous agent of the day, Hyman Zahl, came backstage.

'How long have you two been a double act?' he asked.

I glanced at my watch: 'About two hours and twenty minutes,' I told him.

'Right!' he said. 'I'm going to handle you two (don't get any funny ideas!) and you're going to have some wonderful work.'

And we did!

In the twelve years we worked together Joe and I did the whole of the Moss Empires theatre circuit. We started Crackerjack (CRACKERJACK!) with Eamonn Andrews and we did an innovative television series called 'New Look' with a young director called Brian Tesler, who later became managing director of London Weekend Television.

'New Look' was a very interesting show because of the versatility of all the artists. There was Bruce Forsyth, Roy Castle, Joyce and Lionel Blair, Stephanie Voss, Ronnie Stevens, Gillian Moran and the Vernon Girl Singers, the latter being a bit of a bonus to Joe and I at our age. It was a live, hour-long comedy show, so every change we did we had to do on set, generally crawling underneath the camera at the same time, but it was an excellent training ground. One minute I was playing a seventy-year old man and the next minute I was singing and dancing with Lionel's sister, Joyce. There was never any time for this 'Oh, I must get my motivation' lark that you see with some actors.

Bruce and I were paired off to do quite a lot of novelty pieces together. One sketch in particular was where we were two army officers playing tennis and I said to Bruce's character 'You're limping a bit, aren't you? Are you all right?'

He said 'Oh yes. I've had a bit of a nasty accident. I jumped over the net at the end of the game, but I misjudged it and landed on the net.'

I said 'Oh, Hampton Court?'

And Bruce said 'No, I just twisted my ankle.'

How we got away with a risqué joke like that on television during the Fifties, I'll never know.

Working with Bruce was a marvellous experience and convinced me what a fine talent he was and still is, of course. He's a wonderful dancer and such an elegant and well-dressed man.

I remember when Brian said that he'd got a sketch for Roy Castle and I to do, in which we had to play a couple of country bumpkins.

'I want you to have Cornish accents,' Brian said.

'But how do you do a Cornish accent, Jack?' Roy asked me in alarm.

'Right! I'll pick you up on the way to rehearsals tomorrow morning and from the moment you get in the car we'll speak in a Cornish accent,' I told him.

We did this for a whole week and when we did the show, Brian said to Roy 'I know that Jack's the character actor, but your accent was superb, too, Roy.'

As regards theatre work, Joe and I did two good spots for Moss Empires, so we were put on the circuit with visiting American stars, like Guy Mitchell. Then we were booked to do a three-month stint with Howard Keel and we arrived at our first date in Liverpool. In the morning, Joe Baker and I found our dressing room, unpacked our gear and then went off for some lunch. Afterwards, we spent a pleasant afternoon whiling away the hours at the local cinema.

Do stop me if I'm boring you!

Anyway, we arrived back at the theatre ready for the evening's performance and headed along the corridor to our dressing room chatting happily. Joe opened the door and stopped dead in his tracks.

'What is it, Joe?' I asked, just avoiding a collision with his back.

'I don't believe this!' he exclaimed. 'Oh, we must have got the wrong room,' he added, leaning back to check the names on the dressing room door.

'We've got the right room, Joe, but where's all our gear gone?'

The room was completely empty. Our entire band parts, our stage props, our suits, make-up, everything had disappeared.

'What the hell are we going to do?'

'Well, we can hardly go on-stage looking like two tramps,' I said, gazing down at my slacks and scruffy shirt.

'You look tidier than me,' said Joe pointing to a missing bottom button on his shirt, revealing a glimpse of his substantial stomach.

Just as we were about to report the 'theft' we heard a deep and familiar laugh coming from the corridor. What we didn't know was that Howard Keel was a great practical joker and while we'd been out, he had paid two of the stagehands to move all our stuff into another room.

'We've got to get him back,' said Joe after we'd finished laughing. 'What do you suggest, Jack?'

'I'll think of something, mate, don't you worry.'

It was about a week later when Joe and I got our own back on Howard. During his act he would perform a stirring rendition of a song from the musical, Porgy and Bess, in which the character he was portraying so movingly was a cripple. For more impact, he would actually go down on both knees while performing this particular song and it was always a big hit with the audience. I'd noticed that Howard would face the wings during the song and this gave me an idea. I secretly arranged for the stage manager to lock the door to the stage during this part of the show.

The next night Joe and I stood in the wings in our dressing gowns, waiting patiently for the orchestra to strike up with the introduction to 'Bess, You Is My Woman Now'. At the precise moment Howard went down on his knees, Joe and I disrobed and clasped hands. Howard raised his head slowly and was about to burst into song when he spotted the two of us standing there wearing only our socks and shoes and holding hands. Joe and I must have been a magnificent sight, because we stopped him in his tracks and it's a wonder he didn't 'keel' over. I was tall, lithe, handsome, slim … and modest with it! On the other hand, Joe resembled a cuddly, prototype Tellytubby. I'm sure that they were modelled on him, you know! Suffice to say that neither of us would have had a hope in hell of passing a successful audition for the stage musical, Hair.

Howard's shoulders began to shake uncontrollably and he hid his face in his hands. Being the great professional that he is, though, Howard turned his laughter into tears and got a standing ovation from the spellbound audience. They all thought that it was Howard's most moving performance ever, but then, they didn't know the naked truth, did they?

* * * * *

Joe and I also appeared in Liverpool with Guy Mitchell. Guy had been hoping to make his way back to London by train after the show, but, as it had been cancelled for some reason, Joe and I offered him a lift. We also said that he could stay at ours for the night, as he hadn't booked a hotel. The show over, we all jumped into the car and headed for London. It's a funny thing when you're in a double act, because you develop a kind of telepathy between you, so you don't ever have to voice what you're thinking. I'm sure it must have been the same for the late, great Morecambe and Wise during their long association.

Anyway, we were driving through a dreadful slum area, when I suddenly spotted this run-down house in a dirty old street. I glanced at Joe and he immediately twigged what I was thinking. I pulled up outside the house. The fence was falling down, the front garden was full of rotting rubbish and there was paint peeling off the front door. Its filthy curtains were hanging like rags in the grime-covered windows.

'Here we are!' I announced brightly. 'Home at last.'

Guy Mitchell's face when he looked at this house was an absolute picture, which was all too much for Joe and I and we burst our laughing. Please forgive the language, but Guy looked at the pair of us, joined in with our laughter and said: 'You bastards!'

* * * * *

It's a strange thing, but as soon as I put on the clothes I'm wearing for a part, I instantly change my personality to suit that costume. The late Dick Emery remarked to me once that no matter what costume he put on, he was still Dick Emery.

'You always manage to look different in each particular role, though, Jack,' he said. This 'gift' was put to the test when Joe and I were doing 'Crackerjack'

We went on and my first line to Joe was normally 'How dare you impersonate Alma Cogan?' On that occasion, however, it came out as 'Zow dare you imperzzonate Calma Hogan? Hic!'

Joe Baker walked down to the front of the stage and said to the audience: 'Ladies and Gentlemen! This is going to be very interesting, because the straight man's pissed!'

How I got through the act I'll never know, but when I came off the stage you could have wrung my clothes out, they were sopping wet. Even in my drunken haze Robb Wilton's advice of never having a drink before a show came back to haunt me. Needless to say, I never have since. I've gone cold just thinking about that episode now.

* * * * *

I celebrated a birthday while we were over in France. Well, I say 'celebrated', but it seemed to me that Joe had forgotten all about it and I began to feel more and more dejected as the day progressed. That night, we were just giving our curtain call at the end of the show when Joe suddenly brought the proceedings to a standstill.

'Gentlemen! Thank you for your rapturous applause, but, before we finish, I'd just like you to join in with me now and wish a very happy birthday to my dear friend and partner, Jack Douglas.

'He thought I'd forgotten, so he's been walking round all day looking like a bulldog who's swallowed a wasp, bless him.

'But I could never forget your birthday, old friend,' said Joe, giving me a hug.

I was quite overcome as the house lights went up and some service men appeared from the wings carrying a bottle of champagne and a tray of glasses. A hostess trolley bearing a huge birthday cake, which was wheeled on by the chef, closely followed these. I was choked and I have to admit that I nearly broke down in tears when the whole audience joined in with a hearty rendition of 'Happy Birthday to You'.

'Just come and have a look at the workmanship that's gone into icing this cake, Jack,' said Joe when they had finished singing. 'It's amazing, isn't it?'

'Yes, they've done a fantastic job,' I agreed. 'Thanks, guys.'

'Well, aren't you going to say a few words, mate?' asked Joe.

'Speech! Speech!' clamoured the audience.

I felt too emotional to say anything, but thought that I'd better make the effort after all the trouble everyone had gone to. 'Well, I really don't know what to say,' I began. 'I am completely … '

Before I could finish, Joe had picked up the cake, swung round towards me and, in the best pantomime tradition, splattered it right in my face. This perfectly crafted confection was actually made of shaving foam.

'Let's 'soap' he doesn't swallow any, folks,' said Joe and the auditorium rocked with laughter.

'Oh, you little tinker, you,' I said, after scooping all the froth away from my mouth and eyes. Well, I said something similar to that, anyway!

Joe Baker, Jack Douglas and Mr. Grumble mix their 'Cream puffs' with a KENWOOD FOOD MIXER.

I did get a proper cake later on and it was beautifully made and absolutely delicious. Plus, I had the added bonus of a face as soft as a baby's bum for several days afterwards.

* * * * *

One of the things that Joe and I did when we first started out together was a show at the Astor Club. It really wasn't our scene, but we thought we'd give it a go. The place was filled with people from the Motorshow and, by the time we appeared on stage at 11.45 pm they were all well over the limit, if you'll pardon the pun. When we walked out onto the stage the audience were making more noise than the pair of us could ever hope to generate. Afterwards, Joe and I came off the stage in silence and I turned to him and said: 'Well, I can't stand that racket for the rest of the week.'

'They were well and truly 'revved up',' agreed Joe with a sigh.

'Don't worry, Joe,' I said. 'I've got an idea.'

'Emigrate!'

'No,' I laughed. 'Tomorrow we will go and see our old friend, Major Baptie.'

'Major Baptie! Isn't he the guy who supplies firearms to the film industry?'

'The very same.'

'What the bloody hell are you intending to do, Jack?' asked Joe looking alarmed.

'Trust me,' I said with a sadistic grin.

The next night we walked out on stage and if anything, the noise from the audience was worse than it had been the night before.

I glanced at Joe and nodded 'Okay, partner. Let 'em have it.'

We pulled two .38 revolvers from our shoulder holsters and fired the blank cartridges into the air. Well, the reaction in this small nightclub was amazing and immediate. We didn't notice that a group of men had dived for cover underneath their table.

After the show, the head waiter came to us and said: 'Gentlemen, you have been invited to table five for a drink.'

If my memory serves me correctly, there were about twelve men seated around this table. We shook hands first with two of these smart-suited gentlemen, who were introduced to us as the Kray brothers. Apparently, when we fired the guns they had thought it was a raid by a rival gang.

Lucky for us, though, they saw the funny side and were the most incredible hosts … I've still got my kneecaps to prove it! It was about three in the morning by the time that we'd finished drinking the night away with the Kray brothers and their cronies.

'We've got to be in Shepherd's Bush by nine-thirty to film Crackerjack (CRACKERJACK!),' I said to Joe. 'Why don't we stay in town tonight?'

'There's hardly much point in going home,' he agreed.

We stayed at the Turkish Bath in Jermyn Street and when we walked in and asked for two single rooms, the porter told us that we would have to hand over all our valuables.

'Okay,' I said sleepily, giving him my watch and my wallet for 'safe' keeping, so to speak.

I was just about to remove my jacket when I remembered that we were both wearing the .38 revolvers and shoulder holsters. We'd had strict instructions from Major Baptie not to be parted from them under any circumstances, as the police would have classed them as real weapons. The expression on the porter's face when he clocked the guns was priceless. I bet he thought that we were either a couple of gangsters or members of some elite force, like the SAS. Everyone looked at us strangely at breakfast the next morning, so the word must have got round. We arrived refreshed and ready for our day's filming on Crackerjack (CRACKERJACK!).

'And we don't want any trouble from you,' we said to Eamonn Andrews, opening our jackets and showing him the guns.

I will never forget the look of horror on his face, bless him.

I suppose we started that particular episode off with a 'bang', although it's us who would have been 'fired' if the producer had found out about it.

* * * * *

I can remember another funny incident from the time when Joe and I were working at the Astor Club. We were using up a lot of our comedy material and needed more all the time, so I came up with the novel idea of giving money away to the audience. No, I hadn't won the pools and it certainly wasn't a bribe, but just a gimmick to get them all talking. We had these look-a-like white five-pound notes printed; that's how long ago it was. From a distance they looked exactly like the real thing, but where genuine notes have 'Bank of England' on them, our forgeries had the name and address of the Astor Club. Above our signatures it read: 'Joe Baker and Jack Douglas promise to pay the bearer on demand the sum of £5s worth of laughter', so they could never have been used by the unscrupulous as legal tender.

There was still quite a few left over when we'd finished our stint at the club and, as we were going straight off on a tour with Guy Mitchell, Joe stuffed them inside his suitcase. The train from Euston to Glasgow was packed and after we'd eaten our lunch in the Club Car, boredom quickly set in. As we stared at each other across the table, I noticed a twinkle in Joe's eye.

'Fancy a game of snap, Jack?' he asked, reaching for his suitcase.

Joe winked at me and then indicated with a downward sweep of his eyes that he was about to pass something to me underneath the table. He handed me about two hundred pounds worth of the fake fivers and I guessed immediately that he was intending to put on some sort of show for our fellow passengers. Joe shuffled the cards and our noisy game of snap soon attracted quite an audience, especially when they realised there was a lot of money at stake. The entire compartment was buzzing and even people passing through on their way to the toilet, stopped to watch what was going on. I was doing really well and the money was piling up on my side of the table. Then, in a last ditch effort to win, Joe gambled everything he had in front of him.

'Snap!' I shouted excitedly, leaning over to scoop the huge bundle of notes across the table towards me. Joe looked suitably mortified and the claps and cheers of the onlookers slowly subsided into obvious sympathy for his loss.

'You know your trouble, Jack?' said Joe, jumping to his feet. 'All you can think about is bloody money!'

With that, he reached up, opened the sliding window, picked all the money up and threw it out. I will never forget the sight of those fivers fluttering away down the track or the looks on the faces of the other passengers. Even though we weren't guilty of forgery, perhaps we should have been 'done' for littering. I must apologise for raising the hopes of those maintenance men who may have chased after, what looked like, white five-pound notes blowing tantalisingly along the railway tracks!

* * * * *

When Joe and I arrived at the Glasgow Empire we were thrilled to see that Peter Sellers was also appearing on the same bill. We were both great fans of the Goon Show and never missed an episode if we could help it. Peter was doing a very funny act dressed in a judo suit while being 'interviewed' by one of our great character actors, David Lodge. The Glasgow Empire has always been notorious for its hard-to-please audiences, as Joe and I discovered when we walked out on stage for the first house on Monday night. I thought they must have forgotten to open the doors to let the audience in, because our tried and tested comedy routine raised not so much as a titter.

If we'd imagined that good old Peter would have them rolling in the aisles, we were wrong. His act was greeted by the same stony silence and when he went back out on stage for an encore, nobody even clapped. We were all sitting in our dressing rooms feeling despondent when the show's host introduced the next act.

'Ladies and gentlemen!' said the crackly voice on the speaker. 'Please give a warm Glaswegian welcome (at that, Joe and I looked at each other and laughed!) to … Guy Mitchell.'

These words were followed by a burst of applause like we'd never heard in our lives.

Joe and I watched from the wings in amazement as Guy completely electrified this seemingly unresponsive audience.

'They obviously prefer singing to comedy,' whispered Joe.

'No, that's not the reason,' I whispered back. 'It's because they don't like English comedians.'

'Great!' said Joe in an exasperated tone. 'We may as well leave Guy to do the whole show himself and head off home, then.'

'No, wait Joe. I've had an idea.'

Joe and I went on in the second half and did our entire act in an American drawl. Would you believe it? We got laughs. We got applause. We even got an encore. We kept up the pretence for the rest of the run and at the end of a very trying seven days the last show went quite well for us.

Poor Peter, on the other hand, had died a death every night and when he went back on stage for his final encore, he decided to get his own back. First off, he pretended to pull the pins out of hand grenades and lobbed them into the audience. Then, he finished up by spraying them all with imaginary bullets from a machine gun.

Relieved that our stint at the Glasgow Empire had at last come to an end, we all scrambled into a taxi and sped off to the railway station. Once safely on-board the overnight sleeper, Peter invited us to his compartment to share a well-earned nightcap with him. Out came a bottle of Chivas Regal, one of the most beautiful whiskies in the world. After drowning our sorrows and putting the world to rights till four in the morning, we arrived in London (bleary-eyed, but in high spirits) at seven.

* * * * *

Joe Baker and Jack in Crackerjack 1955

Joe, Jack and Jimmy Wheeler in pantomime

CHAPTER FIVE

It had been during a well earned few days off in the spring of 1947 that I happened to be at a loose end one evening. I decided that I hadn't visited my local haunt for some time, so I put on my best bib and tucker and headed down to the Stork Club in Streatham. It was known as the Stork Club, because by the end of the evening you'd run up a huge 'bill'! Only joking. The club had a pleasant atmosphere, subdued lighting and an exclusive bar/restaurant with a dance floor and resident pianist.

I walked into the bar (no jokes, please) and after a few pleasantries with the manager, sat on a bar stool and ordered my favourite tipple. I was just about to take a sip of my Martini, when I saw a beautiful redhead reflected in the mirror behind the bar. I turned to get a better look, as you do, and noticed that she was dining with an older man and woman.

'Henry!' I said, catching the manager's eye. 'Who's the young lady sitting over there with that couple?'

'That's Frank and Bobbie Williams and their daughter, Rita,' he said.

'Would you like me to introduce you?' he asked politely.

'Would I? I mean, yes, I would. Thank you.'

With the introductions over, Frank asked me if I would like to join them at their table. The conversation flowed like the wine all evening, especially after Frank told me that he'd been a theatre manager for a while and he actually knew my father. At the time of our meeting, he was Circuit Controller for the J. Arthur Rank Organisation.

'My daughter's a dancer, aren't you, darling?' he said, turning to the lovely Rita.

'Really?'

'Yes, I'm currently appearing at the Whitehall Theatre in the Phyllis Dixie Show,' she said, glancing up from her meal.

I nearly dropped my glass at the sight of Rita's large green eyes sparkling in the candlelight as they looked into mine. Wow! I was well and truly smitten by this kitten! (Sorry about that, but all this talk of storks has made me hot under the collar!)

I was twenty years old and although there had been plenty of girls around to stamp my ration book, as it were, this was my first experience of a really earth shattering attraction to someone. To my delight, Bobbie and Frank got up to dance, leaving the two of us on our own to chat. After a while, I asked Rita if she would like to dance and as she stood up I could see that Rita's figure was just as beautiful as her face. She was a lovely dancer and, thanks to Mum's tuition, I wasn't bad either.

At the end of the evening, I offered them all a lift home and when we pulled up outside their house, Frank and Bobbie said goodnight and discreetly went indoors.

'Rita, I was wondering … ' I said, as she went to follow them.

'Yes,' she answered and I couldn't help noticing that her eyes looked even more magical by the light of the street lamp.

'Well, it must be difficult for you to date when you're working six nights a week.'

'It is, yes.'

'I was wondering if you'd mind if I came to the show tomorrow night and then perhaps we could have a meal together afterwards.'

'That would be lovely, Jack.'

'*Yippee*!' I thought to myself, but, not wanting to appear too eager, just said politely. 'Till tomorrow night, then.'

When Rita finished her season at the Whitehall Theatre later in 1947 I was lucky enough to get her into my father's production of 'It's All Blarney', which went on tour around England. I was in the show doing a double act with Bill. Rita was a quiet girl, not at all like the others I'd been out with. I knew that she was such a good catch that I'd better reel her in before some other dashing young 'angler' beat me to it. I had to choose the right moment to cast my net and ensnare her heart forever … or end up looking like a wet kipper, one of the two. We had been dating for just a few short weeks when I finally plucked up the courage to ask Rita for her hand in marriage. I mean, I wanted to marry the rest of her body as well, but her hand seemed as good a place to start as any.

'Um,' I began. Erudite is my middle name, you know. Shall I hang on for a minute while you go and look it up in the dictionary?

'R … Rita,' I stammered.

'Yes, Jack darling,'

'Um, Rita,'

'Yes, Jack?' Rita's green eyes were looking at me questioningly.

'Will you, um? I was just wondering whether you would … um, do me the honour of marrying me, please?'

'Yes.'

'I realise that we haven't known each other for long and I'd understand if you wanted to wait a little … what did you say?'

'I said yes, Jack. I'd love to marry you.'

I was ecstatic, but the only person I told was my brother Bill. Funnily enough, his wife's name was Rita, too.

I was afraid that people might think that we were too young and I didn't want any misgivings our parents may have about the match to put her off. The following week we left for Hamburg, where we began our tour around Germany and Italy for the CSEU of 'It's All Blarney'. I clearly remember (which is unusual for me) going into the jewellers shop and swapping my rations – four hundred cigarettes, two bottles of whisky and two bars of soap – for an engagement ring. It's a good job we weren't in the desert, or it might have been four hundred camels, a couple of water bottles and two shakes, sorry, I mean two sheikhs. When Rita and I arrived back in England, both sets of parents were delighted with the news of our engagement and, not the least bit surprised, I have to say.

* * * * *

After a long season, Rita and I went away for a well-earned holiday. On our return I found a lovely flat at 64, The Woodlands, Beulah Hill, London, which was just round the corner from my old school. I was too much of a gentleman to ask Rita to cohabit (I would have got a resounding clout around the ear from our fathers', more like!) I was soon busy decorating and buying bits of furniture to make a home for us.

During the winter of 1948/49 I was directing the pantomime Dick Whittington at the Kingston Empire for my father. All this was the start of a new phase in my life. Not only had I started up a 'double act' in my private life with Rita, but I'd also met Joe.

At the end of the panto' season Rita I began to make our wedding plans. We were married in the spring of 1949 at St Bede's Church in Streatham and guess where we held our reception? The Stork Club! Unfortunately, when Rita and I came out of the church to pose for our wedding photographs, we discovered to our horror that the wedding photographer had gone AWOL. (Absent Without Letting us have any bloody photos of our big day!) After waiting for fifteen minutes and deciding that he obviously wasn't going to show, a disappointed bride and her disgruntled groom, not forgetting our hundred or so guests, walked over to the Stork Club nearby.

Many glasses of champagne later, the manager of the club came to me and said that there was a man outside asking to see me. I thought for a minute that I'd forgotten to pay the priest.

'Sorry, gov'nor, me car broke down,' explained the red-faced photographer.

'Tell you what! If you and your lovely wife and guests will follow me back over to the church, I'll take the photos now.'

I went back into the reception, taking a deep breath, plus a large slurp of champagne, before making the announcement.

Jack and Rita

'Ladies and Gentlemen! Could I have your attention, please?' I said, tapping the side of my glass with a pen.

A hundred or so faces turned towards me in bleary-eyed anticipation.

'I'm happy to inform you that the photographer has now arrived.'

A loud cheer rocked the room and I put my hands up to silence the by now rather merry guests.

'Would anyone mind if we all went back across to the church to do the pictures?'

All one hundred of them obliged without a fuss and the outcome was some of the happiest and most comical wedding photographs I've ever seen in my life. Talk about 'Say cheeeezzz'!

* * * * *

The summer of 1949 turned out to be a particularly slack time, as far as shows were concerned, and I was sitting in Dad's office twiddling my thumbs.

'Nothin' happening, Jack?' inquired one of Dad's friends, Peter Webster.

'Not really,' I told him with a sigh.

'Oh yes there is,' he said. 'How would you like to do a sixteen-week stint at the open-air theatre at Jaywick Sands, near Clacton?'

'I thought that was your patch, Peter.'

'It usually is, but I'm doing a summer season in Blackpool this year. How does Uncle Jack of Jaywick sound to you?'

'It sounds great.'

Peter took me along to the Odeon on Saturday mornings, where there were always children's shows and films and he taught me how to entertain the kids. I became 'Uncle Jack' on the cinema circuit for two months and I remember that I was paid £3 3s 0d for the Saturday shows and by the end of that time I was ready for Jaywick.

'This is lovely, Jack,' said Rita, when we arrived in Jaywick to find this delightful open-air, one-hundred seat theatre facing the sea, complete with a small stage and 'resident' pianist.

'Sorry, I mean Uncle Jack,' she added with a laugh.

Rita was in charge of the cash desk, but because we would get about a hundred people standing around watching the show from outside the area when we were packed, Rita would go round with the bottling box. This was a box with a handle that she would rattle and people would put their spare coins in as a thank you for the entertainment.

'Right! I need six children to come up onto the stage,' I would say.

These children had to perform a play, a knobbly knees contest and a talent competition, amongst other things. The winner was awarded with a prize at the end of the show and automatically qualified for the finals on Friday. It was quite an undertaking, as there were two shows a day, six days a week and I was whacked by the end of September. However, all the ad-lib certainly kept me on my toes and it was great fun and very satisfying.

I remember on one occasion when an innocent-looking little blonde boy of about six came up from the audience. He played the lead in our horror play and he was fabulous in the role. His last line was meant to be: 'I must leave this house of blood,' so, he stuck his thumbs under the lapels of his jacket and pulled himself up to his full height, all of four feet nothing, to deliver this dramatic line.

'I must get out of this bloody house!' he said authoritatively and everyone, including me, fell about laughing. Out of the mouths of babes, as they say.

I ended up playing 'Uncle Jack of Jaywick' for three summers and I felt wonderfully fit working out in the open all the time. Rita and I were as brown as a couple of berries by the end of each season.

Some twenty or so years later, I was about to go in the stage door at the Royal Variety Performance when a woman approached me.

'It's Uncle Jack,' she said.

'I'm sorry?' I answered, not recognising her. 'Forgive me, but are we related?'

'No,' she laughed. 'I don't mean that sort of uncle.'

'You were Uncle Jack of Jaywick and I was one of the children who came up onto the stage and won a prize. Can I introduce you to my son and daughter?'

As I shook the hands of these tall teenagers, I felt about a hundred years old.

* * * * *

Come October, Joe and I were busy working on our new double act and Hyman Zahl was true to his word, because the work started rolling in. The Christmas of 1949/50 found Joe and I playing the robbers in 'Dick Whittington' at the Chiswick Empire. Married life was great and everything was going swimmingly.

Although Rita hadn't danced since we'd come back from Germany, she worked as a photographic model in London and got plenty of work during the day. Often, she would accompany Joe and I to our various venues at night and, lucky for me, Rita and Joe got on so well we were all as happy as can be in each other's companies.

During the summer of 1950 Joe and I did (I think) a whole season at Butlin's in Clacton. Rita and I locked up the flat in Beulah Hill and headed for the dizzy heights of Clacton, where we rented a house. Rita obviously enjoyed married life and I think I can honestly say that she didn't just put her career on hold, but was actually happy to give it all up. A good job, really, considering that in December 1951 came the wonderful news that we were expecting our first child.

Craig was born on the 24th August 1952 and he was healthy and bonny and all we could have wished for. He ate and slept and rarely cried (he obviously took after his father!) and Rita and I thoroughly enjoyed every minute of parenthood. Rita was the perfect mother and brought Craig along to wherever I was appearing in summer shows and pantomimes.

Our daughter Debbie arrived on the 24th June 1955 and Craig adored his new baby sister. As they grew up, Debbie looked upon Craig as her knight in shining armour.

By now the flat at Beulah Hill was getting a bit cramped, so we sold it and bought a place in Worcester Park with plenty of garden for the children to play in. After Craig started at the local school, Rita and the children could only join me during the school holidays, which meant that Rita had to spend more and more time alone with them.

Sadly, this was when the cracks began to show in what had seemed up till then to be the perfect marriage.

* * * * *

Rita with Craig and Debbie

Our agent at the time, Richard Stone, summoned Joe and I to his office one day to say that he wanted us to do a summer season for him at Butlin's Holiday Camp.

'As it is, you do about three or four changes of programme,' said Richard. 'So it would be perfect for you both to do some comedy sketches, too.'

'Perhaps Joe can try a few production numbers as well, Richard,' I said. 'He has a beautiful singing voice, you know.'

'Good idea,' agreed Richard.

The first one we did was the one in Clacton, which was a great success. The only thing I didn't like very much was going into the dining hall with about a thousand other people.

You may think that this sounds a bit pompous, but when you've been entertaining crowds of people every day, you relish a bit of peace and quiet, especially at mealtimes. Well, how would you fancy having an autograph book thrust in your face when you're about to tuck into a fried breakfast?

'Sorry to interrupt your meal, but it's not for me,' said one man. 'It's for me ninety-three-year old grandmother who's a great fan of yours.'

After listening to a graphic description about the time 'Granny' lost her teeth down the toilet when she was sick from drinking too many sherries at cousin Freda's wedding, my breakfast was stone cold … and strangely unappetising. I poked at my now rubbery sunny-side up egg and pushed a stiff rasher of dried-up bacon aimlessly round in a pool of grease.

'Help!' shouted a partially submerged button mushroom. 'I can't swim!'

I was just about to throw him a fried-bread life raft, when Joe interrupted my reverie.

'Don't you want your breakfast, Jack?' he asked, patting his stomach.

'No, I'm not hungry.'

'Here, give it to me,' said Joe. 'You can't waste it.'

He ate the lot, including my floundering fungal friend. I shouldn't make fun of the food at Butlin's, because they did their best to feed all those hungry holiday makers, it just didn't appeal to my palate, I suppose. I remedied this by treating myself to a little two-ringed hot plate, a steamer and a frying pan.

'What have you been up to?' inquired Joe one morning, gazing suspiciously round the door of the chalet in the direction of the bed.

'I haven't been up to anything,' I said defensively, following his gaze. 'What do you mean?'

'Why didn't you come to breakfast this morning?'

'You won't find any clandestine 'dishes' in here,' I told him. 'Apart from the ones I knocked up on my new toy over there,' I added, pointing to the hot plate.

'You crafty old devil, Douglas,' he said (or words to that effect). 'What's for lunch? I'm famished.'

Needless to say that after that we both ate in my chalet and occasionally, just for appearance sake, we would go and eat in the dining room.

'I fancy something a bit more exotic for lunch,' mentioned Joe, as we were relaxing on a pair of deck chairs outside my chalet one morning. 'I suppose it would be impossible on that small hot-plate, though.'

'Hmm,' I said thoughtfully, taking a few puffs on my pipe. 'Alimentary, my dear Baker. What about chicken in plum sauce?'

'You can cook **that**?' said Joe, his eyes lighting up.

'Course.'

I went across to the little camp shop (the shop wasn't effeminate, it was just in the camp), but no luck. So I went into Clacton and bought some chicken pieces, a jar of plum jam and some rice. I melted the plum jam, painted it on the chicken pieces, placed them in a frying pan with the lid on the top, then put the rice into the steamer. We were just standing outside the door, licking our lips at the delicious smell, when, much to our horror, Billy Butlin and his entourage came walking along the chalet lines. He was accompanied by his first in command, Basil Brown, and next to him was Wally Goodman, who was the Entertainment Manager, and another influential member of the Butlin organisation.

'Good morning, gentlemen,' said Billy Butlin, as the formidable trio drew alongside us.

'Good morning, Mr Butlin,' replied Joe and I in unison, each of us standing to attention as if he were a commanding officer.

'Lovely day,' I added, pulling the door of the chalet shut behind me as innocently as I could.

'You two go on and I'll join you later,' he told his companions and they gave us a cursory nod as they walked away.

'All right, gents,' he said as soon as they were out of earshot. 'What's been going on here?'

'No … nothing,' said Joe, but the telltale aroma of the meal was wafting through the open fanlight of the chalet window, which was now running with condensation.

'I can think of only two reasons why a chalet window would steam up like that,' said Billy. 'And I don't see any women around.'

'Perhaps it's rising damp,' ventured Joe, but our inquisitor seemed unimpressed by his limp excuse.

'Um, we've been doing a bit of cooking,' I admitted guiltily, sensing that we were probably in for a grilling.

'You know that cooking in the chalets is forbidden, don't you?' he said.

'Yes, Mr Butlin. I'm sorry, it won't happen … '

'It smells delicious. What is it?'

'Chicken in plum sauce with rice, sir,' I said.

'Mmm,' he said, sniffing the air. 'Is there enough for three?'

'Yes, Mr Lutbin, Mr Butlin.'

He joined us in the chalet and the three of us sat down on the bed and ate heartily.

'Thanks for the meal,' he said as he left. 'I may be back tomorrow.'

'That's what makes him such a famous man,' I said, as I rinsed the (borrowed) plates and cutlery in the tiny sink.

'Why? Because he eats other peoples food and then doesn't stay behind to help with the washing up?'

'No! Just that, he's so down-to-earth and approachable, Joe. I've heard he drives a Rolls Royce, you know.'

'Oh, that's down-to-earth all right.'

'Ah, but, when he comes to Clacton, the Rolls disappears into the garage nearby and out pops a Ford Prefect.'

'That's not very clever magic, is it? If it were me I'd make it work the other way around … Ford Prefect, Abracadabra, Roller!'

I refrained from throwing the dishwater all over him and tried to explain.

'Listen, Joe. It's quite good psychology, actually,' I said, handing him a tea towel.

'Butlin realises that if the campers see him arriving here in a Rolls Royce, they will think that their hard-earned money goes on keeping him and his flashy motor.'

'Really?' said Joe thoughtfully. 'If I threaten to broadcast it over the tannoy to the campers, do you think he'll put our wages up?'

* * * * *

A question I'm asked frequently is when my Alf character first appeared. He was 'born', if you like, at Butlin's during my partnership with Joe and you've heard the saying about necessity being the mother of invention, well, that certainly applies to this story. We were doing five spots in the show. At times like those, new material is hard to come by, because there are lots of writers for television and film scripts but not so many for the stage. When I was with my father, there was always a wealth of material to draw on. I was thinking the acts through, when I suddenly remembered one that Albert Burdon used to do with Jimmy Clitheroe.

'I'll be the old magician, Joe, and you can be the naughty schoolboy who comes up from the audience and messes up my tricks.

'I think you'll look really funny dressed up as a little boy with this lot hanging over your trousers,' I said, patting Joe's substantial tummy.

'Yeah, should get some belly laughs,' he quipped in response.

The act worked well, until one particular night …

'Would anyone like to come up and help me with my next trick?' I asked.

Normally, Joe would appear from the back of the auditorium and join me on stage. Not on this occasion, though.

'Would anyone like to join me on-stage,' I asked again in a louder voice, in case Joe hadn't heard his cue.

Nothing!

Apparently, the Redcoats had locked the doors because the theatre was full, so Joe couldn't make his usual entrance.

Suddenly I noticed a couple of musicians from Eric Winston's Band were taking a break from the ballroom next door and were in the auditorium. The only reason I spotted them was because their red coats were brighter than the Redcoats red coats, if you see what I mean. They always used to pop in during one of their breaks to watch Joe and I. They knew that Joe was a great ad-libber and that the act always turned into a bit of fun. Anyway, there's me wondering what to do, when I notice these musicians and I remembered that their band leader, Eric Winston, had a bit of a twitch.

'I'm going to show you a little trick,' I said, picking up my tray of magic goodies.

Needless to say, I did a twitch and all the stuff on the tray went everywhere.

The two band boys fell on the floor laughing, because they realised I was taking off their governor, all I was doing was exaggerating it a bit. More importantly, it got a huge laugh from the audience. Ignoring the fact I'd done this twitch, I picked all the stuff up and twitched again, which got an even bigger laugh.

By this time, Joe had kicked the door in (bless 'im) and was running down the aisle from the back of the auditorium as fast as his little legs would carry him. He couldn't believe his ears when he heard the straight man was getting huge laughs. Joe finally joined me on the stage, reacted to the next twitch by doing a well-timed duck and from that day on, we kept 'Alf', as he became known, in the act.

More of Alf, later.

* * * * *

CHAPTER SIX

Joe and I were appearing in variety at the Queens Theatre in Blackpool. Trains weren't very good in those times (what do I mean, in **those** times?) and were pretty expensive (no change there, either!), so we decided to visit the car auctions. I spotted an American Packard, which was rather like a Mafia car.

'This'll suit our needs, Joe.'

'You can't be serious,' he replied, peering inside and pointing to the windup chauffeur's window.

Up came Lot 5, or whatever it was, and the auctioneer said 'Right! Who would like to start the bidding?'

I glanced around the room, but all the other punters just sat there, silent and unresponsive.

'Forty pounds!' I shouted.

Joe fell about laughing, but nobody was interested in buying it, probably because it was heavy on petrol, so my ludicrously low bid remained unchallenged.

'Going, going … gone!' said the auctioneer finally and down went his gavel. 'Sold to the gentleman on my right for forty pounds.'

I knew enough about cars to be able to service one and I almost took that car to pieces and rebuilt it. It ran like a dream, but, of course, Joe Baker was terrible with his practical jokes.

He would say, 'Excuse me, but I don't want the chauffeur to hear what we are saying,' and he would wind up the window between the front and the back of the car.

We had that car for many years and Joe couldn't drive, which meant that I drove everywhere. I didn't mind, though. I eventually taught Joe to drive and he bought his own car, so I sold the Packard for £280, which wasn't bad after all those years.

* * * * *

Early in 1960, Joe and I were summoned to the office of our then agent, Leslie Grade. We'd just finished in the pantomime Robinson Crusoe at Finsbury Park and, as we took our seats in Leslie's London office, we wondered why we were being honoured in this way.

'Right, gentlemen!' he said and I couldn't help noticing that he was looking rather pleased with himself. 'You're about to do a three-month tour of Australia.'

Our mouths dropped open in astonishment and neither of us could speak for a moment.

'But we've only just started making a name for ourselves in Britain,' I said, as my composure returned.

'If we go to Australia now, isn't there a danger that we'll disappear from the scene over here?' added Joe.

'No,' said Leslie. 'Anyway, it's all been organised.'

The star of the tour was David Whitfield, who was very 'hot' at that time, especially in Australia. It was, of course, a wonderful opportunity for us, but I couldn't help worrying that all our hard work at building a name for ourselves would be forgotten. Anyway, I had a cunning plan (like Baldric) and I explained to Leslie that Joe and I hadn't had a holiday for three years.

'If we fly to Australia for this three-month tour, we'll be knack ... extremely tired,' I told him.

'If we were to consider this wonderful offer of yours, then I think it would be better if we go by ship and this will enable us to have a good long rest before the start of the tour.'

This may sound as if I was trying it on a bit, but I was honestly expecting him to say that they wouldn't be able to afford to send us both by ship. I was wrong, however, because he thought that it was a wonderful idea.

'Oh, there's another problem,' I countered. 'Joe and I never share a room on tour because I snore and keep him awake.'

I didn't dare glance across at Joe in case he set me off giggling.

'No problem,' said Leslie. 'I'll book you two single first class cabins.'

He just agreed with everything I said and there was no way out of it.

So, when Joe and I boarded the Orion at Southampton on the 2nd of February 1960, we knew that we had a wonderful holiday ahead of us, with Sydney as our last port of call.

* * * * *

From the moment I stepped on board the Orion, her appearance had fascinated me. By the time we'd docked in Gibraltar, I'd done a bit of research into her history. She had been built for the Orient Line and launched at Barrow-in-Furness shipyard in the early 1930s, when apparently it was unusual for large liners to have just a single funnel and only one mast. Used as a troop carrier throughout the war, the Orion had then been extensively refurbished. In the late fifties and early sixties she ferried emigrants to Australia and I've since found out that she finally ended up at the breakers' yard in Antwerp in the autumn of 1963.

From Gibraltar, our voyage continued on to Naples and I was sitting up on deck one morning sipping a dry Martini and gazing out over the azure Mediterranean when one of the crewmen dashed up to me.

'The Captain wishes to speak to you right away, sir,' he said.

After he'd tapped on the door, I followed him to the Captain's cabin.

'Don't tell me! Our agent's forgotten to pay for our passage and you want us to walk the plank!'

'No, nothing like that,' he said sombrely, politely ushering me to seat. 'I'm very sorry to have to tell you this, but I've received some very bad news from home,' he said, placing a hand on my shoulder.

'Are the kids all right?'

'Yes, yes, but I'm afraid that your father has died.'

It was just like being hit in the face with a brick and I can remember saying, 'Oh, my God! What am I going to do?'

'Now, I don't want you to worry,' he said kindly. 'I've spoken to the ship's company and we've arranged for you to be flown home from Florence once the ship docks in Naples tomorrow. The day after the funeral, if you feel up to it, of course, there will be just time for you to fly back to Florence and rejoin the ship.'

God bless the man for his thoughtfulness and compassion, because that's exactly what happened. At no expense to me, I hasten to add. My brother met me at Heathrow on a cold February morning and took me to his home in Hampstead, from where we attended Dad's funeral. Much of that day remains a blank, but I can remember standing in the crematorium saying farewell to my father and thinking that my mother should have been there. Dear Mum couldn't attend due to her own ill health.

I flew back to Florence, as had been arranged, but my father's death naturally cast a shadow over my long-awaited 'holiday' to Australia and I spent many days sitting on my own, reflecting. Whether the Captain realised that I needed snapping out of my melancholy state, I don't know, but one particularly sad day he summoned me to his office again.

'Don't worry, there's nothing wrong,' he assured me. 'I was just wondering, and I hope you don't think that it's an awful cheek, but would you and Joe like to put on a show for the passengers.

'Yes, of course,' I said, happy for the diversion. 'Just as long as we can also do one for the crew.'

At first he said that it wouldn't be necessary, but finally agreed. So, we entertained the crew as well, albeit with a somewhat broader show and after that they treated us like royalty. They were the best audience we'd ever had.

A few days later, the ship docked in Port Said, then it was on to Aden, and then Colombo and we finally arrived in Fremantle near Perth on the 29th of February. Our tour of Australia was continuing to Adelaide, Melbourne and Sydney. A couple of nights into the tour we were told by the manager of the theatre that our act had been such a success, that we were being made top of the bill. David Whitfield was furious, but there was nothing Joe and I could do and it was all rather embarrassing. The tour continued and Joe and I even appeared in some television shows for Channel Seven. At least, I think that's what it was called in those days.

* * * * *

One day, I received a phone call from Rita.

'Hello, love,' I said. 'How are the kids? What's the weather like in chilly old Britain? It's about ninety degrees … '

'Jack!' she cut in impatiently.

'What is it? Everyone's all right, aren't they?'

'It's Gordon. He's been in a terrible car crash.'

(Gordon was a mutual friend of ours.)

'Oh, my God. Is he going to be okay?'

'It's been touch and go, but he's off the danger list.'

'Thank God for that.' I said with a relieved sigh.

'It's just that, he's got no family and he needs somewhere to recuperate. I was wondering if it would be all right if … '

'Yes, yes, invite him round to ours till he's better. Your cooking will soon put him right.'

* * * * *

After Rita's call, the homesickness I'd been desperately trying to suppress came bubbling up to the surface with a vengeance. It may sound strange, but despite performing in front of huge audiences every night, I was feeling lonely and depressed. Whereas Joe had the amazing gift of being able to party anytime, anyplace, anywhere, as they say, I was a real homebody. Joe was the life and soul of many a gathering. A hugely comical man, who never seemed to mind being away from home.

Losing Dad hadn't helped and I used to dwell on all manner of negative thoughts when I was alone in bed at night. Give him his due, Joe would always try and include me in his social life, but I wasn't interested.

This all changed, however, when I met Matilda. That wasn't her real name, but I shall use it here to protect the guilty.

Matilda was a member of the dance troupe who were touring with the show and the sight of this tall, raven-haired beauty was enough to make any man's 'billy boil', I can tell you. She had legs right up to her bu … sorry, I mean very long legs and luxurious hair hanging down her back. Not that a married man like me noticed that sort of thing, of course. To be perfectly honest, I didn't think I would ever stand a hope in hell and just went back to reading my paper.

Matilda and I became good friends, however, and as the tour progressed we spent more and more of our spare time in each other's company. Any man reading this will understand how a weak male of the species like me could have fallen for such a beautiful woman. All I can say in my defence is that I didn't intend to get involved. Stop jeering, lady readers!

All right, cards on the table, then. We were both to blame and I'm ashamed to admit that me and the lovely Matilda finally got it together and went 'waltzing' on more than one occasion. Matilda was under no illusions, however, and she knew that I was a married man with a family back at home in England. Nevertheless, we had a very emotional parting at the last night party in Sydney.

'It's been fabulous, Jack,' said Matilda, her brown eyes swimming with tears. 'I'll never forget you.'

'I'll never forget you, either,' I said, kissing her tears away and then hugging her close for the last time.

Eat your heart out Mills and Boon!

It had been a wonderful few months, but I made a pact with myself that I would never again accept such a long engagement away from home.

'Nor will I get entangled with anymore extra-marital ladies,' I thought to myself.

The pangs of guilt had begun pricking at my conscience like needles as soon I'd said goodbye to Matilda.

The tour had been a huge success for all concerned and four days later Joe and I boarded the ship. We were homeward bound at last. After going to my cabin to unpack, I shaved and changed. I then headed to the cocktail bar and ordered a Martini. From there, I made my way to the dining room.

'Table 26, please,' I said to the head steward.

'This way, please, sir,' he said.

As we approached the table I was shocked to see a familiar woman sitting there waiting for me.

'Hello again, Jack,' said Matilda, standing up and taking hold of my hand.

'What are you doing here?' I said in amazement.

'Sit down and I'll explain,' she said, leaning forward and planting a kiss on my lips. 'And don't look so horrified, or I'll think that you don't want me here.'

'How … ? Why … ? What … ?' I spluttered.

'I've made a big decision, Jack,' Matilda told me, still clasping my hand. 'I don't want to work in Australia anymore.'

'Oh, I see,' I answered, as thoughts of how I was going to explain all this to Rita began flashing through my mind.

'I'm so excited, Jack. This is a whole new life for me,' she said, gripping my hand ever tighter.

The thought that this beautiful woman had sold her house and given up her life in Australia for me was blowing my mind, but I knew that I'd better play devil's advocate.

'Listen, Matilda, I'm a married man.'

'Oh, don't get the wrong idea. I'm chasing my career, not you.'

My male ego at once took a nosedive.

'I've got an audition at the Talk of the Town in the West End.'

'How wonderful.'

'Just think, though,' she said. 'We've got another month together before we arrive back in England.'

Cruise ships, by their very nature, are designed and organised to offer social recreation, fun and enjoyment for the passengers. Well, I could hardly ignore her, could I? I'm ashamed to say that I was tempted all over again and despite my promises about no more dalliances in that direction, we carried on with our affair for the duration of the cruise. Thankfully, Matilda was nowhere to be seen when I walked down the gangplank to meet Rita and the children.

(I found out subsequently that Matilda found herself a flat in London. I did socialise with her a couple of times and then she headed off for the bright lights of gay Paris, where she eventually married a Frenchman).

As we docked I could see Craig and Debbie waving frantically on the quayside. After receiving some frenzied hugs and kisses from them both, I was quite surprised to be given a mere peck on the cheek by Rita. I was suspicious even then, but assumed that she may have been feeling a little peeved at having to stay home in England for so long. Well, I had been away for several months!

We got home and after the children had opened their presents and gone up to bed I said, 'All right, what's the matter?'

At first Rita pretended that she didn't know what I meant, but she eventually admitted that while I'd been away she and Gordon had become really close. In a nutshell, they had fallen in love and had been having an affair.

Now, I can't say anything against Rita, she was a lovely person and still is, but I'd offered Gordon the hand of friendship and had trusted him in my home when I was away. If he'd found himself falling in love with my wife, he should have packed his bags and moved out, not moved in on her. I can never forgive him for that.

After my admission about Matilda, I'm sure all the ladies reading this will have some sympathy for Rita. Rita and I had got married and had two wonderful children together, but she hated this showbiz thing of going away, which is quite understandable.

'I can't take anymore of this, you're going to have to get a proper job,' she had said to me once. 'What about driving a bus?'

She was deadly serious, but what could I do? Show business is in my blood, as I said before, and it's all I know. I can remember the painful business of sitting the children down and explaining everything to them, because I didn't want them taking sides. How do you tell two young children that their parents are splitting up? I'm getting a huge lump in my throat just thinking about their sad little faces.

* * * * *

I didn't even bother to unpack my cases and checked into a local hotel until I could decide what to do next. Feeling disorientated and depressed, I popped in to see my friend at his office.

'What ever is the matter? You look dreadful, mate,' Jack Keevil said when he saw the state of me.

'Rita wants a divorce and I've moved out of the family home,' I told him.

'Oh, I'm sorry to hear that. What happened?'

'It's a long story,' I said, feeling in no mood for any long drawn-out explanations at that particular moment.

'Well, have you thought about where you're going to live?'

'No, but I can't go back there.'

'Right!' he said. 'Come on. You're coming home to live with us.'

Jack and Diana Keevil had a beautiful house in Horley, Surrey, which was set in huge grounds with a magnificent sweeping drive. Jack, Diana and their children, Carol and Paul, were most welcoming and I quickly became one of the family.

'It won't be for long,' I assured Jack from my comfortable sun lounger on the patio. 'Just until I can buy myself a bachelor pad.'

'There's no rush, J.D.,' said Jack, handing me a Martini. 'Anything of interest in that pile of bumph you got from the estate agent this morning?'

'Well, there are a couple of properties I shall go and view,' I said. 'Here, what do you think of this two-bedroomed flat? It's got 'unrivalled views' according to the estate agent's blurb.'

'I bet it has,' said Jack with a grimace. 'I wouldn't touch that with a barge pole.'

'Why? What's wrong with it?'

'It's been in all the papers.'

'Well, that doesn't matter. They might knock the price down a bit if it's been on the market for a long time.'

'No, I don't mean that. It's been in the papers because the residents have been complaining about the brothel next door.'

'Brothel!' I exclaimed, throwing the paper down on the ground as if it were red hot.

'Yeah, it's run by a Russian woman known locally as Eva Corsetoff.'

'Oh, come on, pull the other one.'

'That's just what she said to her last neighbour,' said Jack with a wicked chuckle. 'Fancy another drink?'

'Honestly, I don't think you want me to find a place,' I said to his retreating back. 'That's the umpteenth property you've found fault with.'

As Jack moved out of my eye-line and went indoors, I noticed two familiar children opening the gate at the other end of the long driveway. A second glance convinced me that these children were none other than my son and daughter, Craig and Debbie. I leapt up off the sun lounger and raced down the drive. Eight-year-old Craig was carrying an overnight bag and five-year-old Debbie had her favourite rag doll slumped over one arm.

'Daddy!' they shouted in unison when they saw me.

'Craig! Debbie!' I cried. 'Whatever are you doing here?' I scooped the pair of them up into my arms and promptly burst into tears.

'We missed you, Daddy,' said Debbie, taking an embroidered handkerchief from her pocket and wiping my eyes.

'I've missed you, too,' I said.

I placed both of them back on the ground and glanced down the drive: 'Where's Mummy?' I asked them.

'Mummy's not with us,' said Craig.

'Oh, did Mummy drop you off and drive away? At least she could have waited long enough to say hello to the Keevil's,' I said, surprised by her rudeness.

'No, Daddy,' Craig answered, as he put the bag down and placed his arms behind his back. 'We came on the train … on our own.'

'Mummy doesn't know,' said Debbie with a sniff. 'Please don't be cross with us, Daddy.'

'We were staying at Nanny and Poppa's house while Mummy was on holiday with Uncle Gordon,' said Craig. 'The journey was my idea,' he added.

For the first time in my life, words failed me. I hugged the children to me, my heart secretly bursting with pride.

'Anything could have happened to you travelling down here all alone like that,' I managed to say eventually.

'We didn't talk to any strangers, did we, Craig?'

'Only a porter when we needed to change trains.'

'Whatever will your mother say when she finds out?

'Oh!' I exclaimed suddenly. 'Nanny and Poppa! They must be out of their minds with worry.'

'It's okay. I left them a note pinned to my bedroom door,' Craig announced proudly.

As it happened, the note had fallen off the door and it had taken Rita's distraught parents a while to find it.

Naturally, they were still frantic, even after reading the note and they were very relieved when I phoned to say that the children were safe.

TO NANNY AND POPPA

PLEASE DO NOT

OPEN TILL POPPA

GETS BACK

NANNY AND POPPA

Dear Nanny and Poppa,

Please don't worry, we are perfectly all right, We are going to stay with Daddy at Horley, on the train, and we will be back Saturday morning about 12-0-Clock.

All our love Craig and Dolly Douglas

P.S. Do not call Mummy.

The rascals had planned their little adventure right down to the last detail. After paying a visit to the Post Office and drawing out his savings, Craig had even packed a picnic for them to eat on the train, including an army drinking can filled with water. The journey from Streatham to Horley was quite a complicated one for children of their age and I shuddered when I thought of them having to change trains at Clapham Junction.

It was during a visit to my daughter's house in Bath recently that Debbie produced the actual note Craig had written to his grandparents all those years ago.

I'm afraid that when I'd finished reading it, the tears flowed unashamedly, just as they had on the day it happened.

* * * * *

As I mentioned earlier in the book, I was certainly my mother's boy. No, not a mummy's boy! I loved her company. We thought alike, acted alike and had the same sense of humour. It was never a surprise for me to see my mother tap dancing at home and I can still see the pair of us now, pirouetting around the kitchen like a couple of lunatics in time to the music on the radio. (Yes, all right! We've all heard the joke about tap dancing in the kitchen and falling in the sink!)

Between these impromptu dancing lessons, dear Mum also found time to teach me to cook and I'm afraid my dancing abilities never quite equalled my culinary skills. To this day, though, I still trip the light fantastic around the kitchen while I'm waiting for the sprouts to boil … especially after I've burnt myself on the saucepan!

My parents had been soul mates during their long and happy marriage. When my father died, Mum suffered some sort of mental breakdown. While I was away in Australia, Bill had taken the initiative and placed her in a home in Brighton. We went to see her as soon as I got back and although Bill had warned me beforehand, I was shocked to see the change in her. She was sitting in a chair gazing out of the window into the garden.

'Mum,' I said quietly, crouching down beside her and taking a small, pale hand in mine. 'It's me, Jack.'

She didn't respond.

'Mum! It's your loving son returned from his Antipodean adventure and I've got some presents for you.'

Still no response.

'Look! Don't you want to see what I've brought you back from Oz?' I probed gently, my voice sounding falsely bright in the silent room.

At last she turned her head towards me, but I was horrified to see that the once lively chocolate-brown eyes were now encircled by black rings and hooded with sadness.

'You said that you'd always wanted one of these hats with the corks round the rim, didn't you?' I said, twisting and turning the hat so that the corks danced dizzily back and forth.

Her steady gaze never left mine.

'I also got you a boomerang with some Aboriginal art on it. Isn't it beautifully painted?

'Just look at the intricate designs … '

The words died on my lips as she gave a deep sigh and, without so much as a glance at my gifts, turned to gaze unseeingly out of the window again.

'Oh, Mum,' I said, choking back the tears and feeling like a helpless child. 'What's happened to you?'

Bill put his hand on my shoulder. 'It's no good, Jack. Come on, the nurse has made us a cup of tea.'

England's answer to everything again.

'She was so full of life, Bill. It just isn't fair,' I said as we left the room.

Suddenly, the floodgates opened and I began to sob uncontrollably. All the hurt of losing, first Dad, then Rita and the children, and now my beloved mother in this cruel and heart-rending way, rushed to the surface. Bill looked confused and embarrassed.

'It's for the best, Jack,' he said. 'How can we take proper care of her?'

'I know, I know. I realise that, of course. It's just that … well, on top of everything else.'

I would have given anything for a reassuring hug at that moment, but Bill was a chip off the old block and unable to show his feelings.

Although the nurses at the home were friendly and welcoming, my heart was fit to burst.

'She's got a lovely sea-view, Bill,' I said mechanically. 'Mum's always liked the sea.'

'She'll be fine,' said Bill, sensing the concern in my voice. 'Try not to worry, Jack.'

'We'll pop back and see her later on,' Bill added tremulously and it was obvious that his heart was breaking, too.

'Come on,' he said, grabbing my arm in a shaky grip.

I was desperate to give Mum a hug before we left, but I knew that the dam welling up inside me would have finally burst and embarrassed everyone, particularly poor Bill. Mum stayed in the home for the rest of her life. Although she sometimes seemed to rally and be more lucid for a while, she was never the same vibrant woman she had been. She died on the 9th of August 1984, when I not only lost my mother, but my best friend. In later years, it was a great sadness to me that Mum didn't live long enough to line up with the rest of the family on 'This Is Your Life'. As the biggest single influence in my life, she should have been there.

* * * * *

Right through the fifties and early sixties Joe and I were gainfully employed. Towards the end of a summer season at Butlin's in Clacton, Norma Lewis, the lead dancer, called me to the side of the stage.

'What are your plans when Joe goes to America?' she asked me.

'Oh, he hadn't mentioned he was planning to take a holiday,' I said, knowing that he was feeling a bit jaded after a particularly long run of work.

'No, silly,' she chuckled. 'I mean when you and Joe split up.'

'Split up! Come on, Norma. He's been having you on.'

My immediate thought was that Joe had been winding Norma up and I let it pass. There ain't no smoke without fire, though, as they say, so I decided to have a quiet word with Joe in the dressing room after the show.

'Look, Joe, it's probably nothing, but Norma said …'

'It was an accident, Jack.'

'What!'

'I didn't mean to, honest. The lights went out and while I was groping in the dark I mistook it for a cherry cake.'

I couldn't help laugh at his witty repartee. Delivered, as always, at lightning speed in an American drawl.

I decided that being direct was probably the best policy, especially in his current (bun) mood.

'Joe! Norma said that you're breaking up the act at the end of the season.'

'Yeah, yeah, she was telling the truth.'

I sat down heavily in a chair and Joe looked at me, his dark eyes suddenly becoming serious for a change.

'Jack, I should have been straight with you, mate. I'm sorry.'

'Yes, you should have, Joe. I had no idea that you were unhappy with the act.'

'I'm not unhappy with the act.'

'Why, then?'

'Because we've done it all, Jack. I think we've taken our act as far as it can go. Times are changing and we should quit while we're ahead.'

'It seems such a terrible waste of all our hard graft, though.'

'I've got to move on. You know that my ambition is to make it in America eventually.'

'Of course I do. That's all you've ever talked about for the past fourteen years.'

'Well then. Be happy for me, Jack, please.'

I realised that nothing I could say or do would make him change his mind. The night of our final show together, I felt as if I were in some sort of trance. I think it was just my way of dealing with the inevitable. Even as we said our goodbyes in the dressing room afterwards, it didn't seem real. How could my partner of fourteen years just shake my hand and walk out of my life forever? I'd spent more time with Joe than I had with my own wife and my marriage had suffered because of it. I knew that Joe was desperate to conquer America, but I presumed that it would be as part of a double act with me. How wrong can you be?

I should mention at this stage that my comic heroes have always been Laurel and Hardy. When Joe dropped his bombshell, Hal Roach, who was Laurel and Hardy's producer in America, had just approached our agent. His idea was to remake the Laurel and Hardy films in this country … and guess whom he wanted for the parts? He'd watched our show and liked what he saw. Anyway, he invited Joe and I out to dinner after the show and Joe said, much to my annoyance at the time, that he'd got a hot date and couldn't make it. He was turning down one of the best directors in Hollywood.

I went out with Hal Roach and to hear him telling all these wonderful anecdotes about Laurel and Hardy, well, I was in my element. Sadly, though, Joe and I were not destined to become the British equivalent of my comic heroes. I suppose you have to leave 'em laughing, as they say, but when Joe left the act, we had been at the height of our success and I was shattered. He had been right to move on, of course, although I couldn't see it at the time. I suppose that he must have thought that the years were slipping by and it was now or never.

* * * * *

CHAPTER SEVEN

After the split with Joe, my agent found me plenty of freelance work as a straight man for comedians like Bruce Forsyth and Benny Hill. I was doing a Variety Bill at Birmingham, standing in as Arthur Haynes straight man while his usual partner, Nicholas Parsons, was in hospital. On the same bill were Lauri Lupino Lane, son of the great Lupino Lane, and George Truzzi. Each Saturday night after the show, I would drive down to London, so that I could spend Sundays with the children.

One particular week, I'd noticed that the car had seemed particularly sluggish when I tried to start her up, but just thought that the plugs and points may have been a bit damp. I prayed it wouldn't let me down, but, on the Friday morning, my worst fears were realised when I tried to start the engine and … nothing. Not even so much as a splutter.

'I won't be able to fix it until Monday at the earliest, mate,' the garage mechanic told me with a solemn shake of his head.

I loved going home to spend some time with the kids and was heartbroken to think that I'd have to spend a lonely weekend in Birmingham without them. I was just wondering how I was going to explain to Craig and Debbie that our planned Sunday picnic would have to be postponed, when Lauri and George heard about my predicament.

'We don't live far from you, Jack,' they said. 'We'll drive you home, pick you up on Monday morning and bring you back.'

'Oh, thanks, guys,' I said.

As soon as the curtain came down on Saturday night's show, the three of us jumped into Lauri's car and sped off towards London. We had been driving along for about five minutes, when George produced a bottle of whisky from inside his hold-all and took a couple of deep, gratifying swigs.

'You want some, Jack?' he asked, wiping the top of the bottle on his sleeve.

I declined his offer and was horrified to see George then hand the bottle over to Lauri. As the journey progressed, George and Lauri consumed more and more of the whisky and with every mile, their speech was becoming more and more incoherent. At one stage, Lauri even suffered a bout of hiccups, which set the pair of them off giggling like a pair of deranged hyenas. I had never been so glad to get home in my life before.

'Um, thanks for the lift guys,' I told them. 'But don't bother about picking me up on Monday morning, because I'll get the train.'

'Oh, why is that?' asked George, giving Lauri a conspiratorial look before they both broke down into an uncontrollable set of giggles again. The penny suddenly dropped, as I realised I'd obviously just been the victim of one of their famous windups.

I grabbed the bottle from George, tipped the dregs onto my fingertips, tasted it and then joined in with their laughter.

It was cold tea!

* * * * *

There are certain debts in life that can never be repaid.

During the sixties I was very friendly with Kenny Earle and his first wife, Barbara. Kenny was one half of a double act called Earle and Vaughan.

The couple lived quite close to me at that time and we had the habit of dropping in on one another unannounced. The three of us got on really well, so much so, that Barbara and I would often go out shopping together, which wasn't Kenny's scene.

I was dating a lovely lady, who I shall call Molly. That wasn't her real name, but I don't want to embarrass her or her family with this story.

One night, I was invited over to Molly's parents' house in London for a meal and after we were seated at the table, her father walked into the room carrying a silver salver, on which were half a dozen oysters.

The three of them preferred smoked salmon, but they knew about my love for shellfish and had kindly bought me some oysters as a special treat.

'These are absolutely delicious,' I said, carefully swallowing each one in turn.

I did notice that the flavour of oyster number five was a little unusual, but I'd already gulped it down so it was too late to spit it out. In any case, it would have been rather ungracious of me to make a fuss, especially after all the trouble they had gone to. Anyway, the rest of the meal tasted fine and I soon forgot about it.

Not wishing to outstay my welcome, I left at about 10.30 and made my way home to Croydon. During the journey home, it began to feel as if someone had been stirring my stomach with a spoon and I was suddenly hot and feverish. When I let myself into my flat I just made it to the toilet in time, where I was violently sick.

I immediately felt much better and thought that was going to be the end of my queasy episode, but this turned out to be merely a temporary respite. For the next three days I wore the carpet out between my bedroom and the bathroom. In fact, I became so weak and dehydrated that I had to crawl there, rather than walk. All this time, my telephone rang in vain and piles of mail lay unopened by the front door.

Meanwhile, Kenny and Barbara had been trying to get hold of me and so they decided to pop round. I heard the doorbell ringing and I was going to ignore it, until I heard Kenny's voice through the letterbox.

'Jack! Are you in there, mate?' he called.

I dragged myself out of bed, pushed the post out of the way with my foot and opened the front door.

'Oh, my God!' exclaimed Barbara, grabbing my arm to support me as I wavered drunkenly from side to side.

'What the hell's happened to you, Jack?' asked Kenny, taking my other arm. 'You look dead.'

'I wish I was,' I answered weakly.

They helped me back into bed and I struggled to tell them about my three-day nightmare.

'Right! You're coming home with us,' Kenny insisted.

'No, no,' I protested. 'Just leave me here to die in peace.'

'We'll do no such thing,' said Barbara.

Barbara cleaned and tidied the flat, which couldn't have been a very pleasant task, while Kenny packed a suitcase for me. Then the pair of them virtually carried me out to the car and on arriving at their house they shepherded me into bed, where I stayed for a further five days.

After a few weeks of pampering, I gradually began to feel better. Barbara cooked some special "invalid" meals for me, like watery soups, and Kenny did his best to cheer me up.

I'm quite certain that without their intervention I would have just given up and died alone in my flat, because I'd definitely lost the will to live by the time that they found me.

The night before I left to go home I asked Kenny what we were having for dinner.

'How about a dozen oysters?' he joked, laughing at the sickly grimace on my face.

After eating a rogue oyster I may have been left feeling a bit "shell-shocked" for a while, but at least I was lucky enough to find **two** pearls.

* * * * *

I remember one episode during my freelance career, which was quite magical. It was in the early sixties when I was compering a Sunday concert at a theatre in Great Yarmouth. I was reading through the list of acts that were appearing on the bill, when I noticed the name of a pop group that I hadn't heard before. I knocked on their dressing room door and was ushered inside by four fresh-faced young men.

'Hello, lads,' I said. 'I'm compering the show and I was wondering how you would like me to introduce you.'

'I remember you,' said one, shaking my hand and introducing himself as John. 'You used to be on Crackerjack (CRACKERJACK) with Joe Baker.'

We started chatting and I found them to be quite a charming and jovial bunch of lads. Throughout the concert, as I introduced the many and varied acts onto the stage, I was aware of a buzz of excitement going through the audience. I just put it down to the fact that they were all in holiday mood, until it was time for me to introduce the four lads.

'Now, Ladies and Gentlemen,' I began. 'We come to a group … .'

That was as far as I got, because the entire audience went berserk. They shouted, they screamed, they clapped, they whistled and I didn't even have a chance to tell them the group's name. I tried to calm the audience down, without much success, so I just shouted above the clamour as best I could.

'Right! What else can I say, but … The Beatles!'

They literally stopped the show and I've never seen anything like it, before or since.

'That was terrific, guys,' I told them afterwards. 'Forgive me, I'm not into pop music and I've never heard of you before.'

'Not a lot of people have, because we're just getting off the ground,' said George.

They were coming back to do another show a week later and I was chatting to a jeweller friend of mine and telling him about the new group.

'My son is a great fan of The Beatles,' he said. 'Could you possibly get him a signed photograph of them, please?'

'Of course,' I told him. 'No problem.'

'Tell you what! If you give me their names, Jack, I'll make them a little keepsake as a thank you.'

The boys kindly autographed an 8 x 10 photo and then I handed them each a beautiful miniature silver tankard, specially made for them by the jeweller. The boys were particularly thrilled to see their names had been engraved on the front of the tankards. I often wonder what became of those silver tankards, because they would be worth an absolute fortune now, as would the signed photograph.

* * * * *

I was extremely grateful to my agent for all the work he'd booked for me, but something had been bugging me for quite a while.

'Leslie! I'm fed up of being a straight man,' I announced in his office one day. 'I want to be a comedian.'

'Oh, come off it, Jack,' said Leslie, shaking his head and flicking through his diary. 'Look! I've got two years of bookings for you in here.'

'Yes, I appreciate that, but I want to be a comedian.'

He looked at me long and hard: 'But you don't even look funny,' he said.

'If I can't be a comedian then I shall quit the business,' I said, folding my arms and huffing petulantly.

'Oh, you'll never do that,' he answered, snapping the diary shut as if that were the end of the matter.

Now, I'm a stubborn Taurean and saying something like that to me is literally a red rag to a bull!

* * * * *

I wondered around in a daze for a while and then an old friend of mine invited me to stay with him. George Wragg was an auctioneer at the car auctions in Blackpool. I'd always felt at home in Blackpool, having spent half my childhood there, so it seemed the natural place to go and reflect on what had happened.

'Are you still into cooking, Jack?' George asked me one morning.

'Yes, when I get the time. Why? Do you want me to rustle up something for lunch?'

'No, no, it isn't that,' he said, looking thoughtful. 'Listen, are you really serious about leaving show business?'

'Yes, I am.'

'Well, how do you fancy going into partnership and opening a restaurant?'

'With you?'

'No, Fanny Craddock! Of course, with me.'

'Sounds like a great idea.'

'I was hoping you'd say that, because I've seen an ex-old folks home in Lytham Road which would be ideal for our purposes.'

(Now, I know what you're thinking, ladies. He wouldn't give up the business for his wife, but as soon as he couldn't get his own way with Leslie Grade … I'm guilty as charged, I'm afraid, but this did turn into an interesting phase in my life.)

George was right about the old folks home being ideal for our purposes, although it needed a lot of alterations. The builders set to work, first turning the ground floor into a bar area, complete with a stage and dance floor. Then, the first floor became the restaurant and kitchen. We let the second floor as a gambling club. See! We had that idea long before Blackpool Council came up with it! The third floor was my flat.

With the alterations completed, the Winmarith was ready for business and we employed some staff. These included Harry the head waiter and our hot-blooded Italian chef. As my theatrical family was well known in Blackpool, the press were more than happy to give us plenty of publicity. So, not only did we have a splendid opening night, but also we were packed to the rafters for weeks afterwards.

Naturally, the first thing that customers would do when they came in was offer me a drink and without realising it, by seven o' clock each evening I would be knocking them back fast and furious. The drinks, I mean, not the customers! My old rule about not drinking whilst working was starting to sink without trace.

'I tell you what, Harry,' I said to the barman. 'If anyone asks me to have a drink, I'll say a vodka and tonic.

2nd left pianist Arthur Black, centre George and Mrs Wragg

'But you just give me the tonic with ice and lemon and keep the money for the vodka, yourself.'

'Cheers, Jack,' said Harry.

By the end of the evening, after downing about ten or twelve drinks, I must have built up quite a reputation for myself in Blackpool as someone who could hold their liquor.

After Winmarith had been up and running for a while, I was approached by a very beautiful half-English, half-Japanese lady called Jean Kamiya. Her father was a wealthy Japanese business man who owned a holiday camp and I knew Jean because I'd once dated her beautiful raven-haired cousin, Heidi Hi, or was it Hodi Ho?

Only joking! Actually, I can't remember her name. Yes, I can. It was Helen.

Anyway, Jean called into the restaurant one lunchtime and said that she was going to be entertaining some VIPs.

'I'm hopeless when it comes to menus and wine lists, Jack. Do you think that you could come up with some sort of extra-special meal, please?'

'Yes, I'd be delighted to, Jean. How much were you thinking per head?'

'Oh, money's no object,' she said with a grimace, as if the whole subject of cost was distasteful to her.

On the arranged date, Jean turned up with her group of important businessmen to feast on the meal I had specially created. The first course was a great success, but how can you go wrong with champagne and caviar? They were just tucking into the second course, when Jean summoned me over to the table.

'Is everything all right?' I asked as I reached the table.

'Oh, don't look so worried, Jack,' Jean replied, seeing the look of concern on my face. 'The meal is fantastic, thank you.'

Jean turned to her guests and said something in Japanese and they all nodded in polite agreement.

'The meal is fine, but I was wondering if you had any soy sauce in the kitchen, please?'

'Certainly, Madam,' I answered, remembering that there was a bottle of soy sauce in my caravan.

Now, you have to remember that this was the early sixties, long before us British had developed a taste for cosmopolitan foods. I dashed out of the back door, jumped in my car and sped off down the road. I then raced back, quickly tidying my hair and straightening my jacket, before casually strolling over to Jean's table and handing her the soy sauce. I have to say that Jean and her guests were most impressed … I'm a poet and I don't know it!

'Oh, so that's where you rushed off to in such a hurry,' George said, when I related the story to him afterwards.

'I just hope she never soya,' he added with a laugh.

'No 'saki' comments, please,' I shot back.

* * * * *

79

Despite running the busy restaurant, George still had his car sales business.

'How would you like a trip to Morecambe?' he asked me one day.

'What for?'

'To pick up a brand new car for one of my customers,' he explained.

George arranged for a driver to take me up to Morecambe, from where I had to collect the new car and drive it back to Blackpool. Needless to say, the car was a gleaming silver dream and, even in those days, would have cost a hefty ten grand. She fairly purred along the road and, all too soon, I reached Blackpool. I was just cruising along the front, when I caught up with a slow-moving circus parade. It would have been a bit frustrating at any other time, but I was in no hurry to part company with this luxurious pussy cat of a car and quite content to tag onto the end of the procession, behind the elephants. There were crowds of people lining the pavements as the parade slowly progressed along the sea front, when a policeman on traffic duty suddenly raised his hand and brought us all to a standstill.

I was leaning out of the window to see what was causing the jam (actually, I was eyeing up a stunning blonde), when a large elephant in front of me decided to put herself in reverse. I couldn't pump the horn for fear of starting a stampede and could only watch helplessly as the elephant's huge backside loomed large in the windscreen. There was a slight thud as she made contact with the car's immaculate front bumper.

'Phew! That was close,' I muttered out loud, but my relief was to be short-lived.

The elephant tossed her trunk in the air, gave a defiant trumpet and then sat down heavily on the gleaming silver bonnet. I heard the terrible sound of metal crunching. The spectators obviously thought it was some sort of stage-managed trick, because they all started to clap and laugh.

'Get up, Nelly! Get up!' shouted her mortified trainer when she realised what had happened.

Nelly reluctantly stood up and the general hubbub was soon replaced by gasps of horror, when people saw the massive v-shaped imprint in the bonnet.

'I'm dreadfully sorry, sir,' said the trainer, walking round to my open window. 'We'll pay for any damage, of course.'

Luckily for her, I had been rendered speechless at that point and was unable to comment. Suddenly, there was the sound of grating metal as the bonnet sprang open, juddered a bit, then hung in mid-air at a crazy angle.

'It must be a broken catch, sir,' said the trainer helpfully.

'C … catch,' I repeated, staring blankly ahead.

'Don't you move, sir,' she said, stretching her arm through the window and patting the back of my hand. 'You stay right there while I go and fetch some rope.'

'S … some r … rope,' I answered feebly, my hands locked in the quarter-to-three position on the steering wheel.

The trainer and her colleagues sat on the bonnet and very kindly lashed it down with a length of rope that would have been thick enough to tether the QEII securely … in a force nine gale. The car no longer purred seductively, but rattled like an old tin can as I headed down the Lytham Road to the Winmarith, where George was waiting with his prospective buyer. They were standing in the car park, but George's smile of welcome dissolved without trace as soon as he clapped eyes on the crumpled heap of metal held together with rope. The expensive dream car he had promised his client had turned into a nightmare.

'What the bleep, bleep happened, Jack?' he ranted as I got out of the car, his face white with shock and rage.

'You wouldn't believe me if I told you, George,' I said.

Goodness only knows what he wrote on the insurance company's accident claims form …

'Vorsprung Urghh Technik' maybe!

* * * * *

All was running smoothly at the restaurant, until I had a little falling out with the chef. I can't remember what it was about now, but it resulted in him walking out and leaving us in the lurch on one of our busiest nights of the year.

'What the hell are we going to do, Jack?' asked Harry, his face as white as the chef's apron.

'I'll think of something,' I said.

I walked out into the restaurant, which was by now filling up with prospective diners.

'Ladies and Gentlemen!' I said. 'Can I have your attention, please?'

All heads turned in my direction.

'I'm afraid that we have a bit of a problem here tonight and I hope that you will be kind enough to bear with us.

'Our chef has been taken ill (a murmur went through the restaurant). No, I can assure you that he hasn't gone down with food poisoning.'

They laughed … nervously.

'I hope you won't mind if I cook for you tonight!'

They all cheered.

'But,' I paused for effect. 'This means that the menu won't be a la carte, more like 'orse and cart.

'No, not really. How about scampi and chips?'

They all clapped and cheered and the evening was, in fact, a great success.

Much to the chagrin of the chef, when he came back the next day.

* * * * *

I was just closing up one night after a particularly busy evening, when the telephone rang. Wondering who could be ringing at one o' clock in the morning, I thought I'd better answer it, in case the call was urgent.

'Hello,' I said sleepily.

'Sorry to bother you at this hour,' said a male voice at the other end of the line. 'But I'm trying to find Jack Douglas.'

'You've found him.'

'Hello, Jack, this is Des O' Connor and I'm ringing to ask if you'd like to come back into show business!'

I nearly dropped the phone.

* * * * *

CHAPTER EIGHT

Career-wise, this turned out to be one of the most important phone calls of my life. I gazed around the now deserted restaurant, suddenly realising something I'd actually known for some time. At the start, each day had seemed like an exciting challenge, but now the business was running smoothly and didn't need my input anymore.

'Jack! Are you still there?' said Des, his voice suddenly snapping me back to reality.

'Oh, yes, sorry Des.'

'Well, what's your answer? Do you want to come back into show business?'

'Yes, please,' I answered, feeling a sudden warmth spreading from the left-hand side of my chest and a weight lifting off my shoulders.

'That's great,' said Des sounding relieved. 'Then I'll get the ball roll … '

'Hang on a minute, Des,' I interrupted him. 'Look, I'll be more than happy to come back into show business on one condition.'

'Oh, what's that?' he asked, probably expecting me to demand some sort of astronomical fee.

'If we are going to work together, can I do comedy?' I held my breath, knowing that my whole future depended on his reply.

'No,' he answered thoughtfully and my heart sank. 'No, I can't see a problem with that, Jack. In fact, you can be as funny as you like.'

I gazed skywards and mouthed a silent 'Thank you, God.'

* * * * *

I must admit, I did have some reservations when Des told me what he wanted me to do.

'You know that 'Alf' character of yours? I'd like you to use him in my new television series on ATV.'

'But, Des,' I reasoned. 'He's a stage character. It would never transfer to television.' Shows how much I know, doesn't it?

* * * * *

I'll never forget the reaction when I first walked out in front of a studio audience as Alf. Des was already in the middle of something when Alf came on.

Alf then, of course, interrupted his act with: ''Scuse me, Mr O' Connor.' To which Des replied crossly: 'Yes, what is it, Alf?'

We couldn't believe the big laugh we got when Alf twitched and Des reacted to it. Des and I went on to do about ninety television appearances together, five panto's, three summer shows, plus a Royal Command Variety Show. In 1966 we even went over to America to do the Ed Sullivan Show.

I was a bit concerned whether the humour would travel and I can remember the director over there asking me to play down Alf's broad northern accent.

He said: 'Can you make Alf sound a bit more mid-Atlantic?'

I pinched my nose and said 'Glug, glug, glug,' but I don't think that drowning Alf in the ocean was quite what he had in mind. Whether the audience understood him or not, Alf went down a storm. Well, I suppose he would if he was out in the mid-Atlantic!

While we were rehearsing for the Ed Sullivan Show I got a call from a producer who presented one of America's top cookery shows. He'd heard about my culinary expertise and wanted me to make a guest appearance on the show.

I racked my brain to find a recipe that they wouldn't have heard of, which wasn't easy, but then I remembered something. Later, I received another call, this time from the first assistant on the programme, asking me what ingredients I would need for the show.

'One whole fresh salmon, one lemon, some fresh dill, a bottle of dry white wine, some silver foil and a dishwasher, please,' I told her.

'Okay, no problem, sir,' she answered politely. 'I will make sure that you have all those things, but we have a dishwasher off-set for you to use. Will that be all right?'

'No,' I said. 'What I need is a dishwasher on-set, plugged in and ready to use, please.'

'Oh, well, okay, sure thing, Mr Douglas,' she said and I could hear the bewilderment in her voice. 'There will be a dishwasher on-set for you, ready to go.'

The poor girl must have thought it was all a bit fishy and I suspect that you are feeling just as bewildered as her.

Let me explain.

Some years previous to my visit to America, I'd read in a W.I. cookery book about a woman who was hosting a large and important dinner party when her gas cooker blew up. After her initial panic, she remembered that the best way of cooking fish was to steam it. The enterprising lady wrapped the salmon, with some lemon, dill and wine, in some tin foil, then placed it in the dishwasher on the shortest cycle.

I'll make no bones about it, I did the same on this programme and afterwards the switchboard was jammed … with irate viewers complaining that when they had tried the recipe at home, their fish had tasted of soap. I'm only joking, so don't get in a lather about it. It really does work.

* * * * *

Another little incident, also connected to food, happened while Des and I were in America. We had decided to eat at a famous restaurant in New York, but when we'd arrived it was packed out and the head waiter asked us to wait in the queue.

'Can I take your name, please?' he said, removing a pen from his top pocket.

'Jack Douglas,' I answered.

'Ah, did you say, Jack Douglas?'

'Um, yes,' I said. 'Is there a prob … ?'

'I'm so sorry, sir. I will find you a table straight away.'

With that, he ushered us quickly over to a table, clapping his hands and rousting up the other waiters as he went. Des looked at me and I could see his mind working. Why had the waiter recognised me, when it was Des who was the star? We took our seats, as the head waiter fussed with the cutlery and napkins, then brushed some imaginary crumbs off the tablecloth.

'We would love you to have a drink with us, Mr Douglas, and the meal is, of course, on the house.'

'Oh, well, that's very generous, but … '

'No, I insist,' he said, with a dismissive wave of his hand. 'I wonder, though, could you just do me a little favour, please?'

I was beginning to think that there must be some truth in the old saying that there's no such thing as a free lunch, when he thrust a book in my hand.

'Would you do me the honour of signing this, please?'

The book was called 'Never Trust A Naked Bus Driver' (on account that he'd have nowhere to keep his loose change, I suppose) by the famous American author, Jack Douglas.

I should have told him that I wasn't in fact the author of this imaginatively titled tome, but the other diners were beginning to glance in our direction and so I thought it would be sensible just to sign the blessed thing. I must apologise to the real Jack Douglas who was the author of this book, but it was worth keeping up the pretence just to hear Des laugh. Plus, it was a delicious meal.

I wonder what culinary delights I can expect on the strength of the book I have written? Oh well, I suppose burger and chips will be quite nice!

* * * * *

I remember that Joe and I had once worked with a very talented musical act called Ted and Barbara Andrews. At the end of the act they would bring on their daughter, who was about eight or nine years old and she would sing with this beautifully clear voice. She always managed to make the hairs on the back of my neck, prickle. We worked with them a few times, over a period of about a year or so.

While Des and I were appearing on the Ed Sullivan Show, in walked this very beautiful young woman who said 'Hello Jack.'

I thought *Wait a minute, I'd never forget someone as lovely as this!*

'Don't you remember me?' she asked, her large blue eyes looking at me questioningly.

'Um, no, I'm sorry, but … '

'We were on the same bill together with my parents.'

The penny dropped. 'Of course! Ted and Barbara Andrews.'

This beautiful young lady was none other than the songstress with a beautifully clear singing voice, Julie Andrews!

* * * * *

Des and I were appearing in a show on the north pier in Blackpool for Bernard Delfont. Bernard had been a dear friend of my father's and it was Dad who'd actually

85

helped him to get started in the business with his brothers, Leslie and Lew Grade. Bernard popped into my dressing room at the theatre one day to say hello. He then went next door to have a word with Des. I'm not normally nosy, but I'm afraid that my curiosity got the better of me that day and I listened at the door.

'Des,' said Bernard. 'I want you to host the Royal Variety Show.'

'Oh, great. Thank you, Mr Delfont,' Des replied.

Bernard explained to Des that they normally had one comedian to do the first half and then a different comedian in the second.

'I'd like you to do the whole show, though, Des.'

'I'd be delighted,' said Des, obviously thrilled. 'As long as I can use Jack.'

'Des, I know that you two are good together, but this is the Royal Variety, you know.'

'Bernard!' said Des with authority and I hoped that things weren't going to get prickly on my account. 'When we come on for the finale of the show, does Jack Douglas go down better than I do?'

'Well, no, of course not.'

'Well then, I'd like to use Jack.'

Bernard was persuaded and I hurriedly returned to my seat and pretended to be reading the paper. Just then, Des appeared in the doorway, beaming from ear to ear.

'You look just like the cat who's got the cream,' I remarked innocently, peering at him over the top of the newspaper.

Des O'Connor and Jack

'Bernard's asked me to host the Royal Variety,' he announced brightly.

I leapt up out of my seat to congratulate him.

'That's great news, Des,' I said, thumping him on the back.

'Yes, but I want us to do the 'Green Eye' together.'

For those who don't know, the Green Eye is a funny rhyme we used to do. Des would stand behind me, put his arms around me (don't get any strange ideas) and do all the arm actions for me. Does that make any sense? Probably not, but you had to be there. The cast list for the Royal Variety read like a veritable Who's Who and Des spent his time rehearsing with Sammy Davis Junior, Dean Martin and Lena Horne.

'We haven't rehearsed anything,' I reminded Des on the day of the show.

'Are you worried about it?' he asked.

'Nope!'

'Well, neither am I, so we'll just make it up as we go along.'

You must be thinking that this would surely be bicycle clip time for most performers, but when you've been in the business for a long time, there's always material to draw on. This is especially true when you trust and respect the partner you're working with. So, make-up, costume, Queen Mother, God Save Our Gracious Queen, and then the show began.

I was in John Avery's office, the manager of the London Palladium at that time, with one eye on the clock to see when I'd got to go on-stage. As we were chatting, I noticed a roll of red carpet in the corner of the room.

'Can I borrow that?' I asked him.

'Yes, of course,' he said, looking a bit perplexed.

I then headed for the foyer, because it was always a good laugh for Alf to make his entrance through the audience from the back of the stalls. On this auspicious occasion at the London Palladium, however, I hadn't bargained with an officious security man. Des was in mid-song, which was my cue to go on.

Just as I put my hand on the door, someone shouted: 'Hey! Where do you think you're going?'

I turned to see this red-faced security man heading in my direction. He grabbed my arm in an iron grip, as I desperately tried to convince him that I was a part of the act that was up on the stage.

He looked me up and down. 'Come on now,' he said. 'I'm afraid that I shall 'ave to ask you to leave the theatre.'

'Don't you watch the Des O' Connor Show?' I ventured, as he began towing me towards the entrance.

Several different expressions swept across his face, before realisation dawned and his hand flew up to his mouth in horror.

'Oh, my gawd, sir. You're Alf, aren't you? I'm terribly sorry, sir. It's this way. If you'll allow me, sir.'

He opened the door for me and I entered the darkened auditorium. The house lights began to go up, almost imperceptibly at first, until there was just enough light to reveal Alf in all his glory. You can just imagine the reaction of the audience.

Most of them were wearing sequin-covered evening gowns and wrapped in the

finest mink stoles, with the most exquisite diamonds dripping from their necks …
and that was just the men! Suddenly, they've got a scruffy workman in their midst,
wearing dungarees, a torn shirt, a belt, cap, glasses and big boots. Added to this, his
hair is all over the place and he's carrying a roll of red carpet under one arm.

I walked down towards the stage, acknowledging people as I passed and stopping
every now and then, to steal someone's sweets and hand them round. All this time, Des
diligently carried on with his song, totally ignoring the disruption in the audience.

I walked up onto the stage, keeping my back to the audience. I studied the curtain
material for a while, before casually chatting to some stagehands that were standing in
the wings. Suddenly, I noticed Des for the first time and walked across the stage towards
him. I began peering into his right ear, which must have been pretty off-putting whilst
he was trying to sing. Understanding the cue, he ground to a halt mid-song.

'Oh, Alf. What are you doing here?' he asked.

'Hello, Mr O' Connor.'

His eyes swept over the red carpet (no pun intended) and I knew my little bit of
nonsense was going to work like a charm.

'Why have you got that red carpet, Alf?'

'Oh, everybody was wiping their feet on it, so I thought I'd better bring it inside.'

To see the Queen Mother laughing heartily and banging a gloved hand on the front
of the Royal Box was a magical experience. We followed that with a rendition of the
'Green Eye' and afterwards, dare I say, we got a standing ovation. The show over, Des
and I were in our dressing room bathing in the 'after glow' when the show's director,
Robert Nesbitt, walked in.

'Great show, guys,' he said, then turning to Des he added 'Right, Des. Would you
like to come and meet the Queen Mother?'

'Of course,' Des replied. 'We'd be delighted, wouldn't we, Jack?'

I was about to follow Des out of the dressing room when Robert put his hand up.

'Ah, no,' he said, shuffling his feet and looking uncomfortable. 'I'm sorry, but we
can't possibly extend this invitation to you, Jack.'

'Why ever not?' demanded Des, stopping in his tracks.

'Just look at the state of him, Des,' said Robert, giving my scruffy costume the
once over. 'He can't meet the Queen Mother looking like that. He'll have to change
quickly.'

'With all due respect, Mr Nesbitt. If Jack gets changed nobody will know who he is,
because he doesn't look anything like Alf in real life.'

Robert was resolute: 'I'm sorry, but he can't meet the Queen Mother looking like
that.'

Robert turned to leave and just when it looked as if that was going to be the end of
the matter, Des piped up with the immortal line: 'If Jack can't meet the Q.M. dressed
like that, then neither can I!'

Robert looked stricken.

'But Des,' he reasoned. 'You've just hosted the show, you'll have to meet her.'

'No, I won't,' said Des, plonking himself down into a chair and folding his arms.

So, Des stuck up for me yet again.

The Queen Mother descended the stairs from the Royal Box, then shook hands with all the glittering showbiz stars as she walked past each one in turn, until she finally got to me. I hurriedly removed my cap, stuffed it into a pocket and bowed awkwardly. Meanwhile, the Queen Mother was looking me up and down, taking in my dishevelled appearance.

'Hm,' she said, with a wicked twinkle in those sparkling blue eyes of hers. 'Well, you may not be the smartest gentleman I've met this evening, but you are certainly one of the funniest.'

Thank you, Your Majesty. You made my year. Credit has to go to Des for standing his ground like that on my behalf and I will always have the greatest respect for him because he's such an unselfish comedian.

If he ever said 'Look, I'm in trouble, Jack. I'm appearing in Shanklin tonight and the rest of the cast hasn't turned up. Will you come and do it?'

'What do you want me to do, Des?'

'Can I leave it up to you?'

'No problem.'

Now, I wouldn't do that for anyone else in the world but Des O' Connor.

* * * * *

A lot of people ask me where Alf's surname comes from. Des dropped that question into a show one day and, as he hadn't asked me before, I had to think of an answer quickly. This famous showbiz joke is about eighty or ninety years old and when Des asked me my name I said: 'It's Alf.' That's not the joke, by the way!

He said, 'No, I know it's Alf. What about your other name?'

'It's Ippititimus.'

'How do you spell that?' he asked, determined not to let me off the hook that easily.

'A-L-F,' I replied.

'No,' said Des impatiently. 'How do you spell "Ippititimus"?'

'Two Ipps, a pip and a Titimus!'

See! Robb Wilton and his invaluable advice again.

'Always remember, Jack. It's only an old joke when it doesn't get a laugh.'

* * * * *

I hope Des will forgive me when I tell you about one little incident that sticks in my mind. We were trying to develop a routine, which for some reason involved us using a high-back chair. Anyway, we were rehearsing this piece of nonsense during a break and Des, being very agile and fit, was standing on this chair. As he put one leg over behind chair, the seat broke and he fell onto the chair back, right on his privates. To say that it made his eyes water would be an understatement, because Des ended up rolling around on the floor clutching his 'possessions' and screaming in agony. Compared to me he's only a small guy (in stature, I mean!), so I picked him up and carried him out to the Gents' toilets. I sent for the first aid man and, ever the helpful and concerned soul I took down his trousers and got down on my knees to inspect the damage. Just as I was having a look, the loo door opened and a man came in to go to the toilet.

'Oh! I do beg your pardon,' he said, turning on his heels with a look of horror on his face and scurrying out again.

Thankfully, Des wasn't permanently damaged, although it's a shame that the same can't be said about our macho reputations!

* * * * *

The northern comedian, Jimmy James, could have been my father! No, it isn't a joke. He was once engaged to my mother, but the relationship didn't work out. I can remember being on the same variety bill with Jimmy, along with his two stooges, Eli Woods and Roy Castle. I'll never forget Eli's stammer, or these immortal lines spoken by Roy and Jimmy …

Roy: (wearing a huge fur coat) I've just come back from Africa.

Jimmy: (looking him up and down) In that coat?

Roy: No, in an aeroplane!

I used to stand on the side of the stage and watch Jimmy every night and I learned so much from him about comic timing.

Years later, Des and I were appearing at Coventry in the Birthday Show for Sam Newsom. Jimmy was also in the line-up, although he was getting on in years a bit by this time. What a lot of people didn't realise was, that Jimmy was one of the biggest gamblers (off the course) in show business. It was nothing for Jimmy to gamble away his entire salary and after "the ghost walked" on Friday mornings, he was straight off round the bookies. Des and I would listen to Jimmy's act over the speakers while we were sitting in our dressing room. He wasn't as good, because by this time he was an old man. One particular night, Des and I were sitting there chatting as usual, when I asked Des to hush for a moment.

'Listen to that laughter, Des,' I said.

We both dashed to the side of the stage and watched Jimmy deliver the funniest act I'd seen him do for at least fifteen years. He completely paralysed the audience. When he eventually walked off stage I said to him: 'You've had a good day, haven't you?'

'I did a Yankee, Jack,' he replied, looking pleased with himself.

Now, I'm not a betting man, but I believe that a Yankee is when you put a certain amount of money on five horses. If the first one wins, the winnings go on the second horse and if the second one comes in, the money goes on the third horse and so on.

If I remember correctly, Jimmy had placed a £100 bet on the first horse, which came in at fifteen-to-one. So, he put fifteen hundred pounds on the second horse and this romped home at ten-to-one … yes, we've all heard that joke. All in all, Jimmy had scooped something like £30,000. That was why he'd walked out on the stage and given the performance of his life.

* * * * *

Jimmy had a funny walk. He would take two steps on his left foot instead of one and I asked him why he'd adopted it.

'I had a pebble in me shoe one day, Jack, and I had to lessen the load.'

'Well, it's very funny,' I told him.

'Thanks, lad. I'll tell you what.'

'What.'

'When I go, that walk is yours.'

Now you know why 'Alf' takes two steps on his left foot instead of one.

* * * * *

CHAPTER NINE

I have had many serious relationships with ladies during my life, but also a few platonic friendships along the way, too. One such friendship was with the famous singer Alma Cogan, who was hugely popular during the Sixties, until her untimely death.

I remember that she phoned me one night and asked me to a party at her home in the West End. Anybody who was anybody was at that party and there wasn't anyone from outside show business. At a certain point in the evening, Alma stood up and said 'Right! It's time for everyone to do his or her bit. If you come here, you've got to earn your keep.'

After about twenty-odd turns, it got down to just Eric Morecambe and myself. Eric was at a loss, because he was always used to working with Ernie Wise in a double act and he needed a straight man. Anyway, I obliged.

I don't think I need to tell you about Eric's comic brilliance, because we must have done about ten minutes and everyone was crying with laughter at his antics. I said to him at the end of the evening that it had been one of the most enjoyable acts I'd ever done in my life and Eric graciously agreed.

'If Ernie ever decides to leave the business, please give me a ring,' I told him.

* * * * *

'Oh, that Max Bygraves is a lovely man,' Alma said to me one day. 'It's so nice to meet somebody in this business who's actually in love with his wife and not having affairs all over the place.'

Now, I'm not an impressionist, but it so happened that I could (and still can) mimic Max's speaking voice, so I thought I'd have a laugh with Alma. I rang her at home.

'Alma, it's Max here,' I said.

'Oh, hello, Max,' said Alma, obviously taken in. 'How lovely to hear from you.'

'Alma, I've got to talk to you,' I said. 'I'm in love with you and I want to leave my wife so that you and I can run away together.'

'What!' said Alma, flabbergasted.

'We can go anywhere you like. I've got the money.'

There was this terrible silence and then she said: 'Max, you can't possibly leave your wife and children.'

'Don't be silly,' I said. 'They mean nothing to me.'

Suddenly, I couldn't keep it up any longer and I started to laugh. In all the years I knew Alma I'd never heard her swear, but she said 'You bastard, Douglas!' and put the phone down.

Lucky for me, Alma had a wonderful sense of humour and she forgave me.

* * * * *

Audrey Jeans

I had another one of these platonic friendships with a beautiful actress called Audrey Jeans, who I'd met in a show. She was just like the sister I'd always longed for and I suppose I was like a brother to her.

I'm sure everyone else in the play thought that we were having an affair, which we weren't, but we loved each other dearly.

Some years later Sue (my wife at that time) and I attended her wedding and waved a deliriously happy Audrey and her new husband off on their honeymoon to France.

A few days later, I was at the studio recording a particularly funny show with Des O'Connor and my wife and my step-daughter, Sarah, were in the audience. I happened to glance across at them and noticed that they were sitting there with glum faces and didn't appear to be laughing at all.

The evening was a brilliant success and everyone was thrilled with the show, but Sue and Sarah were in the bar afterwards, still looking as if the world was about to come to an end. Eventually, I couldn't stand it any longer and I called the two of them outside.

'Honestly,' I said crossly. 'That's the best show we've ever done and you look as if someone's just died.'

'Jack,' said Sue, taking my hand. 'We don't know how to tell you this.'

'Tell me what?' I said, fear gripping at my heart.

'The telephone rang just as we were leaving the house,' she said, taking a deep breath. 'I'm so sorry, Jack, but Audrey has been run over and killed by a hit-and-run driver.'

I began to sob uncontrollably at that point and we just jumped into the car and went straight home.

* * * * *

It was actually Des who had introduced me to my second wife, Susan Street. He asked me to go for a drink with him after rehearsals one day, saying that he'd got to meet up with someone and didn't want to go on his own. While we were standing at the bar, two attractive young models walked over (happens all the time!) and introduced themselves as Jenny and Sue. Sue was the most gorgeous redhead and I was taken with her immediately. She was slim and petite and had modelled for Vogue magazine.

She seemed incredibly quite and shy for someone who'd been involved with modelling and I was intrigued to find out more about this charming lady. As the evening progressed, she slowly began to confide in me. She said that she'd had a very traumatic marriage, as her husband suffered from schizophrenia, and she was naturally concerned about her four-year-old daughter, Sarah.

Sue was divorced from her husband, but it was obvious from the sadness in her huge, dark eyes that she had been emotionally scarred. I asked if I could see her again and although she was a bit reluctant at first, she eventually agreed.

I remember the first time I took her home. Sue had almost jumped out of the car before it was stationary. She didn't trust actors, apparently, but I behaved like the perfect gentleman.

As the weeks went by, her trust in me seemed to grow steadily and we eventually got engaged. I met her parents and discovered that they had been a double act for years and had even worked for my father.

Then, I met Sue's daughter Sarah. She was rather remote and shy and it was strange to hear a four-year-old child calling me Jack. Sarah had blonde hair and large dark eyes like her mother's which were all but hidden behind a pair of thick, pebble glasses.

Sue and I married in October 1965 and moved into my bachelor pad in Waldrenhurst, Croydon.

* * * * *

Jack and Sue – Just Married!

After the wedding, Sue and I spent our wedding night in a hotel.

It's always the same, isn't it? You don't want anyone to know that you are newlyweds and then, as you check in at reception, a shower of confetti falls out of your wallet and gives you away … no pun intended. I suppose that booking the Bridal Suite was a bit of a give away, as well!

I thought that Sue looked stunning in her 'going away' outfit, with her red hair flowing down over her shoulders. I wanted everyone to see my beautiful new wife, so, although we'd already eaten at the reception, we headed off into the dining room.

'Champagne?' asked the Head Waiter, as he placed a huge ice bucket in the centre of our table.

He leant over and carefully lit a candle with his lighter. The two-foot high flame was a bit of a shock for everyone, but my eyebrows soon grew back. (Actually, it wasn't a cigarette lighter. It was the blow torch they used to crisp the top of the Crème Brulée!)

Isn't candlelight romantic, though? It's so becoming, especially when you're in love. The skin looks like porcelain, the eyes sparkle like diamonds, the hair looks glossy and sleek, the teeth look whiter than white … I thought the transformation was amazing when I accidentally caught sight of my reflection in a nearby mirror.

On the next table were another couple of newlyweds, bless 'em. The blushing bride was a dainty little blonde who was all of twenty. Whereas, the 'blushing' groom was red in the face on account of his blood pressure. Well, he was ninety-five!

Obviously, the 'something old' was the groom, the 'something borrowed' was the oxygen bottle and the 'something blue' was the groom's lips.

'If she dies, she dies,' he wheezed at me across the table.

Once we'd retired (gratefully) to the sanctuary of our room, Sue disappeared into the bathroom to slip into something more comfortable.

Quite why she wanted a sleeping bag at a time like that was beyond me. No, only joking, but who would marry a comic? We'd only known each other for a short while, so we were both feeling bashful … and Bashful didn't like it at all! Stop it, Douglas!

I decided to be gentlemanly and use the 'facilities' down the corridor, leaving Sue to her own private ablutions. I was extremely organised. I took my pyjamas, dressing gown, shaving accoutrements, shampoo and shower gel, along with me. After a refreshing shower I headed back to the room, where I knew that my lovely new bride would be anticipating my return.

I walked down one corridor, then down another, then another. All the rooms looked exactly the same and I'd have had better luck trying to find my way round Hampton Court maze. I suppose it would have helped if I'd remembered to take my key along with me.

'It's no good,' I said aloud to myself after twenty fruitless minutes of searching. 'I'll have to go down to reception.'

The night porter was very surprised to see me at that time of the morning.

'Everything all right, Mr Douglas?' he enquired, looking me up and down and obviously admiring my tartan dressing gown.

'Um, I'm afraid I seem to be lost. Could you please direct me back to my room?' I asked sheepishly.

'Yes, of course, sir,' he said.

I guessed that the poor man must have been suffering from a sore throat, because his voice kept cracking up as he spoke.

'Where on earth have you been?' said Sue when I eventually found my way back to the room.

Sorry, darling,' I fibbed. 'I was just showing that old chap the way back to his room, as the poor bloke had got lost on his way back from the bathroom.'

'Silly old fool,' she said with a laugh.

* * * * *

Sarah was still calling me Jack, but I knew that she had been through a great deal in her short life and it would take a while to gain her trust. I devoted an awful lot of time to getting to know her and, one day my patience was rewarded when she called me 'Uncle Jack'.

Her vision was extremely poor, so I took her to see a specialist. He confirmed that Sarah had a problem in both eyes, which would require an operation. Sue and I were naturally concerned about her having to undergo surgery, of course, but afterwards Sarah was able to throw her thick glasses away.

One day, quite out of the blue, Sarah climbed on my lap and called me 'Daddy Jack'. I was absolutely thrilled. Later on, she climbed onto my lap again and called me 'Daddy'. At that moment I knew that I wanted to make it official and adopt her.

Sadly, Sue's ex-parents-in-law didn't want Sarah to be adopted. So me, being as wicked as I am, wrote to tell them that I was sending Sarah to Roedean and from there to finishing school in Switzerland. 'Therefore, if you could please deposit £20,000 in a special account for Sarah's education …'

Right away, a letter came from their solicitor, saying: 'We have reconsidered and have decided that you can adopt Sarah.'

* * * * *

You may be wondering how my own son and daughter reacted to all of this and I was naturally worried about integrating a stepchild. I thought it would be a good idea to take them all up to Box Hill in Surrey for a picnic. When we arrived I asked Craig and Debbie to take Sarah exploring while I prepared the food.

I felt so proud of them both, as they each grabbed a hand and ran off with her, all three of them chattering and laughing quite happily together. A bit later, the children arrived back from their adventures in high spirits, flinging themselves down onto the car rug, red-faced and out of breath. As I watched them devouring the sandwiches and cakes, I knew that I now had a son and **two** daughters.

* * * * *

Craig, Sarah, Jack, Sue and Debbie with Duchess the Great Dane

Jack, Sarah and Sue with Haggis and Muffin

I soon discovered that my bachelor pad wasn't big enough for the family, so I found a lovely old 16th century manor house in a little village between Dorking and Guildford, called Abinger Hammer. Big houses were difficult to sell in those days, so I picked it up relatively cheaply and, with my love of interior design, I knew that I was going to enjoy restoring the place to its former glory.

The previous owner had taken all the beautiful panelled doors off and I found them under a gooseberry bush in the garden. Well, it makes a change from finding babies under there, I suppose! I took the door to the local carpenter, who dipped and restored them for me.

One day, I found a small cupboard in the wall, which had been sealed off. Inside, there were some old shoes. A pair of ladies, a pair of gents and some tiny children's shoes. I had left the little cupboard uncovered ready for further investigation, but when I returned from the studio, I was puzzled to see that the cupboard had been covered up again.

Apparently, the local builder told Sue that it would be better to leave well alone, as every member of the house had put their shoes in there centuries before to keep the house free of the devil. Alarmed by this, Sue had immediately instructed him to cover it up again.

* * * * *

While I was renovating the cellar in preparation for my wine racks, I spotted a floor-level hole in the wall. I looked across and noticed another one in the opposite wall. They were both connected by a shallow channel in the floor and, although I was a bit puzzled as to what they were for, decided to leave them alone. One day, during a terrific thunderstorm, I could hear all this rushing water and I ran from room to room in a panic, fearing the worst.

What a relief, though. When I descended the cellar steps, the storm water was running in through one of the holes in the wall, along the channel and out through the other hole. It was an ancient drainage system and if I'd blocked those holes up, all my precious wine bottles would have ended up afloat.

* * * * *

The sitting room at Abinger had a beautiful York stone floor, but I noticed that one of these stones rocked from side to side when I stood on it. Intrigued, I got a chisel to lift the stone and was astonished to find that I was looking down into the murky depths of a well. I was at first elated and then rather horrified by my discovery. With three children running around the house and a fifteen-foot well in the sitting room … WELL, it doesn't bear thinking about!

I commissioned a local garage to make a sheet of armoured glass to cover the top. Then, as I was too big to get into the well myself, a small electrician friend bravely climbed down and fitted two bulkhead lights for me. He positioned one down near the water and the other one, half way up. It certainly made a beautiful feature in the room and was always a great talking point when we entertained. I had a sample of the water tested and we were able to drink it, as it turned out to be over ninety per cent pure. I believe that sixty per cent is considered excellent, so we were really lucky to have our own supply of health giving spa water.

Talking about running water, there is another side of my life that I've never quite understood. It's all to do with itchy feet.

When I'd walked over the loose slab that covered the well, my feet had started to itch. So much so, that I had to remove my shoes and socks and have a jolly good scratch. Sorry if all this is putting you off your lunch, by the way, but it serves you right for eating when you should be reading my book! This happened again when a friend asked me to re-design an old cottage he'd just bought.

I went down to have a look in the cellar, but as I walked across the floor I had to remove my shoes and socks to try and remedy this terrible itch again. No, I hadn't got athlete's foot. I told him that there must be water running under the floor, which he thought, was unlikely. Then he phoned me twenty-four hours later to confirm my prediction. The builders had been digging up the floor and had indeed found water flowing underneath. Most people have to use hazel twigs to divine for water, but I can use my feet. I suppose it might have something to do with soles and 'eels!

* * * * *

I also did a lot of work on the exterior of the house at Abinger Hammer. If you looked out into the back garden, there was the usual lawn, which then culminated in an amazing fifteen-foot high cliff. There was a small field beyond this that also belonged to the house. The field was only about a quarter of an acre and I thought how lovely it would be to turn it back into an orchard, as it would have been originally. I popped along to the Royal Horticultural Society at Wisley and met this delightful man who was an expert on orchards and trees. I explained that I wanted to recreate the 16th century orchard and he said that he would love to be involved with the project.

He searched the whole of Great Britain and found seven-year-old container grown apples, cherries, pears, you name it. Then, he rounded up a team of people to help him with the planting. Two days later, I had my orchard. As my only access to the orchard was to walk up the road and through a gate, I decided to build a staircase up the 'cliff'.

I then got a very large marine pump and some lovely stone work and built channels into the rock face to a pond at the bottom. I have to say, modestly, of course, that my waterfall rivalled Niagara and even featured in 'House and Garden' magazine. Eat your heart out, Charlie Dimmock!

* * * * *

I employed a gardener to help me out at Abinger and he was a real old character. If he'd have told me that he was a hundred and four I'd have believed him. I mentioned to him that I was thinking of planting a fig tree, because I love fresh figs, which incidentally are good for anyone who suffers from blood pressure. Anyway, the gardener watched me dig this piece of ground that I paved with York Stone, so that the fig tree would grow in a sunny spot up the side of the house.

After I'd finished planting the tree the gardener said 'You're not wantin' any figs to grow in it, then?'

'Why, of course,' I said. 'That's why I've planted it.'

'Well you won't have no figs on that tree,' he told me.

'Why is that?'

'You ain't contained the roots.'

Why he didn't explain it to me before I'd done all my excavations I don't know, but apparently if you don't restrict the roots of a fig tree they grow out for miles and take all the goodness away. I duly took the tree out again and lined the hole. That tree was a source of wonderment and was literally covered in fruit. On another occasion I decided to grow a nice variety of runner beans, so I bought some beans and planted them and went out and got some sticks to support them.

'Tell me Mr Douglas,' said the gardener when I'd finished. 'How tall are you?'

'I'm six-foot-four,' I told him.

'Well, how high are those sticks you've just put in?'

'About five foot,' I replied.

'That means you'll have to bend down to pick your beans, don't it?'

Needless to say, I replaced them with seven-foot sticks instead!

* * * * *

With my love of cooking I splashed out on an Aga. It heated the house and it had three ovens, the idea being that you have an oven to keep things warm, a slow oven and a fast oven. I put the Christmas turkey in the slow oven the night before and the next day I put it in the top oven at about noon to crisp. We'd never tasted turkey like it.

This is another delicious recipe, this time for lamb. You can do this in a conventional oven, as it doesn't have to be an Aga. You get the butcher to bone a leg of lamb for you. Then you stick little pieces of rosemary and garlic all over it and pour some melted butter over the top. You place it in the oven on the rack (shelf) with the roasting tin full of potatoes underneath, so that all the lovely roasting juices drop onto them. You put your lamb onto a plate and keep it warm and put your roast potatoes at the top of the oven to give them a fierce blasting. You've never tasted a meal like it. The good thing about the leg of lamb is that when it's boned, it's uneven, which means that you get underdone meat, medium meat and well-cooked meat all on one piece of lamb.

There are many different forms of cooking, but I'm not a microwave person. I cook on gas, but I much prefer an Aga. Unfortunately, we haven't got room for one in our kitchen on the island.

* * * * *

It may sound a bit of a cliché to mention ghosts haunting an old manor house, but what I'm about to relate is perfectly true. This actually happened just before I discovered the well in the stone floor, when the rest of the family was out one day. I'd been busy in the house, when I decided to pour myself a glass of wine (just the one) and sit in the inglenook to study my designs. I suddenly had the feeling that I wasn't alone and, glancing up, I saw an old lady in Victorian clothes sitting opposite me in the inglenook. The figure seemed to be staring into space, unaware of my 'presence' and although I didn't actually feel scared, it was certainly a shock.

I cleared my throat and stated in an authoritative voice 'Excuse me! I have three children and a wife who will be living in this house. So please don't ever appear again or I will bring in a priest.'

I know that this probably sounds far-fetched, but she vanished. I didn't mention the incident to the rest of the family, but one day Sarah came running up to me and asked: 'Daddy! Who is that nice old lady I just passed on the stairs?'

'Oh, she's just come to have a look round the house,' I fibbed, hoping the slight tremor in my voice didn't betray me.

'Well, she was wearing a funny-looking dress.'

As far as I'm aware, that was the only other occasion our ghost at Abinger Hammer ever appeared again.

* * * * *

My neighbour at Abinger must have been retired. I could see him watching me at various times throughout the day and it never occurred to me why. I just thought that he might have recognised me. One day, I was walking out of the house down to the shops when he called out 'Good morning! Not working today?'

'Not until tonight,' I told him and I could see his mind ticking over.

A few days later I saw him again.

'Got a day off?' he asked.

'No, I'm just off to town and then I'm working after lunch.'

It suddenly occurred to me that he was trying to suss out what I did for a living.

Two days later I appeared on the Dave Allen Show, when for once I wasn't dressed up as Alf. My neighbour must have been sitting in his kitchen waiting for me to appear the next morning, because as soon as I walked outside he rushed into the garden and said: 'You're on television! I thought you were a stockbroker.'

* * * * *

During the winter of 1966/67 I appeared in Cinderella at the London Palladium with Cliff Richard and The Shadows. I was thrilled to be cast as Baron Hardup, alongside Cliff, who was playing the part of Buttons. The Shadows were The Brokers Men, Terry Scott and Hugh Lloyd were the Ugly Sisters, Peter Gilmore was a very dashing Prince Charming and Pippa Steel was Cinderella.

From the opening night to the closing night (three months, twice daily, apart from Sundays) we were packed out at every performance. We would all try and dash out for a meal each afternoon between performances, but the fact that the show was such a huge success brought about a problem. With the added attraction of Cliff being in the panto, the stage door would be heaving with autograph hunters. It was wonderful, of course, to have all these people clamouring for our signatures and we would never have wanted to disappoint anyone. It meant, though, that the ravenous cast had little time left to gulp down a meal before the evening performance. I came up with a solution, which I put to Cliff after a show one evening.

'Why don't we bring our own meals into the dressing room?' I said to him. 'Your room on Mondays and mine on Tuesdays.'

'Yeah, great idea, Jack.'

So, this we did and after a couple of days Terry Scott knocked on the door and came into the dressing room.

'Cor! What's going on in here?' he asked.

Needless to say, Peter, Terry and Hugh cottoned on to our mealtime gatherings. After that, we each took it in turns to provide the food and in no time at all we were trying to outdo one another. It was great fun, as these mealtimes became grander with each passing day and you never knew what to expect. Sometimes it was more like a banquet rather than a snack and we certainly made a meal of that particular panto' season.

* * * * *

There were many stories during that wonderful run of Cinderella and it would be impossible to mention them all. The book will end up like 'War And Peace' at this rate!

The one that always makes me smile when I think of it, is about Terry Scott. Terry was living in Guildford at that time and, unbeknown to the rest of us, he would wear his street clothes underneath his enormous crinoline dress during the show's finale. The show over, he would then take the dress off, put his coat on and dash to catch the train home. I happened to spot him doing this one night and so Cliff and I hatched a devilish plan.

Every night in the finale the entire main cast would stand in line to take their bows in front of the audience. On this particular occasion, however, Cliff and I gave one another a conspiratorial nod. Terry was conveniently positioned between the two of us and, as we all bowed, Cliff and I both grabbed a handful of the crinoline. As we stood upright again, there on view was Terry's rolled up trousers, socks and suspenders. Everyone, including the cast and crew roared with laughter, but the upshot was that Terry didn't speak to the pair of us for a week. Sorry Terry. We didn't mean to be so 'under' hand!

* * * * *

My years working with Des were extremely happy ones. Unusually for this business, it was a period of my life when I never had to worry about where the next job was coming from. Des and I were riding on the crest of a wave, quite literally when we were doing our summer show in Blackpool. After reading a glowing report about us in the local paper, Des called me to his dressing room for a chat.

'Listen, Jack. I'll get straight to the point,' he said. 'We've had a marvellous eight years together and it's been a great partnership … '

I could definitely feel a 'but' coming on.

'Look! Have you seen this write-up about the show?' he continued, opening the paper at the appropriate page.

'Yes, it's brilliant,' I said, without conviction. 'What about it?'

'Quote,' read Des. '"Last night I saw Des O' Connor and Jack Douglas in a summer show in Blackpool and they were hilarious. Watch out **Morecambe and Wise**."'

Des emphasised the last bit and I gave a resigned nod.

'You see what's happened, don't you, Jack?'

'Yes. You didn't want us to become a double act and that's exactly what we've become.'

'Precisely.'

Des was a big star and he could now afford to realise his true ambitions. He always knew what he wanted and what we were doing at that time was **not** it. He went on to explain, in the nicest possible way, that he wanted to go it alone. 'We can still do the odd television series together, though,' he added.

'Go down and ask the gypsy on the North Pier to gaze into her crystal ball, Jack,' Des advised finally. 'I know that she will predict a great future ahead for you.'

How right he was. I mentioned before that Des was the most unselfish comedian I've ever worked with. The more laughs I got, the happier he was. I was grateful that he'd taken me with him to the top.

* * * * *

CHAPTER TEN

I can remember going to see Sid James in the farce "When The Wife's Away" at the Windmill Theatre in Great Yarmouth long before I met him in the Carry On's.

Sid was superb, but he was only there for a trial period, as I think he was taking the play to South Africa. Yours truly was booked to take over Sid's role when the farce opened in Blackpool. I went backstage after the show to have a chat with Sid.

'Sid, I'm very impressed with the actor playing that old gentleman in the play,' I told him.

'He's not old, mate,' said Sid. 'He's a young bloke.'

'Really? Tell me, are you taking the rest of the cast with you to South Africa?'

'No, it's just me. Come and meet John.'

Sid introduced us and I was amazed that such a young actor could have portrayed an elderly gentleman so perfectly. I went back to London to see my brother Bill, who was directing the play in Blackpool, and Michael Sullivan, who was my agent at that time. They were co-presenting the farce and confirmed that they had already recast the part of the old gentleman.

'Has this guy signed a contract yet?' I asked them.

'Well, no, not yet,' said Bill.

'Right! I want the actor I've just seen in Great Yarmouth to have the part.'

'Hang on a minute, Jack. We don't want just anybody, it's quite a strenuous role,' said Michael.

'It's me who's got to work with this guy.' I said. 'After all, he'll be playing my father for God's sake.'

'I'm sorry, Jack, but … '

'For the first time in my career I'm going to say that if you don't cast John in this part, then you haven't got me.' I said, making to leave.

There was a deadly silence and Bill and Michael looked at one another.

'Wait!' said Bill, as I opened the office door. 'Is it really *that* important to you, Jack?'

'I wouldn't have said what I just said unless it was.'

'Okay, you've got him.'

'Thank you. I promise you won't regret it.'

The actor in question was John Inman.

We started rehearsals and John played the part of this eighty-year-old impeccably and the show opened to rave reviews. John and I used to have such fun on the stage and there was one bit in the play when John's character was supposed to be reading "Playboy" magazine. I walked on the stage and said, 'Oh, you dirty old man.'

I thought that I'd have a bit of fun and, as one of the stage hands had a collection of pornographic pictures he would show to everyone, I asked him if I could borrow a few. Anyway, the next night, John picks up the magazine as usual, speaks his line, opens up the centrefold and bursts out laughing. I'd stuck these rude photos inside his magazine!

John Inman, Jack and Pat Starck in 'When The Wife's Away'
at the Windmill Theatre, Great Yarmouth

At the end of the season, my brother came to me and said: 'You'll be glad to know that I've just signed up John Inman.'

I gave an affected little cough and smoothed my hair.

'Yes, all right, Jack,' he added. 'I have to admit that you were one hundred per cent right about him and I was wrong.'

John is known as Mr Humphries in America and he's even bigger over there than he is here … I think I'd better rephrase that!

When my brother took him out to New York he said that it was like walking down Broadway with the President of the United States.

* * * * *

It was while I was appearing in the farce "When The Wife's Away" in Yarmouth, again with John Inman, that I received a call from Alec Fine. Alec was the booker for ATV and he told me that Des O' Connor was doing a seven-part series at Elstree and he wanted me to be in it. Although they were being filmed on Sundays, which was my day off, I explained that I was physically exhausted after appearing twice nightly in one of the heaviest farces I'd done in my life. Not only that, but the road from Great Yarmouth to London was always chock-a-block with traffic and the journey would have taken me hours.

'Yes, I see your problem,' said Alec with a sigh. 'Well, if I think of anything, I'll let you know.'

I couldn't see a way round it, but when Alec mentioned my dilemma to the powers that be, they immediately came up with a brilliant solution. Alec was given instructions to telephone the local airport and flying school (no, the school didn't fly, it was just a place for people to be taught to fly) in Yarmouth. It was arranged that I would be flown down to Elstree on Sunday mornings, from where a car would take me to the studios. On Monday mornings, I would be collected from my hotel, taken to the airport and flown back to Yarmouth. Oh, this heady showbiz life!

Anyway, ATV agreed to pay all my expenses, so the problem was solved. The first Sunday, I must admit to the odd little butterfly fluttering around inside me, especially after Alec told me that the flying school was owned by the Wright Brothers! When I accompanied the pilot out onto the tarmac, though, I was relieved to see that it was a natty-looking, four seater Cessna waiting for me and not a battered old twin-winged relic from World War One. We climbed on board then the pilot started her up and taxied into position. After clearance from the control tower, he throttled up the engine and we zoomed along the runway, my stomach doing a little somersault as we took off into the cloudless sky.

The sea glistened like millions of jewels in the morning sun and Yarmouth bay was dotted with tiny white boats. When the plane turned inland, I noticed that the fields resembled a colourful patchwork quilt, stretching off into the distance as far as the eye could see. Here and there a river snaked its way lazily through the countryside, but then, all too soon, the rural views gave way to a more suburban vista and we began our descent into Elstree. As arranged, a car picked me up from the airfield and I arrived at the nearby studio in a complete state of elation.

I was bursting to tell Des about the flight, but our busy filming schedule meant that any tales of my experience would have to wait.

After three Sundays had elapsed, the pilot asked me if I'd ever flown a plane.

'No, I haven't,' I said.

'Well, would you like to learn?'

The Cessna is quite a simple little aeroplane to fly and once he'd explained about speed and altitude, it was just like driving a car.

'You have to keep your eye on the wind, too,' he said.

If you think about it, that's pretty sound advice, even when you're not flying a plane!

The dual controls meant that with his expert guidance on bringing the nose up and making sure the wings were level, I was able to land at Elstree. Thankfully, it was a glorious summer and we had good weather for the whole of the seven weeks, which is, of course, quite incredible for this country.

When I told Des about my newly acquired skill, though, he declined the offer of a flight on Jack's 'Wing and a Prayer Airline'. I can't think why!

* * * * *

At the end of a successful run of 'Don't Tell The Wife', we were given the opportunity to take the show to Durban and Johannesburg. Apartheid was, of course, still very much in evidence in South Africa at that time, but, as none of the cast were remotely interested in politics, we naively put it to the back of our minds. Besides, any worries I may have harboured on that score were far outweighed by thoughts of visiting such a beautiful part of the world.

The two-week rehearsal went well and on the opening night I walked out on stage in my usual guise as Alf. Despite the fact that this was supposed to be a comedy, and a very funny one at that, we played to complete silence.

Laughter is the lifeblood of any comedian, but we didn't manage to raise so much as a titter from the audience. Only another comedian can understand how utterly dreadful it felt. After what seemed like an interminable first half, I went to find the stage manager to ask him what we were doing wrong. I couldn't believe it when he said that I was the problem.

He said that Alf's cap, overalls, belt and boots were the kind of clothes only worn by black people and the white population wouldn't be seen dead wearing them. I had never worn anything else in the farce and as it was too late to change, I went back on stage after the interval to see that more than half the audience had left. We struggled through to the end of the show and I can truthfully say that it was one of the unhappiest nights of my entire career. To me, this really did seem to be a farcical situation, but, if I wanted to perform, then I was going to have to respect their wishes.

The following day, after I'd drowned my sorrows along with the rest of the cast, I went to the shops to buy an ill-fitting and more appropriate suit for Alf to wear. I was dreading the next performance, but we had a fabulous show that night. Thank God that things have moved forward in South Africa since that time.

* * * * *

Sue and I bought a house in Thames Ditton, where one of our favourite pastimes was watching the cruisers going up and down the river on a Sunday afternoon.

'I'm going to have me some of that,' I said to Sue, one particularly glorious weekend.

'Some of what?' she said, eyeing a bikini-clad blonde, who was stretched out across the bow of a passing craft.

'No, I don't mean some of that,' I said, following her gaze. 'I mean, a cruiser.'

'What!' cried Sue, sitting bolt upright on her sunbed. 'I know you're good with boats, Jack, but could you handle something as racy as that?'

'I play with my submarine in the bath,' I told her. 'Anyway, I'm a quick learner and you can help me with the ins and outs.'

(Sue had previously lived on an island in the Thames, so she was well used to being around boats and water.)

'With a powerful engine like that, it might be more ins than outs if you don't know how to handle her correctly,' she warned.

'It's only a four-mile-an-hour speed limit along here, remember,' I pointed out.

'Precisely! I rest my case,' said Sue, leaning back and relaxing again.

I acquired a Freeman 22-foot, 4-berth, in-board river cruiser. The Freeman's are low-slung, making them ideal for inland waterways, as you can pass safely under bridges without decapitating yourself. These sleek little beauties cost an arm and a leg, but, what the heck, I could still steer with one arm, couldn't I?

The 'Lady Susan', as I called her, looked wonderful in her mooring at the bottom of the garden and I would often sit and pose on deck with my Martini, whilst puffing contentedly on my pipe. I even bought myself a little telescope, which came in handy for bird watching! We joined the National Trust, which meant that Sue and I could take off on a Sunday with Sarah and visit their lovely riverside houses. Once safely moored by the bank, I would rustle up a meal in the galley and there we would sit in our idyllic surroundings, just like Lord and Lady Muck.

I was at home one morning polishing me brass compass when a call came in from Thames Television, asking if I would do a guest spot on the David Nixon Show. The studio was just down river and, as they had their own little docking marina, I thought that it would be fun to cruise down there on the 'Lady Susan'.

'This is the life,' I thought to myself, as my 'dream boat' purred along. Her sleek, pointed bow cutting through the water making hardly so much as a ripple.

The studio came into view and I could see David and the rest of the cast sunning themselves on the balcony.

'Ahoy there!' shouted David, suddenly spotting my approach.

All eyes were upon me as I prepared to nose my pride and joy into the dock.

Everything was going swimmingly, until a piece of rope, which some bright spark had left floating in the water, fouled up my propeller.

There was a high-pitched whining noise and then the engine cut out with a splutter.

'Come on, Captain Pugwash!' shouted one of the spectators. 'You can fix it!'

'Yeah, get your waders on and assess the damage, me hearty,' shouted another.

There was nothing I could do from on-board the boat, especially with my best clothes on, so I dropped anchor and went below to change into my wet suit. Luckily I'd learned to dive during my time in Blackpool and had my wet suit on board. On the way back up, I collected my Bowie knife.

Eat your heart out, James Bond!

'They call him Flipper, Flipper, faster than lightening,' the cast struck up in unison when they saw me emerge from below.

Ignoring their taunts I dived into the water and swam around the back of the boat to survey the damage. Luckily, the propeller had only been turning slowly at that point and so none of the blades had bent. I cut away the offending rope and climbed back up onto the boat again. I held the rope above my head like some sort of soggy trophy and my ears rang with the cheers and applause of the now appreciative audience on the balcony. David Nixon was quite impressed.

'Well done, Jack,' he said, as I joined him later. 'You could try and sell it as a Roman relic you've dragged up from the bottom of the Thames.'

'I don't think so, David,' I said with a grimace, throwing the mangled, slime-covered mess into a nearby bin. 'That literally would be money for old rope!'

* * * * *

I wasn't the type of person who enjoyed drinking the night away at wild parties when I was away touring with a play … well, not all the time, anyway! I was far happier keeping a clear head, so that I could spend the day visiting National Trust properties in the area. I must have been appearing in Torquay, because I can remember one particular visit I made to Berry Pomeroy Castle in nearby Totnes. A group of us were following our guide along the ramparts of St. Margaret's Tower, when this lovely labrador that someone had on a lead, suddenly stopped in its tracks and wouldn't budge. His owner tried to coax him to move, but the dog's paws were firmly rooted to the spot and he was whining and shivering with fear. Liking animals as I do, I walked over to see if I could help and immediately sensed the most dreadful atmosphere.

'Forgive me,' I said to the man. 'I hope that you don't think I'm a crank, but I know why your dog won't move.'

'I feel that there's something quite supernatural here.'

The guide had been listening to this and said, 'Yes, you're quite right.'

'Lady Margaret Pomeroy was imprisoned in the tower and walled up by her sister, Lady Eleanor, because they had fallen in love with the same man.'

'Sadly, poor Lady Margaret starved to death and the White Lady, as the ghost has become known, is said to haunt the tower and ramparts.'

I remember being escorted around another National Trust property and having a distinct feeling of déjà vu, even though I'd never set foot in the place before. The guide showed us this beautiful sweeping staircase of carved oak, before saying that he would take us through to the kitchen. Without thinking, I turned on my heels … and walked straight into a wall. The guide asked me if I was all right and I said I was, but that I had no idea why I'd done it. He said that it was once a doorway to the kitchen, which had been bricked up 150 years before!

* * * * *

I do seem to be able to sense these kinds of atmospheres and I can remember another occasion when Sue and I were house hunting in Thames Ditton. We went along to see this beautiful 16th century house and completely fell in love with it. There was a York stone floor in the kitchen, an inglenook fireplace in the lounge and a wealth of oak beams throughout. Sounds just like the estate agent's blurb!

'It's lovely, Jack,' whispered Sue and I could see that she was just as smitten with the place as I was.

I wanted to make an offer right there and then, but thought it best not to appear too keen.

'May we look upstairs, please? I asked the owner.

'Yes, of course,' he said and we followed him up to the master bedroom, where there was a magnificent four-poster bed and yet more beams.

'I see from the agent's details that there is also a flat on the second-floor, may we have a look at it, please?'

'I'm afraid that it isn't convenient at the moment, Mr Douglas,' said the owner, looking decidedly uncomfortable.

Back in the estate agent's office, I told the sales negotiator that we wanted to make an offer.

'However, the owner wouldn't let us look around the top flat and I will need to see it before committing myself,' I told him.

'Of course, Mr Douglas. I'll telephone the owner and see if it's convenient for you to go around tomorrow,' he promised.

True to his word, he fixed up our second visit and this time we were shown to the stairs leading up to the flat on the second floor. As soon as we reached the door of the flat, I stopped dead.

'What's the matter, Jack?' asked Sue, nearly colliding with my back.

'I can't go any further,' I told her.

'Why ever not?'

'Because there's an atmosphere up here.'

We turned around and descended the stairs again.

'Is there something wrong?' asked the owner.

'I now know why you were reluctant to show us the flat.'

'Um, well, it was rather untidy yesterday and we needed to …'

'It's haunted, isn't it?' I snapped, cutting his explanation short.

His silence confirmed my suspicion.

'Thank you for showing us around your beautiful home,' I told him. 'I wish you luck in selling it, but neither my wife nor I would want our children to live alongside a malevolent ghost.

'Thank you and goodbye.'

This may have seemed a little curt, but believe me, if you had sensed the dreadful feeling of foreboding that I had just experienced on those stairs, then you'd have wanted to get out of there as quickly as possible, too. A little while later I was chatting to an historian friend of mine who was writing a history on Thames Ditton.

'I know exactly the house you're referring to,' he said.

'There was a very beautiful chambermaid living there, who Charles II apparently spotted whilst out riding. He arranged to meet her one night in a lane nearby. However, being the lad he was, he promptly forgot all about their little assignation. The poor girl waited for him all-night and died from hypothermia. People say it's her who haunts what would have once been the servants' quarters.'

Hell hath no fury like a woman scorned and if the atmosphere at the top of those stairs was anything to go by, then that old saying is certainly true.

* * * * *

The BBC used to make a wonderful programme called Spotlight. In the programme, a chosen comedian would perform some of their well-loved routines in front of a theatre audience. Various film clips from their careers would also be shown. Comics like Arthur Askey and Spike Milligan had appeared on the show and, in July 1984, it was the turn of yours truly to strut his stuff. I worked on a suitable script with the talented writer, Lance Percival. I went through my repertoire and, as very few people knew that I could dance, I demonstrated the difference between American and British tap dancers.

'Now, American dancers learned to dance when they were hobos on trains,' I told the audience. 'Where their musical accompaniment would have been a mouth organ. Imagine how difficult it must have been to dance on a moving train, though. They had to stand with their legs apart like this,' I said, getting into a suitable position. 'Dancing from the knees downwards enabled them to keep their balance.'

I was just demonstrating this, when an attractive female heckler in the audience jumped up and joined me on-stage.

'No, no, no! That's ridiculous! This is how you do it,' she said.

She then went into a British tap dancing routine.

It was all in the script, of course.

'Meet my wife Sue,' I said to the bemused audience and they applauded her expert performance.

* * * * *

I remember once that I was playing a character called Doctor Wickstead in a farce.

'You will need a moustache for the part,' I was told. 'Do you want a prop one?'

'No thanks, I'll grow my own,' I said.

I'd never felt comfortable with fake moustaches, because they had a nasty habit of coming adrift during a performance.

'Please don't be offended,' said the director. 'But your bald patch makes you look a lot older than you really are.'

'Oh!' I said, putting a defensive hand to the back of my head.

'You look young in the face, Jack, but how would you feel if we had a toupee made for you?'

'I'd be delighted,' I said. 'I'll take care if it myself, though.'

I went along to Wig Creations in the West End and, after a consultation, was told to come back in ten days time. I was astounded when he held the mirror up to the back of my head. As Eric used to say to Ernie – you couldn't see the join.

'I'll have to get used to wearing it, so I'll wear it home,' I said, feeling twenty years younger.

'Hello darling,' Sue said as I walked in. 'Dinner's almost ready ... Oh!'

'What is it, dear?' I asked innocently.

'Have I seen that suit before?'

'Yes, why do you ask?'

'You look so young in it.'

'Why, thank you, darling,' I said, seating myself at the dining table.

Sue walked up behind me and leant over to place a bowl of soup on the table in front of me. Amazingly, as she chatted about her day, Sue still didn't twig about the wig.

'I can't get over how different you look today, Jack,' she said, jumping up to collect the bowls. 'Hang on a minute! Good heavens!' she said, finally noticing.

By the time it came to doing the play, I'd grown my own moustache and the wig worked marvellously. It was so convincing that I even used to wear it sometimes for things like personal appearances. Sadly, one evening I came home to find my two Lhasa Apsos, Haggis and Muffin, playing a game of tug-o-war with something ...

Let's just say that there was hell toupee!

* * * * *

It was a great joy for me when I was asked to do a play with Arthur Askey, as I'd always been a fan of his from the first time I saw him. We were guests for an amateur repertory company, brought in, dare I say, to draw the audiences in. After working with Joe Baker all those years, who was one of the best ad-lib comics there was, I really missed his witty repartee.

As soon as I discovered that Arthur had the same ready wit, the fun started. Each performance the pair of us would try and catch each other out. So much so, that the rest of the cast used to stand in the wings listening to the banter. It got to a point where we would attempt to outdo each other with the most outrageous things.

One night, I'd come direct to the theatre from the golf course, so my clubs were in the dressing room. I was playing the part of an American variety agent in the play and when I joined Arthur on stage in the second half, he was supposed to be sitting at his desk. Instead, though, he was playing golf with one of my clubs. The next night, I came on with a sand wedge and, as I delivered my lines, I practised chipping an imaginary ball out of a non-existent bunker. Did this throw Arthur? Did it, heck!

'May I borrow your club, please?' he asked innocently.

He then proceeded to walk around the stage holding onto the club with me following behind. The audience loved all this nonsense and so, of course, did we.

Arthur was an amazing little man and it was a terrible shame when he had an accident during a pantomime at the Palladium. The director asked Arthur to step back not realising that the trap door was open and Arthur fell down the trap. He never really recovered from the injuries he sustained and eventually ended up having his leg amputated.

from the injuries he sustained and eventually ended up having his leg amputated.

I remember a friend of mine an agent called Cyril Berlin, telling me that he went to see Arthur in hospital. He was watching television and they were showing the raising of the Mary Rose, Henry the VIII's ill-fated ship.

Arthur apparently piped up 'Oh, good. I've been waiting to see this.'

'Why is that, Arthur?' asked Cyril.

'Because my briefcase was on board.'

It was such a tragic way for someone as brilliant as Arthur to end his days, but despite the pain he was always ready with a witty quip. It's sad to think we've lost so many of our great comedians over the years and I've been lucky enough to work with most of them. Heaven must be full of laughter, don't you think? I do.

* * * * *

CHAPTER ELEVEN

My agent phoned me one day to say that he'd got some good news and some bad news.

'The good news is that you're in the next Carry On film, "Carry On Matron",' he told me.

'What! Oh, that's marvellous,' I said. 'What's the bad news, though?'

'You're not getting paid.'

'Oh!'

He went on to explain that they had cast the film and were already over-budget, but I subsequently received a case of twelve bottles of Dom Perignon champagne for my cameo role.

To me, the Carry On's were the epitome of British visual comedy, which I'd always enjoyed. Hence my love of Laurel and Hardy. I was feeling a little anxious about meeting the rest of the cast when I turned up at Pinewood Studios for the first day of filming. Here was a team of actors who'd made something like twenty-two pictures together before I appeared on the scene, so to speak. I'd only been in the room for a matter of seconds when Sid James approached me.

'Hello again, Jack,' he said, shaking my hand. 'Welcome to the madhouse, mate. Fancy a cup of coffee?'

We were just chatting amiably when Kenneth Williams walked over.

'Sid!' he said, with his usual flourish. 'You haven't offered Jack a biscuit. Where's yer manners, man?' Sid gave a gravelly chuckle as Kenneth flared his nostrils and flounced off to fetch some biscuits.

I needn't have worried about being accepted, because within fifteen minutes the whole team had introduced themselves to me and from that moment on I felt entirely at ease in their company. They were the most unselfish group of people I've ever had the pleasure of working with.

Any one of them would say: 'Look, this joke isn't right for me, but it would be better for you.' If it got a laugh, they were as pleased as I was.

At the start, I'd been especially worried about meeting Kenneth Williams, as I knew he didn't suffer fools gladly. Not that I'm a fool, you understand. Well, not all of the time, anyway. If he liked you, he liked you. If he didn't, it was just an abrupt 'Hello', if you were lucky.

We did a scene together and afterwards, during a quick break from filming, we would sit chatting about Egyptology, which turned out to be a shared interest. We were just talking about young King Tut and the amazing silver plate that had been found inside his skull, when Sid James, who had been listening to our conversation, cut in.

'Actors!' he exclaimed. 'Cor blimey, I've never heard anything like it in me life. You're more like a couple of university professors.'

Jack and Kenneth Williams in Carry On Dick 1974
Photograph reproduced by kind permission of Peter Rogers, Producer of the Carry On films

'Clear off! We're having a proper conversation' said Kenneth, shooing Sid away with a dismissive wave of his hand.

Since Ken's death the media have had a field day over the question of his sexuality, of course. He may have been gay, but you never saw any evidence of this while he was working with the team. He never flaunted his boyfriends in front of us and, as far as I was aware, he was very much a loner. More often than not, he was in the company of his mother.

To the viewing public, Kenny was a funny man with an even funnier voice and they loved him. Kenneth adored Barbara Windsor – she was everything he liked in a person. So much so, that when she married Ronnie Knight and they went away to Spain on honeymoon, Kenny turned up at the hotel. I think Barbara just has this innate ability to accept people for what they are. With Barbara there is no pretence or falseness and that's why Kenny liked her so much.

As for Barbara, I think she's one of the most professional actors I've ever had the pleasure of … Ooh, Matron! I was going to say, 'the pleasure of working with' if you'd given me the chance to finish. However, just why she associated herself with that disgusting television drama, "Cor Blimey", is quite beyond me.

Everyone knows about Sid and Barbara's affair so there's no point in me raking over old coals here. What I will say is, that I have a nose for such things and I can't remember sensing so much as a sniff of a relationship between Sid and Barbara while they were filming at Pinewood. I wasn't even aware there was a friendship between the two of them until we had left the confines of the studio and did "Carry On London" on stage at the Victoria Palace.

I always feel a little guilty that I may have been instrumental in getting them together in the first place. You see, it was me who suggested that it might be better if the cast stayed at a hotel for one night as we were doing an early morning broadcast for the Pete Murray show. That night I first noticed them holding hands underneath the table and I was absolutely astonished. Prior to that, I hadn't even been sure they even liked one another and yet there they were, gazing into each others eyes like a couple of lovesick teenagers.

Anyway, apart from all that business with Barbara and despite his reputation as a womaniser, I can honestly say, hand on heart, that I never once saw any evidence of the so-called lecherous behaviour associated with Sid. In fact, he was always the perfect gent. This business about young women being lured inside his on-set caravan is just a load of old twaddle, as far as I'm concerned. When you have to complete a full-length feature film in just six weeks there simply isn't time for such shenanigans. Apart from the fact that the powers that be at the studio wouldn't have allowed it. While the rest of us retired to the Pinewood bar at the end of filming, Sid would always rush off home to be with his wife Val and the kids. Well, whatever, poor Sid's no longer around to defend his good name, but I always feel extremely sorry for his family, who have to "carry on" listening to all the unpleasant things people say about him.

Sid, like most red-blooded males, myself included, enjoyed the company of pretty ladies and there are always plenty of those around on a film set. Thankfully, there's no law against chatting up women, or I'd have been in prison years ago! Even yours truly became a victim of the gossipmongers during my time with the Carry On's. There was a rumour going around that I was having a torrid affair with the beautiful, statuesque actress, Valerie Leon.

Valerie was, and still is, a stunning-looking lady and she and I spent many a happy hour in each others company while we were filming and yes, we did get on extremely well. Even today, when we bump into one another at a Carry On convention or a Heritage Foundation do, we still hug and kiss like the old pals we are. I make no bones about the fact that I love Valerie … but as a platonic friend, not in a sexual way.

After "Matron" I made seven more Carry On films, including Carry On Abroad, Girls, Dick, Behind, England, Emmannuelle, and Columbus. As well as various successful stage and television recreations like Carry On London and Carry On Christmas.

The Carry On's now have a cult following of fans and the films are still as popular today. I receive more fan mail now than I ever did. I even got one from the Assistant Ambassador at the embassy in Thailand, who said that he was an avid fan and had all the films on video.

* * * * *

Peter Rogers and Gerald Thomas were responsible for all the Carry On films and could make a full-length feature comedy in just six weeks, which was unheard of in the

Valerie Leon

Gerald Thomas, Valerie Leon and Jack

film industry. Peter was the producer and would cast the films, book the artists, arrange the locations and organise the finance. He was, and still is, of course, an expert in all of these aspects of filmmaking.

I can remember the first time that I met Peter. I think his talent must have preceded him, because I was very nervous, which I suppose is normal when you meet someone of his standing and reputation.

Peter was always very charming, but distant, and I had the distinct feeling that no one would ever really be able to get close to this lovely man. Someone had mentioned that it was Peter's seventieth birthday and so I thought it would be nice to break the ice a bit by buying him a little gift.

I was looking round a garden centre when I spotted two standard roses in pots. I knew that Peter lived out in the country and so presumed that he might like gardening. I bought the two of them, attached a little bow and a gift card, and then left them outside his office at Pinewood early the next morning. Later that same day, the team were in the middle of rehearsing a scene when Peter came in. He asked Gerald if he would mind holding up the action for a minute or two.

'Take fifteen everyone,' said Gerald, without question.

We all knew that Peter would never disrupt the filming without good reason and we were all wondering what that reason might be.

'Douglas!' said Peter, looking straight at me. 'I want to talk to you.'

'Oh, my God,' I thought. 'What have I done?'

I followed him outside, fully expecting the worst, but he just turned and put his arm around my shoulder.

'That was one of the loveliest birthday presents I've ever had,' he said. 'How did you know that I like gardening?'

From that moment on our friendship "blossomed" and we would chat together endlessly about plants and soil and such like. I think he's a brilliant man and I just wish that there were a few more like him in show business.

* * * * *

I consider the late Gerald Thomas to be one of the best comedy directors ever. The secret of the Carry On's was the fact that Gerald allowed the actors to behave like naughty school children between takes, letting us laugh and kid around with one another. When he clapped his hands, however, we knew we had to be ready to work. Gerald knew that if he could transfer these offset ingredients to on-set situations, the humour and atmosphere would be ready-made. Add this to the talent of the writer and the subject matter, mix well and cook for six weeks and you have the recipe for a perfect Carry On picture.

I remember when we were filming Carry On Dick and I had to dash into this beautiful church and run up the staircase to the bell tower. I opened the trap door, climbed up into the bell tower and they cut the shot.

'Right!' said Gerald. 'Get the cameras up into the belfry and we'll shoot the rest of the scene.'

One of the camera operators climbed through the trap door and then shouted down 'Mr Thomas! You'll have to come and see this.'

'Why? Is there a problem?' Gerald called back.

'There isn't enough room to swing a cat and if Jack's up here, there's no way we'll get a camera or anything else in.'

Gerald climbed the ladder and poked his head through the trap door.

'Oh, I see what you mean,' he said, climbing down again. 'Well, we shall have to build a replica bell tower back at Pinewood and film this scene at the end of the picture.'

Problem solved!

The following day, Gerald told me that he wanted me to ride a horse and, as we didn't have the luxury of stunt doubles on the Carry On's, I was duly introduced to my equine companion.

'I want a shot of you riding down here chasing Dick Turpin (alias Sid James) through the forest,' Gerald said, indicating the route he wanted me to take.

I climbed on board and awaited further instructions.

'Action!' shouted Gerald.

I squeezed my heels into the horse's sides and we set off at a gentle canter down the woodland track.

What a perfect way to spend a day I thought happily.

It felt great to be back in the saddle again and I was thoroughly enjoying myself. That is, until my mount suddenly swerved sideways, straight into the path of a chest-level branch. The impact swept me clean off the horse and I landed heavily on my back with my legs in the air.

'Ooof!' I said. It wasn't in the script, but there isn't much else you can say with the wind knocked out of you.

'Are you all right, Jack?' shouted Gerald, running over and helping me to my feet.

In the film I was playing the part of Sergeant Jock Strapp, who was on the side of the law enforcers in the Bow Street Runners.

'You didn't tell me my character was in Special "Branch", Gerald!' I said breathlessly.

Needless to say, the scene was kept in.

* * * * *

Four weeks later we were back in Pinewood to film the rest of the belfry scene, but when I walked in, Gerald was pacing the floor.

'What ever is the matter, Gerald?' I asked him, anxiously glancing at my watch to make sure I wasn't late.

'Come and have a look at this,' he said angrily. 'Nobody told the carpenter that you're six-foot-four and the whole of the belfry has been made with six-foot beams.'

I climbed up through the opening and was astonished to see this marvellous balsa wood belfry complete with bells and ropes. I was going to do my Hunchback of Notre Dame impression, but thought better of it.

'It's so realistic Gerald,' I said as I climbed down. I was genuinely impressed with the carpenter's handiwork.

'That's academic if we can't fit you in it,' he said and I could see that he was upset.

Despite the fact that the "chippy" had done a wonderful job, Gerald was extremely agitated by this careless oversight in continuity.

The needless irritation was causing a major hiatus in our tight filming schedule. (Tempus fugit and all that. Or rather tempers fidgeted!) Suddenly, an idea popped into my head and I turned to Gerald and said, 'Can I try something, please?'

'Yes, go on, try anything, Jack,' said Gerald with an exasperated sigh. 'We'll have a rehearsal,' he added, turning to the crew. 'Go on, Jack'.

I climbed up through the opening and turned immediately towards this big beam, hit my head and reacted to it. Then, I came backwards and hit the back of my head on another beam, turned left and hit my head on another beam, turned right and hit my head on a different beam. After that, I crossed my eyes and sank to the floor.

I paused for a bit of comic effect and then said, 'Did you like that, Gerald?'

'Great!' he said.

'Shall we film it, then?'

'No.'

'But why?' I said, reaching for the headache pills.

'Because I've already filmed it.'

That was typical Gerald. He captured a magic and that magic is very apparent in a lot of the Carry On pictures.

* * * * *

When actors joined the Carry On company they signed a buy-out contract, which meant that everybody was paid for the picture and that was it. In those days, of course, the films just did the rounds in cinemas and were never repeated on television like they are now. There were certainly no such things as videos or satellite television and, in any case, no one ever dreamt that the Carry On films would still be as popular forty years later. Peter Rogers did set up a deal with Thames Television for us to do thirteen Carry On programmes, however, which are on video.

These half-hours were the untold tales of history and included such gems as Orgy and Bess and The Case of the Coughing Parrot. As it happened, Sid James was away doing a farce in Australia, which was so successful they kept him on. Gerald asked me out to lunch and told me that he wanted me to star in these thirteen half-hour tales. It was lovely to be at the top of the bill and I really hadn't expected it.

My favourite story during the filming of these was about Joan Sims, who played Queen Guinevere in the two pieces we did about King Arthur and the Knights of the Round Table. The incident itself is emblazoned on my memory, although I can't recall whether it was the King Arthur one we were filming at the time. I even asked Joan and she couldn't remember, either. It had to be a costume drama, or rather a bodice ripping comedy of some kind, so we'll say that it was King Arthur, for the sake of argument.

Whatever, we were a week away from filming when I discovered that it was Joan's birthday on the first day of shooting, so, unbeknown to Joan (that rhymes!), I got the whole cast and crew to join me in a windup. As part of my dastardly plan, we all agreed not to wish her a happy birthday. This may seem a bit unkind, but in my role as Sir Gay I had something up me doublet and hose, so to speak. It didn't half itch, as well!

Poor Joan had spent an hour in make-up, followed by a further hour in wardrobe, because she had to be laced up tightly in a corset. It's called "suffering for your art", although suffering round your parts would have been more appropriate in Joan's case.

Anyway, Joan arrived on set looking stunning in her regal costume. Joan glanced round expectantly, but everyone just busied themselves with their usual tasks and although she looked disappointed that no one had remembered her birthday, like the true professional she is, Joan carried on regardless. Excuse pun.

To add insult to injury, when it came to lunchtime, Joan couldn't sit down in this costume and so the crew built her a special construction. If you can imagine a plank on legs with two arms rests, that's the only way I can describe it. Joan had a tray on there in order to eat her lunch standing up. During the afternoon, Joan was by the throne (don't worry, that joke was in the script!) waiting for her cue.

Gerald shouted: 'Action!' and Joan turned to her page and said, 'Bring on my courtiers.'

The next bit is not for the faint-hearted reader.

The double doors opened wide to reveal Bernard Bresslaw, Peter Butterworth, Kenny Connor and yours truly, clad in only our underpants and wigs … I did warn you. The only things covering our decency were trays bearing a large birthday cake, an ice bucket with a bottle of champagne, and some glasses and sandwiches.

With that, we all struck up with 'Happy Birthday to you' and Joan began to laugh and cry at the same time. For the next ten minutes the cast and crew enjoyed Joan's birthday, then Gerald clapped his hands and said: 'Right! Back to work.'

'I can't!' announced Joan loudly and everyone turned round to look at her with surprise.

'Why ever not?' asked Gerald.

'Because I've wet meself!'

Everybody on the set, including Gerald, was helpless with laughter at Joan's "wee" bit of bother.

'Is that what they mean by a royal flush?' whispered Bernie, as Joan was taken off to wardrobe.

'Good thing it wasn't a Richard the Third,' added the wicked Peter Butterworth.

* * * * *

How's this for a strange coincidence?

I was driving my much-loved Austin Healey 3000 along a country road when I saw a beautiful Jaguar XK 120 coming towards me in the opposite direction.

Suddenly, the Jag hit an oil slick and I watched in horror as it skidded off the road and plunged down an embankment. Applying my brakes and pulling up in the middle of the road, I turned on my hazard lights and went to see if the passengers were all right.

I scrambled down the bank and opened the driver's door, thankful to see that the driver and his female front-seat passenger were dazed, but seemingly unhurt.

'Overtures and beginners, please,' I said, which is what everybody says over the tannoy before the start of a show.

'What the bloody hell are you doing here?' asked Peter Butterworth, blinking his eyes in amazement.

'What's happened, Peter?' asked his wife, the impressionist Janet Brown.

That little incident became a classic story with the Carry On team.

* * * * *

Gerald Thomas had a very strict rule that none of the Carry On actors must drive themselves to work, so there was always a succession of hire cars to ferry the team to and from Pinewood. Mine would pick me up at about five-thirty in the morning and I would go straight to make-up on arrival at the studios. Most locations were nearby and I think my most exotic location in a Carry On, was Brighton. The car would collect me again at the end of the afternoon, usually at about four-thirty and I could learn my lines for the next day during the journey home. You see, this chauffeur driven car stuff wasn't to look flash, it just left us actors free to learn our lines. I must admit, it did make you feel rather important, though.

After my stint in make-up one morning, I was accompanying the rest of the Carry On team across the lot to our location at the back of the studio. (See what I mean about exotic locations?) I think we were filming Carry On Behind at the time, but again, my memory … We were just walking past the largest caravan I've ever seen in my life, when one of its many windows opened and out popped a familiar face.

'Good heavens! It's the Carry On team,' announced Peter O' Toole, who was also making a film at Pinewood.

'Have you had any breakfast?' he asked.

'No, we are just on our way to the Honey Wagon now,' we told him. (You will notice that I have no trouble remembering the name of the catering van!)

'Then come and join me,' said Peter, ushering us all inside. 'Come on, there's plenty of room.

He wasn't kidding! The interior of this "caravan" bore no resemblance to the ones you can hire out at the seaside and it was like stepping inside Dr Who's TARDIS, except for the chandelier. There was a thick white carpet underfoot, a huge television set on a mahogany sideboard, and heavy chintz curtains round the windows. There was also a fully stocked drinks cabinet with its drop-leaf door open to our astonished gaze.

The team sat down on the white leather sofa, which filled three sides of this immense room. We watched in horror as Peter lifted a huge bottle of champagne out of the cabinet. He then fetched some freshly squeezed orange juice from the fridge and proceeded to mix the two together with a swizzle stick in a cut-glass jug.

'What's that?' I asked him.

'Buck's Fizz.'

'Buck's Fizz?'

'Yes, our breakfast,' he answered, as if it were as normal as having a bowl of cereal or a boiled egg and soldiers.

'Oh, Peter,' I said. 'Please forgive me, I don't know about the others, but I never drink alcohol until I've finished work.'

I thought I'd offended him, because he placed the swizzle stick down on the table and fixed me with those extraordinarily blue eyes of his. He then shook his head incredulously and said: 'You mean you go out there … alone?'

* * * * *

Despite that inauspicious start, Peter and I got on extremely well and our paths crossed again a few years later. The team were doing "Carry On London" at the Victoria Palace and when I went forward to do my curtain speech at the end of the show, I spotted Peter.

I'd just been to see the film Lawrence of Arabia, which, in my opinion, is one of the best performances I've ever seen by a British actor. I couldn't resist it, so I said 'Ladies and Gentlemen. We are very honoured this evening to have in the audience one of the finest actors Britain has ever produced. If you haven't yet seen the film "Lawrence of Arabia", then I urge you to go and see it without fail. The star of that film is sitting out in front tonight … Mr Peter O' Toole.'

The audience went wild and I knew that if I left him sitting out in the auditorium he would have been besieged, so I invited him up on stage for our finale. Clasping the hands of the two prettiest girls in the line-up, Peter gamely joined in with our song and dance routine. The show over, he then came back to the dressing room.

'I meant what I said about Lawrence of Arabia,' I told him. 'May I offer you a drink?'

'I thought you'd never ask,' he said.

Afterwards, we chatted for over an hour and I discovered that Peter was an authority on old, English comedians, like Sid Field. To this day, although I haven't seen him for some years, I still consider Peter O' Toole a friend.

* * * * *

This next incident happened when I was, again, being chauffeur-driven, but in a BBC car. I was going to be interviewed on the Pete Murray radio show at Broadcasting House, but the driver said that he had to pick someone else up in the centre of London, first.

A smart gentleman climbed into the back of the car, sat down next to me and said 'Good morning! My name is … .'

Unfortunately, I didn't catch his name, as at that precise moment the driver blasted his horn at someone, who'd not only had the brass neck to cut him up, but also then had the audacity to give him a two-fingered salute. As you know, this kind of hand signalling is rarely observed amongst the agitated motorists that are stuck in the busy London traffic … it's more usually the one-fingered variety.

Ignoring the incident, I was just about to introduce myself to my companion when he sat bolt upright and stopped me in my tracks.

'Wait a minute! Aren't you that chap who appears in all those wonderful Carry On movies?'

'Yes, that's right,' I said, desperately trying to think who my inquisitor might be. 'I'm … '

'No, don't tell me,' he said, snapping his fingers with exasperation and closing his eyes. 'It's Jack Douglas, isn't it?'

'Yes, that's right.' I was surprised he'd managed to recognise me out of my "Alf" guise.

'Tell me, how long does it take to film a Carry On picture?'

'Six weeks,' I answered.

'What! That's bloody impossible.'

'Yes, I agree, but we do it,' I told him proudly. I then went on to tell him about our marvellous producer and director. He listened intently as I explained the ups and downs of movie making and how everything was cleverly put together at the end of the tight filming schedules.

'Do you know, it takes me eighteen months to two years to make a film,' said the stranger finally, as we reached Broadcasting House.

'Make a film,' I thought. 'Who is this man?'

I soon found out when the commissioner at the BBC opened the car door and said 'Ah, Mr Michael Winner. Good morning to you, sir.'

It seems I'd been teaching granny how to suck eggs.

* * * * *

I remember doing a midnight charity concert to raise money for Coventry Cathedral. I was there doing a summer show with Arthur Haynes and when I got to my dressing room, there was a card on the door bearing the name: "Sir John Gielgud".

'Oh, I'm sharing a dressing room with Sir John,' I thought anxiously.

He was absolutely charming, however, and insisted that I drop the "sir" bit as soon as we started chatting.

'What a wonderful career you've had,' I said to him. 'Tell me, you've done so many things, but is there anything you haven't done that you would like to do?'

'Oh, yes,' he answered without hesitation.

'What is it?' I asked.

'A Carry On picture.'

I remember thinking at the time that this was a marvellous compliment from this great man and he wasn't joking, either. If you remember his wonderful performance as the manservant in the film, "Arthur", with Dudley Moore, he certainly had a flair for comedy. I've often wondered why we create such fine actors and comedians in this country … present company excepted, of course!

* * * * *

Another bit of advice given to me by Robb Wilton was to come in useful during the stage version of the Carry On's. His advice was: 'If ever anything goes wrong in the theatre, whether it be that someone misses their cue, a door jams, or a knob falls off in your hand (ooh Matron!), simply tell the audience the truth.'

Barbara Windsor and I were right in the middle of a sketch in "Carry On London" at the Victoria Palace, when I glanced into the wings and noticed an agitated stage manager frantically pointing skywards. I looked up to see that the safety curtain was descending on our performance … no, we weren't that bad.

An expert in these things has since told me, that although a Safety Curtain comes down quickly, it then stops about eighteen inches from the floor. After this, it descends at a much slower rate to ensure that luckless souls, like me and Bar, can get out of the way in time. It's scary, though, when you consider these curtains actually weigh about ten tons.

In those days, a Safety Curtain would have been made of an asbestos sheet surrounded by a steel frame. These days, since the dangers of asbestos have become known, they are made entirely from steel. It's amazing what you can find out when you're researching a book!

Anyway, back to the plot.

'Um, Barbara. Step forward, will you?' I said.

'W … What! What are you doing, Jack?' asked a confused Barbara, realising this impromptu manhandling wasn't in the script.

'You don't want to end up like a fly, do you?'

'What!'

'Squashed,' I said, pointing up at the curtain's menacing progress towards us.

'Oh, my Gawd,' she said. 'What's 'appening, Jack?'

'Follow me down to the front of the stage or it'll be curtains for both of us,' I said.

We couldn't "carry on", as it were, so I decided to put Robb Wilton's advice into action.

'I'm afraid that the Safety Curtain seems to be suffering from a bad case of stage fright,' I told them.

'So, Barbara and I will be keeping you amused for the next twenty minutes or so, while it tries to pull itself together.'

I got a round of applause, not for the groan-inducing joke, but because I'd told them the truth and they appreciated the fact that we'd have to ad-lib for a while. I explained that, like some other theatres in London, the Safety Curtain at the Victoria Palace was controlled hydraulically by water pressure. (When you bought this book, you didn't realise that you were going to get a science lesson thrown in as well, did you?) I suppose they might have run out of water that night on account of someone pulling the chain down at Woolwich. This would mean, of course that the river was only running at a turd sorry, I mean a third of its usual capacity. Actually, the same expert told me that nothing more than a brake coming astray probably caused it. Back to the plot.

As an actress used to working from a script, Barbara was horrified at the thought of having to ad-lib while the stage hands winched the heavy curtain up by hand. Being the professional that she is, though, Bar soon began to relax and have a laugh with the audience. When the curtain was safely back in place, the audience gave us a huge and appreciative round of applause.

* * * * *

I can remember another little incident that happened during the run at Victoria Palace. Sid James and I were just leaving the theatre after the show one night, when we were surrounded by a screaming mob of girls. Still happens sometimes when I'm walking out of Tesco. These days it's usually because I've left some shopping behind at the checkout, though! If I'm honest, it was Sid who was surrounded by the girls. It has always been a complete mystery to me how that craggy-faced charmer was regarded as a sex symbol, when the only cymbal I could ever aspire to, was the one on my drum kit.

Anyway, among this bevy of beauties stood a particularly striking, well-endowed blonde, who was wearing, or nearly wearing, the miniest of mini skirts and a see-through blouse. Underneath this diaphanous top was a thin strip of material masquerading as a bra and I remember thinking that I'd seen more material in my brother's catapult. Not that I was looking you understand. She pouted seductively, fluttered her huge false eyelashes at Sid and said: 'Is Jack Douglas coming out?'

'Yeah, there he is,' answered Sid, pointing in my direction.

I smoothed my hair, straightened my tie and gave her my most dazzling film-star smile.

'Pleased to make your acquaintance,' I said, extending my hand politely. 'Jack Douglas at your service.'

'That's never 'im,' she said. Her heavily made-up eyes giving me the once-over before turning back to Sid.

'It is 'im, darlin',' said Sid with a chuckle. 'Jack looks completely different without Alf's glasses and cap.

'Na, you're 'aving me on. That's not 'im, is it, Tracy?' This last comment was directed at her equally stunning raven-haired friend.

'Na, you're telling us porkies, Sid,' said Tracy unconvinced. 'Lookin' at 'is natty clothes, though, I'd guess 'e was a wardrobe assistant, Liz. Am I right, Sid?'

'He is not the wardrobe assistant, ladies. I'm telling you he's Jack Douglas.' Sid insisted, but his protestations were to no avail. Lovely poetic line, that.

'What a shame, Tracy,' said Liz, as they teetered off down the street in their stiletto heels. 'I was looking forward to showing Jack me little … .'

Their voices were drowned out by the traffic as they disappeared round the corner and out of earshot. Sadly, I never did discover what "little" thing the voluptuous Liz had been planning to show me. It's the story of my life, really. If you happen to be reading this, Liz, then answers on a postcard, please.

* * * * *

It's perfectly true that people never recognised me out of costume and I once received three separate bits of fan mail from the same person. One letter was addressed to "Jack

Douglas", the second was to "Alf Ippititimus" and the other one was to a bishop character I'd been playing. I've heard of schizophrenia, but, as I said to the other two at the time, a three-way personality split is ridiculous! All this confusion was to come to an end, however, when the comedian Dave Allen phoned me up one day and asked me to appear on his show.

'I'd like you to come on stage dressed as a bank manager,' Dave explained when we met.

'Oh, but no one will recognise me without Alf's gear on,' I told him.

'Precisely!' said Dave.

'Um,' I answered feebly and he laughed at my confused expression.

'Let me explain,' said Dave, putting his arm around my shoulder. 'You appear on the Des O' Connor Show every Saturday night. Right?'

'Right!' I agreed.

'Yet you are one of the most well-known people on television, who's unknown.'

I hope you're following this, dear reader, because I hadn't got a clue what he was going on about.

'Well, I've got an idea,' Dave continued. ''You walk on stage wearing your best bib and tucker and I say to the audience 'Do you know who this is?'

'Yeee ... s,' I said.

'I bet the audience won't have a clue who you are.'

'I'll stake my life on it.'

'Ah, but later in the same show, you come back on stage dressed as Alf and I shall say ... '

The penny suddenly dropped and I interrupted him: 'This is the same well-dressed, handsome young man I introduced you to earlier.'

'Got it,' said Dave, clapping me on the shoulder. 'I guarantee they'll be amazed Jack.'

It worked like a charm and the audience just couldn't believe that the dapper chap they had seen before in a blue pinstriped suit was actually scruffy old Alf. From then on, audiences recognised me as Alf as well as Jack Douglas and it was all down to Dave Allen. Thanks mate. My only regret is that he didn't come up with the idea before my stint in "Carry On London". Oh Liz, just think what might have been!

* * * * *

Another little gem of advice from Robb Wilton was never to change a successful comedy format. I think that "Carry On England" was a very funny film, but they unfortunately changed the Carry On format, which I think was a terrible shame.

Kenneth Connor was playing Captain S Melly with Windsor Davies as his sergeant major. In one of the scenes the ATS girls were instructed to stand in line. They were all dressed in slacks and Kenny Connor said, 'They are women and I want to see them in skirts and nothing else.' Needless to say, his orders were misinterpreted and in the next scene the ATS girls were indeed wearing skirts, but no tops.

In previous Carry On films, misunderstandings like that would have been left to the imagination and I had thought at the time, that the camera was going to concentrate on

Kenny's horrified expression. This was, forgive me, completely over the top for a Carry On film and I just had to voice my opinion here and get it off my chest. The same problem arose, if you'll pardon the expression, in the film Carry On Emmannuelle.

In Carry On Columbus there was one scene when I had to go into the cabin and talk to Jim Dale. I decided to play around with the script a bit. I walked in and Jim handed me a glass of wine, so I did an enormous twitch, threw myself at the (balsa wood) door and smashed it down. When I went to see the premiere, however, that entire scene had been cut.

In 'Columbus' there just wasn't the team spirit, as in the earlier Carry On's and that had been a major part of their magic, I think. Despite the popularity of stalwarts like Sid James, Barbara Windsor and Kenneth Williams, there were no stars as such and everyone had been given equal billing. In Carry On Columbus, all the established stars wanted to do their own thing. We were known as 'the Carry On **Team**' for a good reason.

* * * * *

Barbara Windsor and Jack in ATV Series

Barbara Windsor, Terry Scott, Anita Harris, Jack and Bernard Bresslaw
Photograph reproduced by kind permission of Peter Rogers, Producer of the Carry On films

Jack and Barbara Windsor in 'Aladdin'
Photograph reproduced by kind permission of the Daily Mirror

Jack, Joan Sims and Sid James in Carry on Abroad, 1972

Carry On Behind 1975
Photographs reproduced by kind permission of Peter Rogers, Producer of the Carry On films

Jack in Carry on Behind 1975
Photograph reproduced by kind permission of Peter Rogers, Producer of the Carry On films

Carry On England 1976
Photographs reproduced by kind permission of Peter Rogers, Producer of the Carry On films

*Jack as a German soldier left
behind after the war was over.*

*Pilot programme with
Andrew Sachs and Amanda Barrie
– never to be shown!*

Peter Rogers, Producer of the Carry On films

CHAPTER TWELVE

Pantomimes are, of course, a uniquely British institution and I never tire of doing them. However, the Americans in particular find our tradition of the Principal Boy being a girl and the Ugly Sisters being men, a rather puzzling concept. They've obviously never walked down a London street on any **normal** Saturday night!

There's a magic about pantomimes, though, and it's great for a performer to hear the children calling out excitedly and joining in with all the fun. I remember one incident that happened during the ghost gag, when I was appearing in "Puss In Boots" (or, Cat In The Chemist, as we like to call it!) at the Hippodrome, Birmingham in the winter of 1972/73.

The "ghost gag" is where the ghost floats around the stage and whoever happens to be on there at the time, pretends they can't see it. This then results in the audience shouting out the familiar line: 'He's behind you!' I was in the middle of this particular scene and the children were getting themselves into quite a frenzy, because I was always looking to the right when the ghost was on my left and vice versa. Suddenly a little five-year-old girl ran up onto the stage, took hold of my hand and pointed to the ghost.

'There he is, you silly man!' she said, which brought the house down.

The audience clapped and cheered as I thanked the little girl and took her back to her parents who were sitting in the front row. When I went off-stage, I asked the theatre manager to bring the girl and her parents backstage after the show. This he did and I then arranged for them to come back the following day for tea with the cast.

My first entrance in the pantomime was on a Raleigh bike, which they had supplied for advertising purposes, so I rang Raleigh and told them the story of the little girl. The family duly arrived that afternoon for their special tea with the cast and when we'd all finished eating, I called for a hush. I took hold of the little girl's hand and walked her over to an object, which had been in the corner of the dressing room covered with a sheet. No, not the ghost! I whipped off the sheet and there was a brand-new Raleigh bike.

'This is for you, sweetheart,' I told her.

She was so surprised that she burst into tears, as did everyone else in the room, including yours truly. It's like I said before. I never "tyre" of pantomimes!

* * * * *

During the summer of 1975 I was playing a character called Stanley Pickersgill in the third series of "Not On Your Nelly" with Hylda Baker. In one scene, Hylda was chasing me around the bar of the Brown Cow pub when she slipped on all the spilt beer and hurt her ankle. Poor Hylda went down with a heck of a thump and her foot had soon swollen up to twice its original size. The first aid man was duly summoned to the set and Hylda was whisked away in a wheelchair, with the director, Bryan Izzard, in hot pursuit. We all thought that it was probably a bad sprain, but by the expression on Bryan's face when he reappeared on set, this clearly wasn't the case.

'I'm afraid that Hylda's injury is far more serious than we first thought,' he announced as we gathered round him. 'She's going to be in plaster for weeks and won't be able to finish the series.'

The awful news was greeted by groans from the cast and crew and it looked as if five weeks work would have to be cancelled. To my great surprise, however, Bryan turned to me and asked if I would be prepared to take over the lead role in the show. The future of the series was hanging in the balance, so it seemed to me that the others were collectively holding their breath awaiting my response.

'Yes, of course,' I answered and a gratifying cheer went up from the studio floor.

Hylda was in the first episode and then her character's subsequent absence from the series was explained by saying that "Nellie" had returned north. Nellie's cousin, Stanley, played by yours truly, was left pulling pints in the Brown Cow pub, amply assisted by his lovely barmaid, Big Brenda. Big Brenda was portrayed by the talented actress, Sue Nicholls, now of Coronation Street fame. "Not On Your Nellie" was the most enjoyable series to do and has recently been repeated on one of the satellite channels.

* * * * *

I was thrilled to be asked to do a pudding recipe on the "Pebble Mill At One" programme. When I arrived at rehearsals, however, I was horrified to see that I was going to be joined by two famous chefs. I wondered how a lowly amateur cook like me could ever impress them with new ideas. It would be like teaching granny how to suck eggs. Or, how to cook them, at least! I suddenly had a brain wave and rushed off to get my ingredients, which I then prepared myself … in secret.

It was an old, unfailing recipe of my mother's for brown bread ice cream with a special sauce. On the final rehearsal before the show went out, I was preparing my secret sauce ready to pour it over the ice cream, when one of the chefs came over. He sniffed the air appreciatively and then asked me what it was. I explained (with my fingers crossed) that it was an old family recipe and that I would rather not divulge its contents.

'Oh, I quite understand, Jack,' he said.

Just then, the other chef joined us and I let them both have a tantalising taste. Even though the pair of them raved about the flavour, I still wouldn't tell them what was in it. We did the programme and I explained to the viewers and the small studio audience that this delicious sauce was simply a melted Mars Bar. After the show, my culinary colleagues bought me a drink in the bar and we all had a good laugh about my little bit of subterfuge. I suppose it means I'm qualified to appear as a judge on MARSterchef!

* * * * *

After one of my appearances on Pebble Mill I was delighted to be asked if I would like to write a cookery book. I wrote down all the recipes I could think of and then it

occurred to me how funny it would be to have a selection of "Alf's" recipes, along with some old country cures. A cartoonist did all the pictures and the "Wey Hey Guide To Better Cooking" was born. It wasn't exactly what you'd describe as an international best seller, but it was fun to do and I still have a copy of it among my much-loved collection of about three hundred cookery books.I didn't write the rest of them, I hasten to add!

* * * * *

Jack shopping

The untimely death of that talented young actor, Richard Beckinsale, came as a great shock to everyone in show business. He is probably best remembered for his superb portrayal of the naïve and endearing character, Lennie Godber, in the classic seventies comedy series, Porridge. Early in 1979 I was lucky enough to work with Richard in a two-part thriller for television called "Red Saturday".

At our very first meeting it soon became obvious to me that he was just as down-to-earth as he appeared to be on-screen. Richard and I seemed to click right away and it's always gratifying for actors when that chemistry between them comes across to the audience. On reading through the script, I discovered that Richard and I had a big and dramatic scene together. This was to be filmed on location, somewhere outside London at two o' clock in the morning. Who said that showbiz was glamorous?

'Prepare for a rehearsal, please!' the director called out, once all the cameras and lights were in position.

I turned to Richard and asked if he would like to do the scene "live" and he agreed. We both felt that this would give the scene more immediacy (eat your heart out, Sir Michael Winner!) rather than going through it all beforehand. It went without a hitch and at the end of the scene the whole crew applauded our performance … much to the annoyance of all the neighbours at that time of the morning, I should think.

'That's one of the best scenes I've ever done,' I said to Richard..

'Me, too,' he agreed, shaking my hand.

A few weeks later I was horrified to hear on the radio that Richard had died of a heart attack. I waited for the next news bulletin in a complete daze, thinking (and hoping) that I must surely have misheard the announcer. Sadly, of course, I hadn't misheard and it was such a shock to think that I had been working with this seemingly fit and healthy young actor only weeks before. Apparently, Richard never realised that he was ill, but I believe that an unusually high cholesterol level caused his death.

Richard's young daughter Samantha had visited the set and I can remember thinking at the time that she was the mirror image of Richard. Today, of course, Samantha is a talented actress in her own right. Her appearances on television never fail to remind me of the brief but enjoyable friendship I struck up with her father.

* * * * *

Jack and the Lotus

My love affair with cars had continued and it was a proud day when I was able to afford to buy a Lotus Elan. I then bought an Austin Healey 3000, which was the most wonderful car of my life. When Eddie Pedder, who was the editor of the T.V. Times, phoned me to ask if I would like to take part in the Dubai Grand Prix, I didn't need asking twice. I was doubly thrilled when he said that they also wanted me to host the World Champions Dinner. Sue and I flew out to Dubai and were taken to our sumptuous hotel.

'You won't be getting involved in anything reckless, will you?' asked Sue.

'I doubt it,' I told her.

'**Promise** me you won't,' she said.

'I promise,' I told her … with my fingers crossed, out of sight behind my back!

On the morning of the first Arabian Gulf road race I was shown to my car and it was so exciting to glance across and see Juan Manuel Fangio, the Argentinean Motor Racing World Champion driver, sitting in the next car to me. There was also Brazil's Emerson Fittipaldi and Australia's Sir Jack Brabham, as well as our own James Hunt and Stirling Moss. Adrenaline and testosterone fought for dominance in my bloodstream as I listened to the throaty roar of engines all around me. As it happened, there had been so many famous faces on that racetrack, that they couldn't possibly insure them to race. All we could do was drive in procession and I never got out of second gear! It was all so frustrating. A bit later that same day, I had been running an appreciative hand over the gleaming prototype of the BMW sports car.

'Fancy taking her for a spin?' asked its owner.

'I'd love to, but I've promised the wife I wouldn't race,' I told him with a resigned sigh.

'You'll be quite safe on this track.'

'Oh, I don't know whether I dare,' I said, glancing anxiously up towards the stand from where I knew that Sue would be watching my every move.

'Tell you what! I'm here at six in the morning, so why don't you come down here and have a go then?'

'Could I?'

'Course.'

I sneaked out of bed at five-thirty the next morning and headed for the BMW spot. He was there, true to his word.

'Here you are,' he said, handing me the keys.

I climbed inside, started her up and drove her out onto the track, where I wound that little beauty up to one-hundred-and-sixty miles an hour. What an experience! I thought my adrenaline level would never come down again. I went back to the hotel and was just opening the bedroom door, when Sue woke up.

'Where have you been?' she asked with a yawn.

'Oh, I couldn't sleep, so I thought I'd go for a stroll.'

'See anything exciting?'

'No, not really. Just some idiot in a BMW driving like a bat out of hell!'

'Mad fool,' she said, before turning over and going back to sleep.

I couldn't agree more, I thought contentedly.

* * * * *

Jack at the Dubai Grand Prix

CHAPTER THIRTEEN

I had a call from Francis Essex, who was the Head of Central Television during the seventies. Over lunch, he asked me to take a script home to read. 'Let me know what you think of it, Jack,' he said at the end of our meal. I was intrigued, because I didn't recognise the name of the writer and I sat up in bed till after twelve reading it through. I knew that it was late, but I just couldn't wait till the morning to telephone Francis and tell him what I thought.

'Francis!'

'Oh, it's you Jack,' he answered sleepily, recognising my voice. 'What's up?'

'Sorry to ring you so late, but this script is wonderful. If you give the part of Jake the farmer to anyone else, I may kill you,' I told him excitedly.

The script was for a one-off comedy/drama called The Shillingbury Blowers. Although I didn't know it at the time, Francis had, in fact, written it himself under a pseudonym. He had given me the script because he wanted me to play the part of Jake.

It was a lovely genteel comedy about a village brass band, who were the "blowers" of the title, and it was to star Diane Keen, Robin Nedwell, Trevor Howard, John Le Mesurier and yours truly.

Robin was playing the part of Peter, a professional musician who had just moved to the village with his wife Sally, played by Diane. Trevor was Old Saltie, the founder member, conductor and a cornet player in the Shillingbury Brass Band. The band had been formed in 1945 to commemorate the disbandment of the local Home Guard. John was the head of the local council, whose character's name now escapes me, and I was Jake, the bandleader and trumpet player.

Now, I hadn't got a clue how to play the trumpet, but I managed to get one of our finest trumpet players, Kenny Baker to double for me. Although he was going to be doing all the blowing, so to speak, he taught me the rudiments of playing.

He showed me how to hold the trumpet correctly and to make sure that the valves were free before I began to 'play'. I got loads of phone calls after the first programme was aired, all along the lines of: 'Oh, I didn't know you could play the trumpet like that, Jack. It was marvellous.' It wasn't me, though. It was the brilliant Kenny Baker.

Anyway, when I turned up for the first day of filming in the beautiful village of Aldbury in Hertfordshire, who should be sitting next to me in the make-up room but my hero, Trevor Howard. I've always regarded him as one of the greatest actors of our era and I was literally star struck when I saw him.

'Oh, Mr Howard,' I said. 'How lovely to meet you.'

'No, no, call me Trev,' he insisted. 'Actually, can I ask you a favour?'

'Who do you want killed?'

'No,' he laughed. 'It's just that, although I've done a lot of movies, this is my first television show. Is it **that** different to making pictures?'

'It is in a lot of instances, Mr How … Trev,' I told him.

Jack 'playing' the trumpet

'Well, I would be grateful if you could tell me if I ever do anything wrong.'

'You want **me** to tell **you**?' I asked him incredulously.

'No, I'm serious, Jack,' he said earnestly. 'I want to get things right.'

Anyway, he was once doing something wrong, which is a bit difficult to explain, but I'll try. In television, you have two cameras. For example, one on Trevor Howard and one on me, if you like. I do the whole of my speech with him interjecting then they stop that camera and do the same thing again with him doing his speech and me interjecting. After that, they cut it and marry the two bits of film together. I'd observed that Trevor was overplaying his reactions to my speech when he wasn't on camera, so I mentioned this to him.

'Oh, thank you, Jack,' he said, obviously grateful for the advice. 'I'll remember that.'

Trevor was later able to return the compliment when I had a very big scene of three pages to do with John and I had been up all night long learning my lines. John and I did the rehearsal and when I'd finished Trevor came over.

'That was really good, Jack,' he said. 'But why don't you ask the director if you can do that scene with your back to the camera, while looking out of the window?'

Now, I had no intention of asking the great man why, so I went up to the director and put the idea to him.

'Oh, you've been speaking to Trevor,' he said.

'Yes, I have. How did you know?' I asked him.

'Because Trevor Howard is the greatest "back of the head actor" in the film industry.'

I hadn't realised this, but as a viewer you can put the expressions on my face far better than I could ever hope to do. Everybody came up to me after it went out on the air and said how moving that particular scene had been. It wasn't my idea, though it was dear old Trevor's.

In acting, it's wonderful to be able to pick up tips from one of the greats in the industry and Trevor Howard was certainly one of the greats. If you think of the other parts that he'd played, like, for example, a Member of Parliament, when he was always so immaculately dressed. It was remarkable that he could be entirely believable as this scruffy village man. Sadly, I think that Shillingbury may have been one of the last things he did before he died.

* * * * *

Shillingbury Blowers was such a success that they commissioned a whole series. Shillingbury Tales, as it became called, was still set in the beautiful and picturesque village of Aldbury on the Bucks/Herts border. In my continuing role as a farmer, it was lovely to be surrounded by all the animals on the farm.

During one particular scene, which we were filming inside a barn, a pregnant cow was standing in the background. Because of the unpredictable nature of the situation, Robin Nedwell and I had to ad-lib the entire scene. There were actually two vets standing by in case the cow needed some urgent attention. We had just started our bit of dialogue when the cow gave out a huge bellow, stopping us in our tracks.

'That's it!' I said. 'She's going to give birth.'

'Can we stop the filming, please?' said one of the vets, pulling on one of those elbow-length gloves, which later became a familiar sight to viewers of "All Creatures Great And Small".

'I'm afraid that this is going to be a breach birth,' the vet announced after a closer examination of the cow. 'The calf is the wrong way round and I shall need a rope, please.'

He attached one end of the rope to the calf and handed the other end to me. This is where my early lessons on Mrs Clark's farm in Meridan came in handy. Filming resumed and with a bit of tugging from me, out popped this delightful little bull calf, which thankfully landed softly on the straw-covered floor behind his mother.

'Cut!' said the director. 'Print that! I don't think we'll need to film that again.'

I'm sure the mother cow must have been relieved to hear that statement! It was a magical and moving experience for all of us, even the vets, who must have witnessed the births of hundreds of calves before. Mother cow turned round and gently licked the calf with her warm, raspy tongue as he drunkenly staggered to his feet. The crew gave Robin and I a round of applause for our performance ... although I think they were applauding the cow, really.

The farmer stepped forward from where he had been watching the scene and said: 'How would you like to christen him, Jack?'

'Oh, I'd be honoured,' I replied.

'May we call him Milo?' I asked.

'Yeah, that's a nice name, Jack,' the director agreed. He then turned to Robin and said 'Your expressions throughout that scene were one hundred percent believable.'

With that, Robin promptly turned round and threw up.

While I may have been familiar with animal births, poor Robin certainly wasn't. It was the first time he'd ever witnessed a birth and yet he'd valiantly carried on with the scene without complaint, bless him. I feel honoured to have worked with Robin and it was a great loss to the acting world when he died so tragically young.

* * * * *

There is a rather touching footnote to the story of Milo the bull. Some years later, I went back to Aldbury and paid a visit to the farm where we'd filmed the birth scene. I was busy chatting to the farmer in one of his fields, when I suddenly noticed a movement away in the distance, to my right. Glancing over, I was horrified to see the biggest bull I'd ever seen in my life galloping towards us.

'Look!' I exclaimed, gathering myself for a hurried exit from the field. 'I think we'd better make a run for it.'

'No,' the farmer answered calmly, placing a restraining hand on my arm. 'Just stand your ground, Jack.'

I was naturally apprehensive, but bowed to his superior knowledge of this animal and did as I was told. The bull approached and I could see the muscles rippling in his massive chest. To my amazement, he looked me straight in the eye and then nuzzled me like a pet dog.

'Milo has grown a bit, hasn't he, Jack?' said the farmer with a grin.

'You mean, this is little Milo?'

'That's him,' he confirmed. 'You see, Jack. Milo will always associate your scent with his mother and he will never forget you.'

As this huge beast gently licked my hand I was overcome with emotion and my eyes are leaking again now, just remembering that touching little scene.

Jack and Milo the bull

* * * * *

I mentioned earlier in the book about working with the black stallion called Blackie from the Lloyds Bank advert. The pair of us spent three months horsing around together on the set of Shillingbury Tales. My four-legged friend and me became very close and every morning, before I went into make-up, I would go to his stable to give him a cuddle and a stroke.

'Got any mints, Jack?' he would ask, as I tickled his soft muzzle. We were on first name terms by that time!

I would feed him his favourite treat, all the while glancing over my shoulder to make sure that no-one saw me. One morning I decided to see if I could get into his stable without him noticing, so I crept quietly along the corridor that led to his stall. I was just anticipating the lovely warm smell of hay and Blackie nuzzling through my pockets in search of the mints, when I suddenly heard the most blood-curdling scream.

If you've ever heard a horse scream, then you'll know that it's the most horrible sound in the world. I ran into the stable to see one of the grooms beating Blackie with a yard brush. Blackie's halter was tethered to the side of the stall and his eyes were rolling in terror as he tried in vain to back away from this broom-wielding brute. The next thing I remember is four stagehands holding me back. They told me afterwards that if they hadn't come along when they did, that I would have probably killed this groom. Now, I'm not like that about people and I have infinite patience and very little temper. But, if I see anyone hurting an animal, especially when that animal happens to be a dear friend of mine, then they had better watch out.

* * * * *

Only once did Blackie try to steal the limelight. Diane Keen and I had a dramatic scene together, which involved us riding towards each other down a hill. We had to meet at the bottom (which was appropriate, given what was about to happen!) and then dismount. It was a beautiful day to be horse riding and the patchwork of fields around Aldbury looked a picture in the sunshine. Blackie was chewing at his bit, impatient to be off at full gallop, as I think he was rather taken with the pretty filly that Diane was riding.

'Whoa, Blackie,' I said, pulling gently on the reins. 'We've got to wait for our cue, old buddy.'

I saw the director raise his hand and we were away down the hill, Blackie's tail streaming out behind him. I know this because I watched the day's film rushes afterwards. Blackie tossed his handsome head and whinnied a greeting to Diane's mount as we ground to a halt beside them. Sadly, the filly was seemingly unimpressed by Blackie's approach and ignored him completely. Blackie snorted in disgust and lowered his head to eat some grass. Diane and I had just started on the dialogue and the tension of the scene was building nicely, when Blackie turned his rear end towards the camera. *'He's doing a "Trevor Howard",'* I thought to myself, smiling inwardly.

Stalwarts that we were, Diane and I ignored his fidgeting and 'carried on regardless', so to speak. That is, until Blackie lifted his tail and passed wind … loudly!

'Blackie!' I exclaimed in disgust. 'There was no need for that.'

Blackie glanced up from his eating, as if to say: 'What's all the fuss about?'

The entire cast and crew were helpless with laughter and, despite the director's pleas to resume filming, it was impossible to carry on with the scene. It had to wait until the next day when we were all feeling much more composed. Well, I suppose the programme was supposed to be about the Shillingbury **Blowers**, after all!

* * * * *

Many years later, I was visiting our famous Garlic Festival here on the Isle of Wight with my partner Vivien. We were completely engrossed in looking at one of the exhibits I can't remember what it was now, when I heard a familiar whinny. I turned to see a handsome black stallion standing about a hundred yards away, outside the Lloyds Bank tent. He was staring straight at me, scraping his front hoof impatiently on the grass. I walked over to him and, as I encircled his neck with my arms, Blackie gave another welcoming whinny of recognition and blew through his lips – made a welcome change from somewhere else!

'I've never seen him behave like this before,' said the grey-suited gentleman hanging onto Blackie's halter for grim death.

'Ah, well, we're old friends from way back, aren't we, Blackie?' I said, patting his shiny, muscular flank.

Blackie nodded his head, as if he understood and then began nuzzling my pocket.

'Got any mints, Jack?'

* * * * *

I loved Shillingbury Tales and judging the response from the public, they loved it too. After the initial programme had been such a success, we'd done a further seven and I honestly thought that it was so popular that it would go on forever. Sadly, though, it ended up on the archive shelves and there is has remained ever since. I even took a compilation tape of it over to America with me, to try and 'blow me own trumpet', as it were, and sell it out there. I thought that they would be bound to love something so typically English. They weren't interested, however.

For some reason, Shillingbury had a magic for the actors and for the fans, but not, it seemed, for the programme planners in the offices upstairs. It seems a shame that they have never brought it back, although I did do a follow-up series called Cuffy with Bernard Cribbins. Sadly, we never managed to recapture the special magic of Shillingbury.

* * * * *

Jack with Diane Keen ...

... and Mona Washborn

CHAPTER FOURTEEN

It doesn't matter how proficient you become in this business because there will always come a time when you need a helping hand. A classic example of this, happened to me in 1981.

In the theatre, someone who makes people laugh is called a red-nosed comic. Whereas those who act in plays, are known as actors. They are an entirely different breed to us comedy types. With my "Alf" character, of course, I'd always been classed as a red-nosed comic and would never be considered for a part in a straight play.

In 1981 the wonderful Michael Frayn play, "Make and Break", was being presented by Bill Kenwright in the West End, with Leonard Rossiter starring in the lead role. When Bill secured the touring rights, however, Leonard was unable to continue playing the part, probably because of other commitments.

'I'm going to recast the role,' Bill said to Michael Frayn. 'And I'm thinking of approaching Jack Douglas.'

'Jack Douglas!' said Michael in horror. 'But this is a very heavy and dramatic part, Bill, and he's a red-nosed comic.'

'Yes, but he's also a wonderful actor.'

(This may sound as if I'm on an ego trip here, but this is how Bill related the story to me … honest!)

I was just eating a leisurely breakfast one morning when the telephone rang and, after a brief exchange of pleasantries, Bill hit me with his idea. I was dumbfounded.

'But, Bill,' I reasoned. 'I'm a comic.'

I will never, ever forget his words.

'Comics are actors, too, Jack. You can't play Buttons in a pantomime without acting and it's much easier to act than to make people laugh. It's even harder to make children laugh. If it's funny, they laugh. If it isn't, they want to go to the toilet.'

With my confidence suitably boosted I told him that I would love to do it.

'Before you accept the part, I'll send you the script to read through,' said Bill.

An hour later, a messenger duly arrived on my doorstep carrying a large envelope and, after opening it with all the eagerness of a child unwrapping a present, I sat down to read the heavy manuscript.

'Oh my God,' I said aloud, as I flicked through page after page of dialogue … which was **all** me. 'This is a marathon.' Although I was in every scene, by the time I'd finished reading it I knew that I wanted to give it my best shot.

'Great!' said Bill when I phoned to tell him. 'You've got ten days before the start of rehearsals, so get learning.'

Well, I spent every spare minute learning that script, even burning the midnight oil while Sue slept soundly in the next room, but I was determined to be word-perfect.

On the first day of rehearsals I walked in to be met by Bill Kenwright, Jack Watling and Diana Copeland. The rehearsals went well and then it was time for the dress rehearsal.

I was so nervous that I messed everything up and if I had been directing the production I'd have sacked me on the spot. Afterwards, I walked dejectedly over to Bill, fully expecting to receive a deserved dressing down. However, the ever patient Bill was philosophical about my dreadful performance.

'Don't worry, Jack, you know what they say. Bad dress rehearsal, good show.'

'But I was hopeless, Bill,' I said, staring at the floor.

'I know you can do it, so prove it to me.'

I didn't sleep at all that night so utterly convinced was I that I'd bitten off more than I could chew. Thankfully, as the grey light of dawn gradually began to filter through the small chink in the bedroom curtains, my confidence started to build. Call it self-hypnosis, if you like, but I didn't want to let the rest of the cast down and I was determined to justify Bill's unwavering faith in me. It was literally "Make or Break" time!

Our first night opened and I'm proud to say that I didn't make one mistake. What's more, we received a rousing standing ovation, which made me feel ten feet tall. Bill has since reminded me, that the actor who played my boss in the production had fluffed every line he threw at me. He'd even called me "Jack" instead of the character's name. I did a quick rewrite of his lines and we got through.

Apparently, Bill and Michael watched this from their seats up in the box, completely helpless with laughter. Again, this is Bill's version of events, not mine. We had a wonderfully successful tour with "Make And Break" and, from then on, my CV stated that I was an actor as well as a red-nosed comic. It was all down to Bill Kenwright and I can never thank him enough.

* * * * *

During "Make And Break", I had to have a heart attack on stage. Wanting to make it as realistic as possible, I made an appointment with my GP, who was also a mate of mine, and he said that he would be happy to advise me on the symptoms. Anyway, the doc and I were sitting on the bed in his surgery while he showed me the appropriate way to react.

'Imagine your heart is being squeezed in a vice-like grip, Jack,' he said, clutching his chest and grimacing horribly with the make-believe pain.

I was just emulating his moves and adding the odd groan or two for dramatic effect, when in walked the nurse. We must have been putting on a very convincing performance, because she thought that we were both genuinely (and coincidentally!) in the throws of a massive coronary and she screamed out in fright. I think the poor woman nearly had a heart attack herself, before the doctor was able to pacify her and explain what we were doing. The lengths we actors have to go to provide you with entertainment!

* * * * *

It was a delight to work with Jack Watling in "Make And Break", as he had a long and very moving speech that I had to sit and listen to. Normally, it's easy to let your mind wander off once you've heard the speech a couple of times. Jack was so good however, that I was transfixed by his words every single performance. Sadly, of course, Jack died during the writing of this book. Yet another great loss to our profession.

The part I played in "Make And Break" was a very brilliant company director (not like me at all!) so I had to develop the character. This meant that I took my work home with me and Sue got very unhappy about me ordering her around. I had to remember to switch the character off when I left the theatre.

* * * * *

In the spring of 1985 I noticed that Sue was acting rather oddly. If I walked in while she was talking on the phone, her conversation with whoever it was at the other end of the line would come to an abrupt end. This had happened so often that I was beginning to feel paranoid. The final straw came when I arrived home one afternoon, put my key in the lock, opened the front door and had caught her "at it" yet again.

'I can't talk now,' she was whispering into the phone. 'I'll speak to you later.'

'Right!' I exploded, as she replaced the receiver and turned to greet me with a guilty smile. 'What the hell's going on, Sue?'

'Why? What do you mean?' she said innocently.

'I mean, all these unfinished telephone calls that I keep walking in on.'

'Oh, that,' said Sue, looking at the floor.

'You've got another man, haven't you?'

'What! Oh, Jack, is that what you think?' she said, walking forward and putting her arms around my waist.

I disengaged her arms and looked her straight in the eyes. 'Just stop insulting my intelligence and tell me what's going on.'

'Oh, all right, then,' she said, the playful tone in her voice totally confusing me. 'It's your birthday soon, isn't it?'

'Yes, but what's that got to do with anything?' I said crossly, stubbornly determined that I would not be distracted from my path of righteousness.

'Well, I'm arranging a birthday party for you. Do you want me to tell you all about it and spoil the surprise?'

'Oh, I'm terribly sorry, darling,' I said, instantly contrite and feeling like a right chump into the bargain. 'Please forgive me.'

'I just might,' she said with a laugh.

A little while later I was working in a very funny farce called "Love At A Pinch" with Ruth Madoc. As I went forward to do my curtain speech at the end of the play, I glanced off-stage and noticed, what looked like, my double standing in the wings. Well, it was someone dressed as a double of Alf, at any rate. Then, I caught sight of a little glint of light in the audience, because I've always been able to see right to the back of the theatre. I spotted this man with a camera and made a mental note to sort it out once I went off-stage, as no-one is allowed to film a show without the permission of everyone involved. I was just finishing my speech when the "Alf" character standing in the wings came out of the shadows and walked towards Ruth.

It was my old pal Eamonn Andrews holding the Big Red Book! I even stood back so that he could hand it to Ruth, but, to my astonishment, he turned to me and said 'Jack Douglas! Man of comedy! This Is Your Life!'

My mouth dropped open and that's where they froze the camera shot, with me looking totally stunned. There was a taxi waiting outside to take me to the theatre at Shepherd's Bush. All my clothes were laid out and ready for me in the dressing room, which Sue had organised. They were the clothes I would have picked if I would have chosen them myself. Walking onto that show was one of the most magical moments of my career, but, as I sat back to enjoy my evening of surprises, I couldn't help wondering who my last guest would be. Finally, Eamonn said: 'Here's someone you've known for quite sometime … '

This "someone" put their arms around me from behind and literally lifted me off my feet. Now, I'm 6'4" and I weigh 14 stone, so there aren't many people who could manage that, but I guessed immediately who it was.

'It's Howard Keel!' I said, without having to look.

That familiar deep laugh in my ear was confirmation enough. As I swung around to embrace this wonderful, unpretentious Hollywood star, the years since our previous meeting just dissolved away. It transpired that Howard had been in his agent's office in America when the call had come through from the programme in England.

'Hold on just a minute, will you?' said his agent. 'Howard, it's the "This Is Your Life" programme on the line and they want you to go over to England to appear on the show as a guest for Jack Douglas. There's no money in it, so shall I tell them that you're too busy?'

Howard had said 'I'm doing it! Jack's my old mate.'

Howard Keel is a big man in every sense. All the subterfuge at home had been the "This Is Your Life" team ringing Sue to do their vital and, of course, top secret research about me for the show. Sue had very cleverly thrown me off the scent with her story about a surprise birthday party. The researchers had even discovered what my favourite tipple was. When I went into the bar for the after-show party, a waiter presented me with a Martini cocktail on a silver tray. It was complete with a shaker, a spoon, a glass and even a slice of lemon. What a perfect end to a perfect evening.

* * * * *

It was tidying my bookshelves and finding a copy of the book "Treasure Island" that reminded me of this next story: During the winter of 1984/85 my agent phoned me to say that I'd been offered the part of Long John Silver at the Repertory Theatre in Birmingham. I was thrilled, because the old film with Robert Newton playing the part of Long John had always been a great favourite of mine. My main concern was how I would keep my left leg out of sight. Especially while walking on a crutch with a live parrot sitting on my shoulder.

As I climbed into my car one morning and "clunk clicked" the seat belt, a marvellous idea suddenly hit me like a belt, sorry, I mean a bolt from the blue. I rang the seat belt manufacturers to tell them about my dilemma and they invited me along for a chat. To my delight, they were able to design me a quick-release harness (in case of cramp) which would fit discreetly underneath my costume.

The next problem was finding an amenable parrot, so I phoned my local branch of the RSPCA in Godstone, who I'd done some charity work for in the past. They introduced me to Jim, a handsome, bright-green Amazon parrot, who looked me up and down with his beady black eyes and then climbed on to my shoulder like an old pro. Lesser parrots might have felt a little nervous at the prospect of starring as Captain Flint in such a prestigious production, but not Jim. His feathers were completely unruffled by the thought of his imminent stardom.

'Been there, done that and bought the cuttlefish, mate,' he said in my ear.

Some local disabled people helped me to design a suitable looking crutch of the period and the carpenter built it in the theatre workshop. There was still a couple of weeks to go before the start of rehearsals, so Jim moved into my place and we practised at home. With my harness in place (it makes me sound like a horse) and Jim on my shoulder, I would walk round the house on the crutch. The postman must have thought that I'd finally lost it when he came to the door one morning, although his face didn't betray him. He even held onto my crutch for me (no rude comments, please!) without question, while I leant against the wall and signed for a Recorded Delivery letter.

'Nothing for the parrot, I'm afraid,' he said nonchalantly, slotting the crutch back under my arm and then handing me the rest of the post.

I was determined to teach Jim to talk, but even though I repeated the words: 'Pieces of eight! Pieces of eight!' to him over and over, he would just stare at me blankly. His contract had obviously stated that his was strictly a non-speaking part. The two-week rehearsals for Treasure Island went smoothly and Jim and I enjoyed sharing a dressing room together. At first, Jim was in a cage and then I bought him one of those parrot stands from a local pet shop in Birmingham.

The opening night arrived, which is always a nervy time for everyone and Jim was to be no exception. I had to make my entrance from the audience, via a ramp up to the stage. Well, you should try and tackle stairs with a crutch! Unfortunately, when the audience spotted me they began to applaud, which was an entirely new sound to Jim. During rehearsals the auditorium had, of course, been empty. It hadn't occurred to anyone, least of all me, that the presence of an audience would frighten this wily bird. Jim squawked loudly, which was deafening for me. He then began to bob up and down frantically before venting his anger on my defenceless ear lobe. Apart from the fact that the pain was excrutiating, I hadn't really planned on going the whole hog and having my ear pierced for the part of Long John. Besides, earrings don't suit me!

I managed to persuade Jim to part company with my bloodied lobe and climb onto my finger, but his sudden and unexpected outburst had completely thrown me. My mind was a blank! The rest of the cast was assembled on-stage awaiting my grand entrance and they were all looking at me, waiting for me to speak. I searched through my memory banks in desperation … nothing. This was the first and only time I'd ever forgotten my lines and all I could think of was the old adage about never working with animals.

'What's the matter with you lot? Ain't you ever seen a one-legged man with a parrot on his shoulder before?' I ad-libbed, much to the horror of the cast on-stage, who were

Jim ~~Hawkins~~ 'Squawkins'!

still anxiously waiting for my opening gambit. Thankfully, by the time I reached the stage, the first line had magically popped into my head and we were able to continue.

We all had a good laugh about it in the bar after the show while the lady from the Red Cross patched up my ear. Although I forgave Jim, he decided to retire from showbiz at the end of the show's run, due to pressure of work. He said that he wanted to concentrate on the much more fulfilling role of being a pet. I hated having to part with my feathered friend, but, much to my delight, the RSPCA had found him a good home. Funnily enough, although Jim had remained stubbornly silent during his time with me, he never stopped talking to his new lady owner. Apparently, he kept repeating the words: 'Pieces of eight! Pieces of eight!' Now I wonder who could have taught him to say that?

* * * * *

An agent is the life-blood of any performer. No matter how good a comedian you are, you're still dependent on your agent, because he (or she) has his finger on the pulse of everything that's going on in the world of showbiz.

He will ring you, usually very early in the morning and say 'Can you get down to Pinewood or Elstree (for example) by eleven o' clock? They are casting for so-and-so and I've put you up for it.'

George Truzzi had been a particularly good straight man to me and I remember once when we appeared together in a club and stopped the show. My agent at the time, Peter Pritchard, rushed backstage after the show and said 'Right! From now on you're going to be doing the clubs.'

'But I don't like doing clubs,' I told him. 'All this *pies for sale* business and people milling around while you're on stage is just not my scene.'

'No, no, no,' said Peter. 'I've got a year's work for you in the clubs.'

This depressed me greatly. It was then that I met up with an old friend of mine from way back called Michael Sullivan, who was the most wonderful agent. Peter agreed, amicably, to release me from my contract and it was Michael who got me into the Carry On films.

When Michael married the lovely Dani Robin, all she wanted was to be the perfect wife to Michael, so she didn't work much, but he did. In time, though, they decided to retire and move to a flat in Paris. One day Michael went to light a cigarette and 'Boom'! The whole place went up, tragically killing them both instantly. Apparently, there had been a gas leak. Everyone in the world of showbiz was completely stunned.

* * * * *

After the drunken fiasco with Joe in France, I'd always kept to my strict rule of never drinking before a show. I went on tour with a play called "Fur Coat And No Knickers" and, on the opening night, the four young men who were appearing with me, asked me to join them for a pint.

'Oh, I like to keep my wits about me, so I never drink before a show,' I told them and they all looked at me askance.

With a play title like that, I didn't want to make any bloomers! At a certain point in the play, we were all seated around a table exchanging some very heavy dialogue. I had my back to the audience (Trevor Howard again!), but the boys were on the other side of the table facing the audience. Suddenly, I noticed that a piece of the scenery had come adrift from its moorings and was about to fall on top of the other actors. If it had hit them, they would have had more than just a hangover headache to contend with, so I

The wedding of showbiz agent Michael Sullivan to Dani Robin

leapt out of my chair and grabbed the offending "wall". A ripple went through the audience and, for a split second, the boys wondered what on earth I was playing at.

'Give me a hand will you, lads?' I said.

When it was secure again, we all went back to the table to resume our dialogue, but I could see by the looks on their faces that the boys had completely lost the plot, so to speak. I walked casually down to the footlights and apologised to the audience for the unscheduled intermission. This was yet another chance for me to put Robb Wilton's good advice into action.

'If something goes wrong on-stage, Jack, always be sure to tell the audience what's going on, so then they can share the joke with you,' he'd say, rubbing his chin in that inimitable way of his.

'This should be interesting, folks,' I said, folding my arms and tapping my foot. 'Let's see if any of these guys can remember what the next line is and who has to say it.'

When I turned back to the rest of the cast, four blank faces confirmed that they hadn't got a clue what came next, so I gave them the line. Just as Robb had predicted all those years before, the audience really enjoyed being part of the fun. I was back in my dressing room after the show when there was a tap at the door.

'Come in!' I called.

The door opened and in walked the "lost boys"!

'Yes, lads. What can I do for you?'

'Um,' said their spokesman, clearing his throat. 'We just wanted to say that we now know why you never have a drink before you go on-stage.'

'Oh, good,' I said.

'From now on, we are never going to drink before the show, either.'

I was so proud that I took them all out to the pub to celebrate!

* * * * *

CHAPTER FIFTEEN

After flying high for a while and having a bit of money in the bank, I went into business with two gentlemen. One was a managing director of a twenty-two-and-a-half-million pound company and the other guy was a barrister. Between us, we organised a massive loan and bought Shakespeare's pub, which was The Falcon at Bideford-on-Avon. It seemed like a marvellous investment opportunity and the picturesque timbered buildings had a great deal of potential.

Our idea was to turn the ground floor into antique shops with dimpled glass in the windows and a cobbled yard in front, then let them out to traders. The first floor was to be an old English restaurant and the upper floor was going to be two penthouse suites. The basement, where the Bow Street Runners would keep their prisoners when they were taking them to London, was going to be a wine bar. I'd even arranged with the Tourist Board that they would use The Falcon as their stop-off point for coaches en route to Stratford-upon-Avon. It was a wonderful idea and everything seemed to be falling into place perfectly.

Unfortunately, however, one of my partners fell in love with his secretary, left his wife and four children and disappeared. Then, things went from "bard" to worse, when the other guy, on hearing what had happened, cleared off to live in Gibraltar, leaving yours truly to face the creditors. My house was up as security for the loan and I had to pay the loan back. All the money I'd earned in show business up to that point was gone.

This was to be the final nail in the coffin as far as my marriage to Sue was concerned.

* * * * *

When we'd moved to Thames Ditton, I'd opened an account at the local branch of the National Westminster Bank. On my first visit, I was shown through to the office of a pleasant-looking bank manager called Mr Merryfield and noticed immediately that the name suited his cheery disposition perfectly. He said that he recognised me from the television shows with Des O' Connor. Although we always kept our dealings on a business-like surname basis, we got on really well and, as the months progressed, he and I became friends. It was nice to feel that my finances were in such safe and trustworthy hands.

'What ever is the matter, Mr Douglas?' he asked, when I walked into his office one morning with dark circles under my eyes from lack of sleep.

I explained about the fiasco with The Falcon and how all the plans had gone belly-up.

'Oh, my God,' he said. 'You put your house up as collateral and stand to lose every single penny you've got at this rate.'

'Yes, but what can I do?' I said, close to tears as I remembered the sight of Sue's stricken face when I told her what had happened. Her initial shock had swiftly turned to anger and who could have blamed her?

'I know it's easy for me to say, Jack,' said Mr Merryfield, calling me by my first name for once. 'But try not to worry, we'll think of something.'

He placed his elbows on the desk in front of him and cupped his face in his hands.

'Right!' he said after several moments had elapsed. 'Bring me all the paperwork pertaining to your dealings with these so-called business partners and we'll try and sort this mess out.'

He was wonderful.

Sue and I had to sell our house in Thames Ditton and buy a smaller place, but thanks to the quick thinking of Mr Merryfield and my solicitor, at least we didn't end up destitute. I called in to see Mr Merryfield just before we moved.

'I can't thank you enough,' I said, shaking his hand warmly. 'If there's ever anything I can do for you, please let me know.'

'There is something you can do for me, actually,' he said.

'Really?'

'I promised my mother that I would stay in the bank until I retired which I'm just about to do,' he explained.

'Congratulations!' I said, a touch mystified as to where this conversation was leading.

'It's just that … I've always wanted to be an actor.'

'Oh, I see,' I said, my heart sinking into my boots. This man had been such a good friend to me and I didn't want to have to knock him back. Sitting at a desk counting money all day is hardly an ideal launch pad into show business. Unless you want to work behind the scenes as an agent, of course. Sorry, Phil!

'I will have to see you working,' I told him, trying to think on my feet.

'That's no problem,' he said. 'I'm playing the lead in the bank's production of "Me And My Girl", so I'll get you a couple of tickets.

For the life of me, I couldn't imagine this man, charming though he was, actually acting. But, Sue and I went along to see the show. From the moment he walked on-stage, our Mr Merryfield was absolutely brilliant, however, and Sue and I just looked at one another in amazement. I managed to get him his Equity Card and for those who still haven't guessed yet …

My bank manager was none other than **Buster** Merryfield, who went on to become the much-loved be-whiskered character, Uncle Albert, in television's "Only Fools And Horses"! Sadly, of course, dear Buster is no longer with us, but I will never forget his kindness to me. God bless you, Buster, and thank you for what you did.

* * * * *

Despite the fact that Sue had been in show business herself and so understood its demands, she still resented the idea of staying at home with Sarah while I was away working. I can remember one freezing cold day when the central heating broke down.

'Can you fix it, Jack?' asked Sue.

'The show starts at eight and I haven't got time,' I said, grabbing my coat and dashing out of the door. 'Sorry, love.'

'Jack! Wait! You can't … '

'Call a plumber in, darling,' I yelled over my shoulder.

You can understand why people in the business describe it as the worst mistress in the world, can't you?

Sarah blossomed into a beautiful young woman, leaving Sue with more time to concentrate on her own career. I managed to get her some showbiz work and this led to voice-overs and eventually to a part in a West End play.

I can remember going along to the first night of "Elephant Man" and being knocked out by Sue's performance. I was delighted to see that she certainly hadn't lost any of her acting ability in the interim years at home. I must admit to having being a little shocked by the content of one particular scene in the play, simply because it was entirely out-of-character for the Sue I'd come to know. In an intimate moment she had to bare all (well, the top half at least) to her leading man.

Don't get me wrong! I'm not the kind of guy who would lay down the law and jealously forbid his wife to do such a thing. It was just that, being a modest lady, Sue had always insisted that she would never take her clothes off in front of an audience.

At the end of the evening I went backstage to join Sue and the rest of the cast for drinks in the theatre bar. Full of congratulations for their superb performances, I shook hands with Sue's leading man and I suppose it sort of registered at the time that he couldn't look me in the eyes. I felt a bit suspicious, but pushed it to the back of my mind, reasoning that not everyone is hot on eye-to-eye contact.

* * * * *

During my marriage to Sue, I'd bought her a longhaired dachshund. Geordie, as he was called, because of my Newcastle roots, absolutely adored Sue and would follow her everywhere. He would even wait for her outside the loo! His favourite spot was sitting next to Sue on the sofa and one particular day she asked me if I'd join her in the living room.

'Come and sit down, Jack,' she said. 'I've got something to tell you.'

'Can I just … ?'

'No, this is important,' said Sue, indicating that she wanted me to sit down in the armchair next to her.

'Right! What is it?' I said, totally unprepared for the bombshell she was about to drop on me.

'There's no easy way to say this,' she began. 'I've met someone else and I want a divorce.'

My mouth dropped open in shock and I couldn't say anything.

At that moment, I suppose to diffuse the intensity of the situation, Sue stretched out her hand to stroke the ever-present Geordie. Geordie, who was obviously in no mood for such pleasantries, suddenly swung round and promptly sunk his teeth into her finger.

Forgetting Sue's momentous revelation, I leapt out of the chair and grabbed her hand to examine the deep puncture wound, which was now bleeding profusely and in urgent need of medical attention. We rushed to the local hospital, where Sue was given a tetanus injection and her finger swathed in a huge dressing. I brought her home again and from that moment on, Geordie would have nothing to do with the woman he had once adored.

It was really strange, but it was just as if he'd said to himself: 'Divorce! Leaving my old man! No you're bloody not!' Now I know why dogs are called a **man's** best friend. Sorry ladies!

When Sue and I eventually parted, I had custody of Geordie. What with the pressure of work and going away on tour, though, I found him a lovely home on a farm, where there were other dogs to keep him company. Despite being the smallest, he soon became top dog and he's still there to this day.

* * * * *

CHAPTER SIXTEEN

So, I had failed again! Or that's how it seemed to me after my marriage to Sue had ended.

'Okay, mate,' I said aloud to the bleary-eyed reflection staring back at me from the shaving mirror one morning. 'No more long-term relationships for you.

'From now on, you are going to be a bachelor gay … well, a bachelor, at any rate!'

After a lonely night spent drowning my sorrows, my tongue was feeling like the bottom of a parrot's cage, only with an extra helping of grit. (We've all been there, haven't we, folks? We kid ourselves that waking up with a head like a bucket and feeling a little "pail", as my father used to say, will somehow solve our problems!)

'Who's a pretty boy, then?' I asked the dishevelled image in the mirror. 'Ugh! Certainly not you this morning, Douglas,' I added, turning away in disgust.

I knew that drinking wasn't the answer. What I really needed was a shoulder to cry on, so I picked up the phone and dialled my brother's number.

'Morning, Bill,'

'Oh, hello Jack. You sound a bit rough. Is there anything wrong?'

'I wondered if I could come and see you for a chat.'

'Um, well, yes, of course, Jack.'

'Look, if it's inconvenient, it doesn't matter,' I said, feeling hurt that my own brother obviously hadn't got time for me. 'I'll leave you to it if you're busy.'

'No Jack, wait. I'm sorry. It's Rita.'

Rita was Bill's wife and while I'd been wallowing in my own self-pity I'd forgotten about her recent illness.

'Oh, Bill, please forgive me,' I said, instantly contrite. 'How is Rita?'

'Not good, I'm afraid. We've just been given some devastating news by the doctor and I can't take it in.'

I sat myself down in a chair, fully expecting to be told that Rita had some sort of inoperable cancer.

'Rita's got Alzheimer's Disease,' continued Bill. 'She's got to go into a home.'

'Oh, I'm so sorry. I didn't realise that Rita was that ill. There's me expecting you to listen to my stupid problem.'

'That's what families are for,' he said. 'If brothers can't help each other out at times of crisis, there's not much hope for anyone else, is there?

'You know I'm always here for you, Jack. Now, what's this problem?'

I was too choked to answer him.

'Listen, why don't you pack a case and get over here as soon as you can? I think I need you as much as you need me.'

I stayed with Bill for a fortnight and during that time all the years of distance and awkwardness between us simply melted away. Some months later, when I sold my house after the divorce and had nowhere to live, Bill suggested that I move in with him for a while. We lived together for a month until I bought a house in Godalming, Surrey.

Despite our mutual problems, it was marvellous to get to know one another properly at last. Sadly, though, Rita stayed in the home until her death in 1994.

* * * * *

During his lifetime, Bill had been a personal manager to many big stars, like Hylda Baker, Pat Pheonix, Sid James, Billy Burdon and, of course, John Inman. In 1984, he had a heart by-pass operation and made a good recovery.

When I met Viv and moved to the Isle of Wight, we invited Bill over for a holiday, which was great fun. In later years, though, Bill suffered from failing health and although he was a strong guy and put up one hell of a fight, he died in March 2000. I thank God that we became close in his final years. I would implore everyone to sort out any misunderstandings they have with the people they care about, before it's too late.

There was a good turnout for Bill's funeral, as he was well-liked and respected by many in our profession. John Inman's address was both moving and humorous and it was so uplifting to hear laughter echoing around the crematorium. Thank you, John. Bill would have loved that.

As so often happens on these occasions, you meet up with people at the wake who you haven't seen for years and have a good reminisce about the departed loved one. Have you noticed how these kinds of reminiscences are always funny? The opening gambit is invariably, 'Do you remember the time when so-and-so did such-and-such?' It's this strange compulsion us humans have to only remember the good times … or it could just be the effects of the sherry, I suppose! Either way, it certainly helps to ease the pain a little and lighten the burden of grief at a funeral.

One of the stories we remembered about Bill was of the time that he and Rita parked their car in a multi-storey car park. After shopping, Rita and Bill jumped in the car and were just driving down the ramp when Rita shouted: 'Whose is that ladies umbrella on the back seat?'

'I don't know,' said Bill.

'Have you had a woman in this car?'

'Of course not.'

Bill looked around and then opened the glove compartment.

'Oh my God!' he exclaimed. 'It isn't our car.'

Bill drove the car out of the car park and then straight back in again.

Unfortunately, the space that the car had been parked in was now occupied, so they parked it a few spaces further along the row. Bill eventually found his car on the next floor up. You can imagine the owner of the car he'd taken in error, returning to his vehicle and saying 'Hang on a minute! I'm sure that I didn't park it here.' What made the story so amusing to people who'd known Bill well, was that he was normally so meticulous about everything.

I was so proud of my elder brother Bill. He was the best brother anyone could have had and this book is dedicated to his memory. I miss you, Bill. Sleep well.

* * * * *

As I mentioned earlier in the book, I'm always happiest in the company of ladies. One of my few close male friends, however, is a lovely guy called Arthur Dakin. Arthur was a drummer in an army band throughout the war and we first met when he'd joined in with my quartet's jam session on the steps at Blackpool Town Hall on VE night.

'Are you left-handed, Jack?' he'd asked, as he sat down behind my drums ... but we won't go into all that again.

A few days later we met up again outside the Feldman's Theatre.

'Let me introduce you to a friend of mine, Jack,' said Arthur. 'This guy is an up-and-coming singer and his name is Dickie Valentine.'

The years went by and I lost contact with Arthur. Then, in the pantomime with Cliff Richard at The Palladium, I went along to the musical rehearsal and spotted Arthur sitting in the orchestra behind the drums. It was such a lovely surprise to see him and we resumed our friendship during the run of the panto, although we lost touch yet again afterwards. Many years later, when Sue and I moved to Thames Ditton, who did I bump into in the local newsagent's one morning?

'Arthur!' I exclaimed. 'What on earth are you doing here?'

'I live just around the corner, Jack. What are you doing here?'

Anyway, we used to enjoy the odd pint together in the local pub, but then I went away on tour and came back to discover that Arthur had moved.

The years passed and when my marriage to Sue ended, I bought an ex-mill worker's cottage in Godalming. Knocking hell out of the place and restoring it to its former glory was all part of the healing process, I suppose. Mentally, I felt like a failure and had sunk to my lowest ebb at that time. Feeling particularly down one evening, I decided to go and cheer myself up at the local watering hole across the road. A few people looked up from their drinks as I walked in, but I couldn't believe my eyes when I saw who was standing at the bar.

'Fancy a drink, Jack?'

'This is incredible, Arthur,' I said, thumping him on the back.

'We seem to have a knack for turning up like a pair of proverbial bad pennies.'

'It's definitely déjà vu,' said Arthur with a laugh. 'I live just along the road. What brings you to this neck of the woods?'

He listened sympathetically as I explained about the traumatic break-up of my marriage.

'I'm so sorry to hear that, Jack. I thought that you were looking a bit down when you came in.'

'Yes, and not only that, but things are pretty tight at the moment, finance-wise.'

'Here,' he said, reaching into his top pocket and taking out a cheque book

'This will help to tide you over.'

'No, really Arthur. I wouldn't dream ... '

'I insist,' he said. 'And there's no rush, just pay me back when you can.'

Dear Arthur loaned me five-hundred pounds. You know what they say about a friend in need, don't you? Well, it's certainly true in Arthur's case.

* * * * *

CHAPTER SEVENTEEN

When Gerald Thomas told me that the next picture was going to be Carry On Emmannuelle, he explained that he wanted me to play the part of her butler, Lyons. I was delighted, but then came the bombshell. He wanted me to play it as a typical butler and this meant, of course, no "Alf", no glasses, no cap and, definitely, no twitch.

Gerald brought in a real butler to teach me how to butle in the correct way. That is, how to conduct myself, how to hold a laden tray with one hand and how to address (no, not undress!) Emmannuelle, in the proper manner. With my new skills as a butler and my elegant persona, I didn't feel quite so naked without Alf. Plus, it was a real joy to work with the lovely Suzanne Danielle and we got on really well together … not that well. One scene that sticks in my mind was when I went to Emmannuelle's bedroom to wake her up. (I wonder why that simple bit of information has just woken up all the male readers, too?)

I coughed politely and said: 'Madam, there is a phone call for you.'

I handed Emmannuelle the receiver and, as she pulled the phone towards her ear, she pulled me with it, as the phone cord was wrapped around my neck. I ended up "lyon" on the bed with my face pressed into her bosom.

She was bra-less at the time (excuse me a minute, my glasses have steamed up and I can't see what I'm writing!) and the tragedy of the situation was, that I was forced to stay in that position for the duration of the call. As my concentration was understandably broken (along with my nose) and what with me being a perfectionist and all, I insisted (pleaded, more like) that we do several more takes in order to get the scene just right.

Gerald Thomas laughed and said 'No, Jack. That was perfect.' He'd obviously been keeping abreast of the situation.

Anyway, it took me four days to regain my composure after that little episode … and several more to straighten my nose. Even today, the trauma of having to relate it all again for your benefit is making me feel hot under the collar. I don't know! The things I put myself through for show business. I watched Carry On Emmannuelle quite recently and I think that scene had actually been cut.

* * * * *

I seem to have played a lot of policemen in my time, presumably because of my stature, I suppose. I was "promoted" to Chief Superintendent in the Cannon and Ball film, "Boys In Blue", and, as we had a very early call one morning, the wardrobe department asked me to take my uniform home with me. During the drive home, I suddenly heard a police siren behind me, so I pulled the car over into a convenient lay-by.

'Did you know that you were doing forty-five miles and hour in a thirty mile an hour speed limit, sir?' asked the fresh-faced policeman peering in through the car window.

'Um, no, I didn't. I'm sorry, Constable. I was engrossed in the radio,' I replied sheepishly, hoping to defuse the situation by being as polite as possible.

He was just about to start scribbling in his notebook, when he glanced into the back seat.

'Oh, um,' he stuttered as the colour drained from his face. 'I'm t … terribly s … sorry, s … sir.'

The young constable had clocked the police uniform folded up neatly on the back seat, complete with its impressive array of medals along the pocket. By now, beads of sweat were beginning to form above his top lip and, being a kind soul I thought it best to put him out of his misery.

'Well done, Constable,' I said, in a more authoritative tone. 'You behaved correctly. Now, may I take your name and number so that I can put in a good report about you?'

'Oh, thank you, sir,' he said, clearly relieved.

After I'd written his details in my own notebook, which was thankfully conveniently to hand, he actually stopped the traffic and beckoned me on my way. This acting lark can certainly come in handy at a time like that, although I wouldn't advise that you try impersonating a police officer.

* * * * *

I had another call from Eddie Pedder at the T.V. Times.

'I need a favour, Jack,' he said.

'Name it!' I replied without hesitation. Eddie and the magazine had been very, very good to me over the years.

'I need you to model some ski clothes for me in St Moritz.'

'That's a favour?' I said, completely gob smacked.

As arranged, a hire car picked me up the next morning and took me to the airport. From there, I flew on to Zurich, then took a train to St Moritz, where I was met by a taxi for the drive to my hotel. My suitcase safely in the boot, I was able to relax in the back seat while the car steadily wound its way up the mountain road. One minute, I'd be enjoying the magnificent scenery, then the next, gasping at the sight of yet another stomach-churning sheer drop down to the valley far below. The car suddenly came to a halt and the driver twisted round in his seat to tell me that this was as far as he was going to go.

For a moment I was reminded of one of those old cowboy films, where the superstitious locals refuse to continue along the pass because the restless spirit of "Scar-Faced Pete" haunts it. Then, once they've galloped off with terror in their eyes, our handsome hero is left alone to find his own way through the treacherous terrain and bravely confront the dastardly villain who killed his best friend … Sorry! I got a bit carried away then.

Before the driver could explain further, my future mode of transport suddenly appeared from around the next bend. After exchanging pleasantries with the fur-coated man holding the reins, the taxi driver transferred my suitcase into the most beautiful horse-drawn hackney carriage. I sat back in the leather-clad seat, pulled a blanket over my legs and silently thanked God for the unexpected delights my career sometimes brought me. As the horse tossed its handsome head and trotted merrily along the mountain pass, I could just imagine myself in a scene from that other classic film, Dr Zhivago, only without the sledge, of course.

Climbing ever higher, the views literally were breathtaking, especially when I felt the crystal clear air pricking my lungs like a million sharp needles. The altitude had begun to make me feel quite light-headed and that was before I'd even been on the piste! By the time we drew up outside the hotel, the snowy mountain peaks were tinged with pink. Eddie was waiting to greet me and gave me instructions to go out and buy four different outfits to model in the photo shoot.

'You know about clothes and you're a smart chap, Jack,' he said, handing me a wad of notes. 'Go and choose what you want, but make sure they are colourful.'

The next morning I went to a shop where I was delighted to find that the manager spoke perfect English … well, he was from Birmingham! When I explained what we were doing in St Moritz, he helped me to find some eye-catching outfits with matching accessories. A bit later on, Eddie took me to the lower slopes, where a ski instructor was waiting for us.

'Let's try these skis on you,' said the instructor. 'How do they feel?'

'I don't know, I can't ski,' I replied.

'Oh, you English,' he chuckled, giving my arm a playful punch and glancing down at my impressive ensemble.

Seeing my outfit, he obviously thought I was a professional skier, so I must have been "looking the part", as usual.

Eddie, who had been a little way away chatting to the photographer, suddenly walked over and said: 'Right! We're ready for you now, Jack.

'Can you go to that slope over there, please?' he added, pointing quite a distance away.

I followed the line of his finger and gulped: 'But how am I supposed to get right over there, Eddie?'

'Well, ski over, of course.'

'But I can't ski!'

'What!'

'You never asked me **that**,' I said, the front of my skis beginning to point precariously inwards. 'I just thought that you'd invited me out here to model the clothes.'

'Oh, my God. What are we going to do?' said Eddie, his face horror-stricken.

'Can you get some labour from somewhere?' I asked, thinking on my feet, or rather, on my skis.

'Well, yes,' he said. 'Why?'

'Because I've had an idea.'

When Eddie reappeared with four of the off-duty crew from the hotel, I asked him to point out the exact spot where he wanted me to go. I got the four men to pick me up, carry me over and set me down in the right place. It was then simply a case of them manoeuvring me into the correct position.

'Can you hand me my sticks now, please?'

'Sticks!' said Eddie, looking confused.

'You know, those pointed things that skiers use to push themselves along,' I answered.

'You certainly can't ski, can you?' he said with a laugh.

(You know, to this day, I still don't know the correct name for those "sticks"!)

At the end of a successful afternoon's filming, Eddie asked me to ski down towards the camera for the final shot. After a bit of persuasion, I allowed my "minders" to gently push me down the slope and Eddie got his last shot, which really looked quite effective in the finished portfolio. When the feature came out in the T.V. Times, all my friends kept phoning me up to tell me they hadn't realised that I could ski.

'You looked like a professional,' remarked one.

I never did pluck up the courage to tell them about the four burly hunks just off camera, who'd gallantly acted as my own personal "ski lift"!

* * * * *

I was asked to appear in an eighteen or nineteen week run at the Watersplash Theatre in Jersey. I rented a beautiful house for the summer and I was chatting to a coach driver in St Helier.

'I'm appearing at The Watersplash,' I told him.

'Oh, well, I'm afraid that we won't be coming to see you.'

'Why ever not?' I asked him.

'Because we've fallen out with the management there and all us coach drivers have agreed to boycott it.'

I was horrified, because the theatre was right at the other end of the island and if people didn't have transport, they wouldn't be able to get to the theatre. Anyway, I organised a sponsor on the island who dealt with food and drink and then I invited all the coach drivers to a cocktail party. At the end of the evening, I did a little speech...

'Listen, guys. Whatever differences you've had with the management, I hope you won't rule me out.'

A murmur went round the room.

'If you do, I'll be dead in the water.'

Thankfully, they didn't. For the whole of the run we were packed to suffocation.

* * * * *

While I was in Jersey, I had a call from Channel Seven, which is their television programme over there.

'We saw your cookery slots on Pebble Mill At One,' they told me. 'And we were wondering whether you would consider doing one, here.'

With all the wealthy tax exiles living on the island, I thought we could have some interesting people on the show. My first guest on the programme was novelist Jack Higgins, who wrote The Eagle Has Landed. When I interviewed him at his home I asked him what was his favourite meal.

'Well,' he said. 'I never write during the day, because the phone rings and people are always coming to the house.

'So, I get up at three o' clock in the morning, go downstairs and write until seven.

'Then, I have my favourite meal of the day … '

'Oh, good. Here it comes,' I thought, getting ready to make some notes.

'A fried egg sandwich!'

'Don't you ever have anything more adventurous?' I asked him.

'No! I'm a beans, sausage and eggs man.'

My next guest was golfer Tony Jacklin and he was very interesting, because he loved food and cooking.

The next guest was Oliver Reed and I was rather worried about his boozy reputation. He appeared as a guest on the programme and he was very good, even though he'd obviously had a few.

'What's in that jar?' Oliver asked, during my cookery demonstration.

'I make my own mustard,' I told him.

'What's in it?' he said, opening the jar.

'It's Dijon and whole grain mustard mixed together with honey and lemon juice.'

'May I try it?'

'Yes, of course,' I told him.

He ignored the spoon I handed him and dipped his finger straight into the mustard. He then proceeded to wipe it all down the bridge of my nose and I thought *No, I'm not going to bite.* I ignored it completely and carried on with what I was doing. I asked him to taste the mustard and he said that it was very nice, before wiping the rest of it down my nose as well. I must admit that my nose was feeling a little warm by this time, but I still ignored his antics and continued with the recipe.

After he'd left the scene, I told the studio audience that I was going to show them how to steam mussels in white wine with spring onions. I placed the mussels in an electric pot and said 'Right! While they are heating up … '

Suddenly, out of the corner of my eye I spotted Oliver Reed crawling across the floor towards me. *Oh no* I thought to myself, but he looked up at me and put his finger to his lips. He then reached forward and switched the electric pot on, because I'd forgotten to do it. Bless 'im!

* * * * *

I made some good friends on Jersey while I was over there and one day I was invited out on a boat for a bit of scuba diving.

'We'll have a competition to see who can bring back the best bit of flotsam and jetsam,' suggested Dave.

Phil went over the side first and brought up an old shoe. Dave went next and brought up a large shell. Mike was third and brought up a crab, which nearly nipped his nose as he held it up triumphantly out of the water for us to see. It was now my turn and I managed to bring an old loo seat up to the surface. So, I was declared the winner and felt thoroughly flushed with success!

* * * * *

People often ask me about the large gold ring I wear on the little finger of my right hand. Many years ago, I managed to help a jazz band to get their first professional gig. The leader of the group was a titled guy who asked me to go and see him up at his huge house.

'I'd like you to have this ring,' he said and I was amazed by the sheer weight of the thing.

I was a little bit reluctant to accept it after he'd told me that the ring had been in his family for generations, but he insisted that I take it. The ring had his family's crest on, so a jeweller adapted it for me and it now bears the legend: "J.D." Thanks, mate.

* * * * *

38–40–42–44 ins. Chest
97–102–107–112 cm   616 10p

Lister/Lee Target

"CARRY-ON-KNITTING"
WITH JACK DOUGLAS
DOUBLE KNITTING QUALITIES

Modelling knitwear designed by Sara Percival

171

*More knitwear modelling
with Barbara Windsor*

CHAPTER EIGHTEEN

One of England's favourite actors was, of course, the late, great Terry Thomas. I saw him on stage with Sid Field when he first started in the business and I can remember thinking that this funny guy was heading for future stardom. Over the years, I became a huge fan of Terry's and just thinking about his plummy accent and his wide, gappy smile never fails to make me laugh. I was lucky enough to meet him once at a charity concert and he really was the most charming man.

Usually cast as the upper-class bounder, Terry even conquered Hollywood and one of my favourite films from the sixties has to be "Those Magnificent Men in Their Flying Machines". Many years later, I heard from Richard Hope-Hawkins that Terry was suffering from Parkinson's Disease.

In desperation, he'd travelled to various clinics all over the world in the false belief that he would find a cure for his illness. There is, of course, no cure for Parkinson's Disease and Terry eventually wasted all his hard-earned money on this fruitless search. He returned to England completely penniless and the church at Barnes in London kindly fixed him up with a rent-free flat. They did their best, but the meagre funds at their disposal could only stretch so far and the basic accommodation was wholly unsuitable for someone as poorly as Terry.

When Richard and I decided to pay him a visit, we were totally unprepared for the havoc this cruel and degenerative disease had wreaked on him. His wife showed us into a tiny box room, where, sitting in front of a one-bar electric fire shaking from head to foot, was my hero Terry Thomas. He was wearing a balaclava and an army greatcoat, which completely swamped his now emaciated frame. Taken aback by his appearance, but determined not to reveal how shocked I was, I knelt down beside his chair and took hold of his frail hand.

'Hello, Terry,' I said quietly. 'Remember me? I'm Jack Douglas. We met once after a charity show.'

He looked at me and although he was unable to speak, I saw a flicker of recognition in his rheumy eyes. We sat with him for an hour, but as we stood up to leave I was horrified to discover that my knees had locked into position. If the damp atmosphere in that chilly room had caused my limbs to stiffen in so short a period of time, imagine the effect it would have been having on poor Terry.

'It's me old war wound,' I said to him, vigorously rubbing my cold knees to get the circulation flowing again.

Once we were out of the gloomy flat and standing in the street, my emotions got the better of me and I broke down and cried like a baby. As a Christian, I couldn't help but wonder about the unfairness of it all. How could a man like Terry, who'd brought such pleasure to millions of people, have ended up like that?

'You're a lucky chap, Douglas,' I thought to myself. *'That could be you sitting there.'*

I knew that my conscience wouldn't allow me to leave a fellow artiste languishing in those awful conditions and decided to do something about it. On arriving home, Richard and I immediately phoned John Avery. He was the head of Moss Empires at that time and we told him about Terry's predicament.

'That's terrible,' agreed John. 'I didn't realise that things were so bad for poor Terry.'

'Listen, John,' I said, crossing my fingers. 'Richard and I have had a terrific idea. We'd like to do a charity show for Terry and raise money to get him out of that bloody awful flat and into a proper nursing home.'

'That's a smashing idea. How can I help?'

'Well, we were wondering if you could let us have the London Palladium, please?'

'Unfortunately no,' said John and my heart sank. 'Simply because the show we've got in there at the moment has such big scenery. You can have the Theatre Royal, Drury Lane, though.'

'What! Oh that's fantastic. Thanks, John.'

'No, it's the least I can do.'

'Um, how much are you going to charge us?' I ventured tentatively.

I won't repeat his answer, but suffice to say that he said that we could use the theatre for free, just as long as I paid the staff.

Richard and I sorted out a date for the concert and wracked our brains on how to raise enough sponsorship for the event. We knew that with the best will in the world our names wouldn't carry much clout, so we phoned Michael Caine's agent. After telling him all about Terry's situation and our idea for the concert, he gave us Michael's telephone number without hesitation. We were delighted when we spoke to Michael and he kindly agreed to become patron of the charity. We will always be grateful to Michael for that, because mentioning his name when ringing round for sponsorship opened many doors which otherwise would have remained closed to us.

* * * * *

For those of you who remember "Sunday Night at The London Palladium", then you will also recall those high-kicking dancers who used to open the show every week. I phoned the lead dancer of the Tiller Girls and asked her if she was still in contact with the rest of the legendary dance troupe. After my initial call, she came back to me and said that she'd managed to trace fourteen of the original sixteen dancers and they were all willing to do the show.

I phoned "Hello" magazine to see if they would be interested in this unique photo opportunity.

'We will need to get an up-to-date photo of them,' said the editor. 'I'm sure we'll have no trouble getting hold of an old one, so we can have a then-and-now feature.'

He arranged for a photo of the girls, but after studying the two pictures side-by-side, he said, 'We can't use these.'

'Why ever not?' I asked.

'Because in twenty years they haven't changed a bit'

* * * * *

A few days before the show I was in the study at home when the telephone rang.

'I'd like to speak to Jack Douglas, please?'

'Speaking,' I answered.

'Hi! This is Phil Collins.'

Now, Phil Collins was one of the biggest names in show business at that time.

'Yes, yes, and I'm Richard Burton,' I said crossly. 'Look, I'm extremely busy, so please don't waste my time. Who is this?'

'It's Phil Collins.'

Something about his voice made me realise that it was indeed Phil Collins at the other end of the phone.

'I'm so sorry,' I blustered. 'I thought it was somebody messing about. How can I help you?'

'I've just read in the paper that you're doing a benefit for Terry Thomas.'

'Yes, that's right.'

'Well, he happens to be one of my favourite comedians and I was wondering if I could appear in the show, please?'

The humility of a performer of Phil's calibre actually asking for permission to appear in the show really touched me.

'Phil,' I said. 'If you do that concert for me you'll guarantee a full house.'

'Then you've got me.'

'Great! Thanks Phil. I'll have to phone you back with the arrangements.'

'That could be a bit difficult, Jack.'

'Oh, why is that?' I asked him.

'Because I'm ringing from Sydney, Australia.'

'What should we do then?'

'You just give me the date and time and I'll be there.'

'But what about music, Phil?'

'Just give me a grand piano on the stage and I'll accompany myself and sing a few songs.'

As soon as Phil rang off I was straight on the phone to the Press Office, which had a twenty-four hour Hot Line number. The next day, the national newspapers ran the headline: "Phil Collins to star in Terry Thomas concert" and the box office was besieged with people clamouring for tickets. Thanks Phil.

* * * * *

Funnily enough, just before the final rehearsal on the day of the show, I'd been standing alone on the stage of the empty theatre. I was just checking for any last minute hitches when I suddenly spotted a figure in grey at the back of the stalls. Incredibly, it disappeared through a solid wall and no, I hadn't been drinking! Feeling a little shocked and somewhat perplexed by this vision in grey, I rushed into the wings to find the stage manager.

'Is this theatre haunted?' I asked him.

'Yes, by a figure in grey,' he said. 'Why? You haven't seen it have you?'

175

'Yes, as a matter of fact, I have,' I said, quite expecting him to then tell me that seeing this spectre was a terrible portent of death and destruction.

'Your show will be sold out.'

'What do you mean?'

'It only ever appears when the show's going to be sold out.'

When I arrived back at the theatre before the concert, I was astonished to see that someone had glued a sticker diagonally across our advertising poster by the front doors. In five-inch high lettering it proudly declared "Sorry – Sold Out"!

The show went brilliantly. Such luminaries as Lionel Blair, Ronnie Corbett, Barbara Windsor, Hannah Gordon, Roy Castle, along with many other showbiz personalities, all gave their time for free. Her Majesty Queen Elizabeth swept into the Royal Box, much to the astonishment of the audience, who'd had no idea they were going to be in the presence of royalty. That is, until the impressionist, Janet Brown, all dolled up in a tiara and jewels, leant over the side of the box and shouted: 'Everyone all right? All enjoying yourselves, are you?' It was a wonderful moment and the whole theatre erupted in laughter.

As the curtains opened and the Tiller Girls went into their high-kicking routine, the audience jumped up and gave them a rousing standing ovation. Thanks, girls, you did Terry proud. Needless to say, the appearance of Phil Collins brought the house down. We were clearing up the rubble for weeks afterwards!

* * * * *

The Terry Thomas Benefit Concert raised a staggering £75,000. There was no creaming off of profits to pay for expenses and I'm proud to say that every last bit of that money went to the Terry Thomas Trust and the Parkinson's Disease Society. I arranged for him to move into a comfortable nursing home near to where I was living in Surrey and four extremely beautiful young nurses attended to his every need.

He may not have been able to speak, but as those women fussed around him his delight was obvious. I went to see how he was settling in and found him sitting up in a comfortable bed wearing a smart red-check dressing gown. I took hold of his shaky hand and was relieved to discover that this time it felt warm, instead of icy cold.

'This is to pay you back for all the laughter and entertainment you've given to us over the years, Terry,' I told him. 'But no chasing these nurses, mind.'

He gripped my hand and smiled with his eyes.

* * * * *

I visited Terry as often as I could and it was heartbreaking to watch his condition gradually deteriorate. He died in January 1990. I consoled myself with the fact that at least he'd been able to die with dignity, knowing that his showbiz pals had been there for him in his hour of need.

* * * * *

176

TERRY THOMAS
BENEFIT

**A NIGHT
TO REMEMBER
AND A TIME
TO HELP**

Artistes appearing include

**PHIL COLLINS · DANA · ROY CASTLE · ROY WALKER
JULIA McKENZIE · LIONEL BLAIR · RONNIE CORBETT
JIMMY CRICKET · JANET BROWN · ALAN STEWART
BARBARA WINDSOR · RICHARD BRIERS · RUSS CONWAY
JOAN REGAN · HOPE & KEEN · GARY WILMOTT
HANNAH GORDON**

plus a host of showbusiness personalities

Seats £10 to £50 Available from the Theatre Box Office and usual Agents

**ALL PROCEEDS TO THE TERRY THOMAS TRUST, THE PARKINSON'S
DISEASE SOCIETY, AND E.A.B.F. CHARITIES**

Organised by   Directed by
JACK DOUGLAS & RICHARD HOPE-HAWKINS   JACK DOUGLAS

SUNDAY 9th APRIL at 7.30 pm (One Night Only)

THEATRE ROYAL DRURY LANE

A STOLL MOSS THEATRE

CHAPTER NINETEEN

In 1991, I was appearing in "Wife Begins At Forty" with Debbie Watling at Paignton. A dog had to be on-stage with me throughout the play and the director decided to hold some canine auditions for this demanding role. All these dogs and their owners turned up at the theatre and, needless to say, when the dogs clapped eyes on one another, there was so much noise and excitement that we nearly went "barking" mad.

Anyway, one particularly good-natured dog called Lady caught my eye. As soon as the pair of us met, we struck up an instant rapport and there was plenty of licking, snuffling, pawing, yapping and tail wagging … the dog made quite a bit of fuss, too!

I was playing the part of an eighty-year-old in the play and on the opening night in Act One, Lady was sitting beside me on the sofa. I was supposed to be watching television, but when I glanced sideways, I realised that the dog was completely engrossed in the telly as well.

Of course, this kind of rare occurrence is an absolute gift to a comedian and, much to the delight of the audience, I began firing ad-lib comments at Lady about the programme we were watching. She was an excellent foil and never once took her eyes off the screen.

Jack and Lady

We were all enjoying this immensely, but the time had come to continue with the scene. Lady, however, had other ideas. As I bent down to switch the television off, Lady threw her head back and howled. The audience gave us a standing ovation. From then on, I could do no wrong.

The following day, the newspaper headline said: "Dog Steals Show in Paignton"! It just goes to show, that the old adage about never working with animals is actually based in fact.

* * * * *

It's a strange thing, but quite a few theatres in England are supposed to be haunted. It's no surprise really, when you think of the heightened emotions that are experienced inside theatres. These feelings not only affect the actors on-stage, but everyone seated out in the audience, too. That's a potent cocktail of emotions flying around.

I was once in a play in Torquay and we'd just finished a performance one night when the most extraordinary thing happened. There were two 'limes', which, as I explained before, were the spotlights in the front of house. I walked forward to do my curtain speech and suddenly, down a shaft of light from one of these 'limes', fluttered the most beautiful butterfly I'd ever seen.

The audience went berserk when I extended my hand and it settled on my palm. The delicate creature opened and closed its colourful wings, presumably relishing the warmth emanating from both the light and my hand. I raised my hand to offer it up into the light, if you like, and the butterfly fluttered back up the beam and disappeared.

It really was one of the most magical moments I've ever experienced on a stage and it left me feeling serene and happy for hours afterwards. A stage hand later told me that butterflies are the souls of dead ballerinas who come back to watch over the theatre. What a charming belief.

* * * * *

Still on the subject of ghosts, it was while I was appearing at the Tameside Theatre in Ashton-under-Lyne that I saw "Ernie". I was walking across the empty theatre chatting to my co-star, the ventriloquist Keith Harris, when we both became aware of a man beckoning us from the upper circle. We didn't pay much attention at first, but he seemed in *dead*ly *earnest* (sorry) and so we went up to see what he wanted. As we approached him, however, he disappeared into thin air. Apparently, Ernie is a regular visitor to the theatre and many people have seen him over the years.

* * * * *

Like most parents, my children have always been a great source of pride for me. When Debbie married Chris and produced a son, Daniel, I was over the moon at being called "Granddad" at last. Funnily enough, though, Daniel calls me "Uncle", because he doesn't think I look old enough to be a granddad, bless 'im! After Daniel, came Joanna.

My son Craig, who lives in Spain, then married Rosie and they produced a beautiful daughter called Jasmin.

Sadly, Debbie's marriage broke up and she did a wonderful job of bringing the children up on her own. Joanna left school and went on to train as a hairdresser. Her boss was a very handsome fellow and when Joanna discovered that he wasn't married, the clever girl devised a way for her mother to meet him. Debbie took one look at Rob and "ting", she suddenly found herself falling deeply in love. Happily, he felt the same way and they eventually married.

I remember Debbie ringing me up a couple of years later, saying, 'What are you doing at this very moment, Dad?'

'I'm standing here talking to you, of course,' I told her.

'Well, can you sit down, please?' she said.

'Why? There's nothing … ?'

'Sit down, please, Dad,' instructed Debbie.

'Right! I'm sitting down.'

'I'm pregnant!' she announced triumphantly.

'What! Oh, that's wonderful … '

'Yes, Dad. I know I'm forty, but I feel marvellous,' she said, picking up on the note of concern in my voice.

Jack and daughter Debbie with her children Daniel and Joanna

Craig's daughter Jasmin

Jack's newest grandson Harvey

Seven months later, little Harvey appeared on the scene and I know I'm biased, but he's one of the most beautiful little boys you could ever hope to meet. I'm so lucky to have such a wonderful family.

* * * * *

I've always been interested in history since I was a child. Now that my daughter and her family live in the beautiful city of Bath, there are two good reasons why it's a place I never tire of visiting.

I was extremely lucky to meet a lady called Marion Carter, who was the curator of the old, original Roman city of Bath.

Amazingly, it was discovered by accident during the excavations for a bank vault. One of the workmen had thrust his pick-axe into the ground when, through no "vault" of his own, it slipped from his grasp and disappeared down a hole. This was closely followed by a loud splash and so he and his colleagues rigged up a spotlight. When they shone it down into the void they found a Roman baths along with a colourful mosaic.

After a period of time, a descent was made into the hole, where they discovered a complete Roman city hidden beneath the modern one. I felt extremely privileged when Marion offered to show me around the excavations before they were open to the general public. It was incredible to see all the streets with their shops and hotels still intact and even the odd brothel or two, with their sexually explicit wall paintings. I should think that the Roman equivalent of Mary Whitehouse would have had a field day!

Call it a flight of fancy, but to me it seemed as if the streets were still teeming with people, even though Marion and I were the only ones there.

Marion explained that the Romans had these huge, seven-foot high sewers built, because their black Nubian slaves had evidently been over six-feet tall. When the Romans left Britain, our typically English ancestors decided to fill in all the sewers, which meant that when the floods came, the city was completely overwhelmed by water. Over a period of years, of course, earth and soil had eventually covered the ancient remains and subsequent inhabitants of Bath had simply built over the top.

I'm always amazed at the seemingly up-to-date technology found in Roman ruins, not least their sophisticated form of central heating. Especially when you remember that this was still a time when we were walking around wearing furs and carrying spears.

* * * * *

I saw a busker in London recently and it took me back to an incident that happened fifty years ago. I was great friends with the American actor Bonar Colleano and we'd been out celebrating his success in the film, "While The Sun Shines". Bonar and I were just leaving the restaurant when we spotted the busker on the other side of the street.

We crossed over to watch him, but it looked as if his efforts had been in vain. The cap he'd been using as a collection box, lay empty on the pavement beside him. We guessed from his appearance that "business" must have been bad for quite a while.

'Poor guy looks half starved,' Bonar remarked. 'Come on, Jack. We should help him out.'

We stepped forward to join in with his tap dance routine and his face lit up with a huge smile. Our presence seemed to instil a new lease of life into his emaciated frame. An appreciative crowd of onlookers soon gathered around us and it was heartening to hear the continual clink of coins, as they threw their money into the upturned cap.

After a while, we said our goodbyes to the busker, but, as we made to go, he said, 'Hold on a minute, fellas. You've got to have your divvy.'

'No, no,' said Bonar, holding up his hands.

'We wouldn't hear of it,' I added. 'It's all yours, mate.'

'You're a couple of toffs,' he said with a laugh. 'Thank you very much.'

Perhaps I should have added the word "busker" to my c.v.

* * * * *

'Did you say you wanted my autograph?'

CHAPTER TWENTY

After the traumatic break-up of my second marriage, I had been sitting dejectedly in the bar of the Harrow pub in Godalming.

'You're looking a bit depressed, Jack,' said the concerned publican. 'Anything the matter?'

'I've just had to sell my house and I'm looking for somewhere to live,' I told him with a sigh. 'Apart from that, everything's dandy.'

'Oh, I'm sorry, Jack,' he said kindly. 'There's a room upstairs going begging if that's any help.'

Needless to say, I moved in and stayed there for a month while the local estate agent kept me informed about properties for sale in the area. The agent finally found me a delightful 16th century ex-mill workers cottage with oak beams, which was very run down and dilapidated. It's true what they say about buying houses, you know. As soon as I walked in and started looking around I felt completely at home there. Something clicked inside (probably me knee caps) and fell into place. I also knew that I'd better make an offer pronto, before someone else beat me to it.

Happily, the sale went through without a hitch and I decided that it would be the perfect therapy for me to set about restoring the cottage. Out came the tool box (ooh, Matron) and on the very first morning I did that classic thing of tapping along a wall with my chisel. You know, when one bit of wall sounds solid, then you move further along and the other bit sounds hollow.

In films, they usually find a secret passage or a dead body walled up behind the hollow bit, but, in this case, the hollow bit turned out to be a wooden petition. I wrenched it away and shone my torch inside.

'Wow!' I exclaimed, as the torch beam fell upon, not a skeleton, thankfully, but a beautiful dust-covered inglenook fireplace with two seats either side.

I couldn't help wondering how long it had been boarded up and hidden from sight. The original dog basket was still sitting faithfully in the middle, full of cobweb-covered logs and a now vacant mouse nest. As I shone my torch around I could see that the whole fireplace was littered with small sticks, probably dropped down the stack by nest-building jackdaws up on the chimney pot.

'That will have to be swept before you can think of lighting a fire, Douglas,' I said to myself, shining the torch beam up into the soot-filled flu. I began by clearing the centuries of dust away and was delighted to discover ye olde bread oven and some large hooks that would have been used for smoking bacon joints. All this hard work, plus the imaginary smell of newly baked bread and sizzling bacon, was making me feel hungry. (Sorry! I've just made you feel hungry as well, haven't I?)

It was a glorious day and rather than eat in the dusty atmosphere indoors, I decided to sit outside in the garden. I was just tucking into some bread and cheese, which I was washing down with a glass of red wine, when, much to my astonishment, a dog fox casually came trotting up the garden towards me. He stopped just a few feet away, endearingly tipping his head over on one side as I spoke to him and readily accepting the bread titbits I threw on to the lawn. I subsequently discovered that "Reynard's" den was actually beyond my garden, down on the river bank.

The cottage was one of four, still served by a dilapidated row of privies at the bottom of my garden. There was, in fact, a right of way through my garden to these loos, which was written in my deeds. With the advent of indoor facilities, however, they were long since defunct and so I went round to ask the neighbours if they would mind me turning them into a workshop. (The loos, that is, not the neighbours!)

I read somewhere that when our predecessors used these privies many years before, they would have probably chucked a dead sheep down there. This meant that the maggots would not only devour the sheep, but "everything" else as well. I wonder if that's why they call it a "ewe" bend? I suppose that instead of pulling the chain, it was more like "pulling the wool"! It's a good thing that the loos were at the bottom of the garden, because the smell would have been unBARable! Enough of these sheep, sorry, I mean, cheap jokes, Douglas.

Anyway, I restored the rest of the cottage bit by bit. I designed the kitchen as much in keeping with the old property as I could and was delighted when a company called "Upstairs Downstairs" offered a free fitting in exchange for an endorsement of their product. I was just about to start on the attic, when I got a phone call from my agent to say that the Summer Season I had been booked to do down in Torquay had fallen through.

'How does a Summer Season in the Isle of Wight grab you, though,' he said.

'Great! What's the show Phil?' I asked him.

'It's "Me And My Girl" and they want you to play the part of Sir John Tremayne.'

I was thrilled, because "Me And My Girl" has always been one of my favourite shows. I was even more thrilled to find out that the show was to preview all over the Easter break. It was then going to run for the whole season at Sandown Pavillion, which has since closed down … but not because of the show, I hasten to add.

I secured a flat in a little place called Winford, just outside Sandown and three weeks later, I drove down the A3 and boarded the ferry at Portsmouth.

My agent's then girlfriend, Debbie, was also going to be in the show and, as she'd had terrible problems finding digs, I said she'd be welcome to share the flat with me. No, there was nothing like that going on! Remember that Phil was my agent and if there had been any hanky panky, my next job would have been in the Outer Hebrides!

Our first day's rehearsal was at the Shanklin Theatre and after being introduced to the cast and crew I knew that it was going to be a most enjoyable summer.

The director said 'Jack! Let me introduce you to Vivien Russell who's playing the Duchess, opposite you.

'Hello, pleased to meet you, Jack,' said Vivien and I was immediately struck by this petite, blue-eyed blonde.

As the rehearsals progressed, her talent and her happy zest for life, which was extremely infectious really impressed me. We got on really well and many a time the director had to check us for giggling like a pair of school kids. It was obvious that we were falling in love, although I subsequently found out that Viv had been a little

Jack and Viv

confused at the start, when I'd turned up to rehearsals with young Debbie in tow. Especially when she found out that we were sharing the same flat.

After a bit of discreet detective work, though, Viv soon discovered that the coast was clear and that it was safe to woo me. This was what we both wanted, of course, and it was lovely being wooed together.

Like me, Viv had had a great deal of unhappiness in her life, relationship-wise. She'd been married twice and although her first marriage had ended in divorce, her second had ended tragically when her husband died of a stroke. Poor Viv nursed him through months of ill health and after his death and all the heartache she'd endured, she vowed never to become romantically involved with anyone again.

Viv was very settled on the island and had a lovely home in Shanklin, plus a steady job in the theatre. It seems that, like me, she had come to terms with being on her own. At the end of the Easter preview I returned home to Godalming, but not before asking Viv to come over and celebrate my birthday, which was just a couple of weeks away. Despite our promises never to become involved with anyone, we both knew that we were destined to be together.

I put my cottage on the market and then moved down to Shanklin on the Isle of Wight, where "me and my girl" Viv still live today. In a more practical sense, we both have qualities that compliment each other. For instance, I love cooking and shopping and Viv loathes cooking and shopping. I hate accounts and office work, whereas Viv loves doing accounts and getting to grips with work in the office. My fan mail and personal finance have never been in such a good state of affairs, which is wonderful.

On a more personal level, we are both crazy about one another and Viv has sorted my life out in every sense. I just want to say Viv that I fell deeply in love with you the first time I clapped eyes on you and that I'm still deeply in love with you now. Thank you, darling, for making me the happiest man alive.

* * * * *

One of my prized possessions when I was a kid was a cap gun. Rightly or wrongly, I've always had a love for guns and over the years I'd collected a beautiful array of weapons. I remember once when Joe Baker and I did the Wyatt Earp Show and I was in my element when one of the "cowboys" agreed to teach me to do gun twirling. I picked it up fairly quickly and in later years I was able to astonish the audience on the "Spotlight" programme with my skills.

I had my collection of guns for many years and they were my pride and joy, but when I opened the trunk and showed my vast collection to Viv she went berserk. She was petrified, as she has a morbid fear of guns and I had no choice but to get rid of them. That's obviously what they mean by "gun slinging"!

I kept my air rifle with its telescopic sight, which still hangs on my study wall. Guns are wonderful pieces of equipment, the trouble is that they can fall into the wrong hands and be used by people with wicked intent. I couldn't resist buying an old cavalry sword, which I found in a junk shop, but Viv doesn't mind that because she's never seen it out of its scabbard.

* * * * *

It was a great thrill in the early-nineties when David Graham asked me to become a director of the Dead Comics Society, as it was known then. The idea of the Society was to honour all those comedians that had made us laugh like Sid James and Tony Hancock. We thought that as you often see blue plaques dedicated to people who had built bridges and written poetry, then why not to our great comics?

I'm sure that those people who were around during the forties will agree that the war effort owes more than it can ever say to Tommy Handley. His radio show, ITMA (It's That Man Again), helped to boost our flagging morale and kept us all laughing through the darkest days of the war.

After a while, there was a bit of a split in loyalties within the group. The Dead Comics Society became The British Comedy Society, which we thought had a much nicer ring to it. David Graham changed his society's name to Comic Heritage. Morris Bright, who Carry On fans will know as one of the world's leading authorities on the subject, asked me if I would like to be President of the revamped British Comedy Society. One of the first things I did in my new post, was to pop and see my old friend Steve Jaggs, who was (and still is) the Managing Director of Pinewood Studios.

'What can I do for you, Jack?' said Steve, shaking my hand.

I explained that the society was a charitable organisation and I asked him if we could use the studio for society functions.

'We can put on a nice meal and entertain the public,' I said. 'Which, with your permission, we could do in the ballroom and dining room.'

'Certainly!' said Steve. 'No problem.'

On my way out through the fireplace … yes, I did say 'fireplace'. The administrative building at Pinewood has a huge, magnificently carved Elizabethan fireplace as a doorway. Just think of all the famous people who might have "swept" through that fireplace. Robert Stack! Heartha Haynes, Fluella Benjamin! Basil (flu) Brush! Gratie Fields! Pokermon! Coal Porter! Arthur Ashky! Ann Thracite! Even Sooty and Sweep! Now you're just being silly, Douglas! Seriously, as I was leaving I spotted a long corridor opposite the fireplace, sorry, I mean doorway. I think I'm right in saying that this corridor leads to the sound department and then on through to all the main film stages. Whatever, it gave me a fantastic idea and I dashed back upstairs to Steve's office.

'Could I just have another quick word with Steve, please?' I asked his secretary, just as Steve appeared in his office doorway.

'What is it, Jack?' he said.

'That corridor opposite,' I said, pointing over in its general direction.

'Yes, what about it?'

'I'd like to turn it into a Hall of Fame.'

'You've got it,' said Steve without argument. 'But what do you want to do with it?'

'Could we put the British Comedy Society's logo on the front, then place our blue plaques along its length, to honour all the famous people of Pinewood Studios and British films?'

'I don't see why not. That's a great idea.'

Our first event at Pinewood was a plaque unveiling to honour the director of all the Carry On films, the late Gerald Thomas, who had been such a dear friend to me. The next plaque honoured "Doctor" films. We were even graced with the presence of Dirk Bogarde at the unveiling, in one of his rare public appearances. Since those early days, plaques have been unveiled to the wonderful Sir Norman Wisdom, the Carry Ons and to the marvellous cast of Last of the Summer Wine. As well as some other locations around London and at Elstree Studios.

It's a tragedy to think that we've lost Gerald Thomas, Betty Box, who produced the "Doctor" films, Dirk Bogarde and dear Bill Owen. At least it's a comfort to know they will live on in the hearts and minds of their many fans. God bless them all.

Sadly, what with living so far away on the Isle of Wight and a degenerative hip problem, I had to give up my post in the British Comedy Society. David Graham's charity organisation, Comic Heritage, has gone from strength to strength and has now branched out into The Heritage Foundation. This encompasses Music Heritage and Sports Heritage.

Viv and I have attended a lot of his plaque unveilings, which are followed by the most wonderful get-togethers at top London hotels. Celebrity members and fans attend David's well-organised events, and they include a three-course meal, a charity auction of showbiz memorabilia, plus a charity raffle. Its functions raise thousands of pounds for charity each year and I think that we are very lucky to have bright, far-sighted people like David Graham in this world.

* * * * *

During the latter part of the nineties, I'd been suffering more and more with my hip. The doctor provided me with some painkillers to get me through the 1998/99 pantomime season when I was appearing in Solihull, but promised me a visit to the specialist at the end of the run.

The panto' went really well – a touch of what we performers call "Dr Showbiz" helped me through. It's simply a case of being so focused when you're on stage that you forget all about what ails you. That is, until you leave the stage and fall into a heap in the dressing room! Anyway, as soon as I returned to the island in January 1999 my doctor sent me for an X-ray.

There was certainly a lot of wear and tear to my left hip joint, but the specialist thought that with a combination of rest and gentle exercise it might just settle down again. A lovely summer on the island that year meant that the garden had never looked so good and I really enjoyed pottering around.

Then the good news came that I would be working with that wonderful Welsh actress of Hi-De-Hi fame, Ruth Madoc, the following winter. The pantomime in Southampton was something to look forward to, but for the time being at least, I was glad that my ailing hip joint could soak up the warmth of the summer sunshine. Come the dampness of October, though, the gnawing and now debilitating pain in my hip began again in earnest, which prompted yet another visit to my doctor.

After a further X-ray the news wasn't so good. When the specialist told me that the only option was a hip replacement operation and that it would have to be done ASAP, my first thought was for the pantomime. I phoned the director, Peter Frosdick, as soon as I got home, but he was marvellous about it. I still felt awful about having to renege on my contract, though. Well, it was the first time in my long career in showbiz that I'd had to back out of a show.

Vivien and I enjoyed a quiet Christmas at home and, just as we raised our glasses to welcome in the new millennium, a call came through to say that I was to be admitted to St Mary's Hospital in nearby Newport on January 4th. Naturally, I felt a bit anxious about it, as everyone does before surgery, although I was glad that I wouldn't have to go over to the mainland for the operation. However, the wonderful staff at St Mary's, who immediately put me at my ease soon dispelled my pre-op nerves.

After the operation was over, I came round from the anaesthetic to find my hip covered in a thick plaster, but at least the awful nagging pain had disappeared. By the time Vivien came to visit me in the evening, I was sitting up in bed and not feeling in the least bit drowsy. The ward staff were pretty busy the following afternoon and so I decided to make my way to the bathroom unaided. Big mistake!

'What on earth do you think you're doing, Mr Douglas?' said the nurse when she saw me shuffling along the ward.

You should have seen the look on her face as she helped me back into bed – talk about Carry On Matron. I'm just thankful that she didn't have a daffodil!

I stayed in hospital for ten days and in all that time I was spoiled rotten by the nurses. At first, I had to get round in a wheelchair and then I had to learn to use crutches, which was a scream. I had to persevere with my exercises to get the hip joint mobile again and, as exercise is not usually a word in my vocabulary, it wasn't easy. Viv was by my side throughout the long convalescence and I can never thank her enough for looking after me so well.

During the summer of 2000, Viv and I were both offered parts in Cinderella at the Playhouse in Weston-Super-Mare. Viv was to be the Fairy Godmother and I was Baron Hardup and we were both thrilled at the prospect of working together again that coming winter. I had a few minor setbacks with the hip during the year and this pantomime was going to be it's greatest test so far. Hippily, sorry, I mean happily it was a fairy tale ending … We had a successful season and my new hip performed like a star.

* * * * *

Although I'm now completely recovered from my hip operation, there is still something that I'm unable to do. No, not that … thankfully.

My doctor advised me not to play golf anymore, which, as you can imagine, was a bit of a blow. Swivelling the hips, it seems, is definitely not recommended after an operation for a replacement hip joint. Seeing my redundant golf clubs languishing in the cupboard only served as a painful reminder of my limitations, so I decided it would be best to donate them to charity. They managed to raise £250 in the charity auction, which meant that at least some good came from my disappointment.

It's an ill wind …

* * * * *

Baron Hardup and the Fairy Godmother

JACK DOUGLAS

Since I've moved to the Isle of Wight, Viv and I have made some lovely friends. One in particular, who's been so kind and helpful to me, is a top journalist called John Hannam. He writes for The Stage and has his own radio and television programmes on the island. He's even written about his experiences in the world of show business in a book called "Stage Door Johnny".

John has interviewed both Viv and me and if I ever need to advertise any of the various charity things I've been doing, John's always the first person to give me a plug. We are also friends with Tina and Derry, who are the proprietors of our friendly local pub. The Crab is a delightful old building with a thatched roof and oak beams, which is reputed to date from the 16th century.

Viv and I make our way down to the older part of Shanklin every Tuesday night during the winter months, in order to team up with our friends, Chris and Jeff, in the pub quiz. We always have a good laugh and there's such a lovely atmosphere. I have to admit, though, that I'm only an asset to our team if the questions are about old films or the history of Egypt, or cooking.

Thank you Derry and Tina for making our Tuesday nights so special.

* * * * *

CHAPTER TWENTY-ONE

I had a call from that wonderful musician, Rick Wakeman, asking if Viv and I would like to do a charity show over on the Isle of Man.

'It's going to be at The Gaiety Theatre in Douglas and all your expenses will be paid,' Rick told me.

As promised Rick was there to meet us at the airport.

'What about our bags?' I asked him as we shook hands.

'No need to worry, Jack, because I've arranged for a porter,' Rick replied.

'You seem to have thought of everything,' said Viv, highly impressed by his efficiency.

He'd arranged for a 'porter' all right! We both burst out laughing when we spotted Norman Wisdom heading in our direction, complete with his trademark cap. Norman proceeded to throw our luggage onto a trolley and everyone was in stitches as he made his way through the passengers at the busy airport. He was weaving this way and that in his usual crazy fashion, causing, as you might expect, utter pandemonium as he went.

It was an unforgettable welcome to the island. Not just for us, but all the other visitors who were lucky enough to be at the airport. After all, it isn't every day that you can get treated to a free show by one of our top comedians.

I've known Norman for most of my career and we've been together at many social events. We even did a cruise for the T.V. Times.

In the show at the Gaiety, Rick wanted me to compere "Beat The Clock", which is that old quiz from Sunday Night at the London Palladium. Rick asked Norman what he was going to do and he looked blank.

'I don't know,' he said. 'I need a straight man.'

'Well, you've got one,' I told him. 'And whatever you want me to do, I'll do it.'

'Right!' said Norman. 'We won't rehearse, we'll have a bit of fun.'

'If you have confidence in me, Norman, I definitely have ultimate confidence in you, so let's do it,' I said.

Anyway, I was doing "Beat The Clock" and before I could say, 'Here's the next contestant,' on came Norman in his usual "gump" suit and cap. He was carrying the biggest pot plant I've ever seen in my life. Goodness only knows where he got it.

We did ten minutes on that stage together and Norman walked off to a huge round of applause. He's a great comedian and a national treasure. Norman's still as funny now, as when he first started.

* * * * *

In show business, of course, you can involve yourself in lots of charities. You have to be selective, however, because if you're not careful you might end up with no time for yourself.

Being an animal lover, one charity I am more than happy to be involved with is called "The Friends of the Animals". It's run by a very caring lady called Helen Sinclair and

Martin Gomez and I was extremely chuffed when Helen asked me if I would become Patron of the charity. The charity's head office is in the West Midlands, but they also have branches in Southsea and Ringwood in Hants, plus one in Ryde, here on the island.

Some of the reports in their magazine do make for depressing reading, like the puppy thrown out of a car window onto a motorway, or some boys playing football with a hedgehog.

The good news is, that "Friends of the Animals" are on-hand when there is no-one to look after a deceased person's pets. Helen and her team will find these animals loving homes. They also help owners who can't afford to have their pets treated by a vet. The "Friends" do a fantastic job and I'm very proud to help them whenever and however I can.

"FRIENDS OF THE ANIMALS"

❖ ❖

HEAD OFFICE **408 Bearwood Road** Reg. Charity No 1000249
Bearwood Warley
West Midlands B66 4EX
0121-420-4201.

Also At

P.O. Box 141 "Cobbs Cottage" P.O. Box 4
Southsea Kingston Common Ryde
Hants. Ringwood Hants. Isle of Wight
PO4 8TL BH24 3AY PO33 4ED
01705-255262 01425-471471 01983-616144

NEWSLETTER NUMBER 27

Jack Douglas, our patron with some of our rescues (I'm not one of them!).

FRIENDS OF THE ANIMALS Page 1

Jack with Helen Sinclair and some of the rescue animals

Dear All,

Welcome to our first newsletter of the bright New Year 1998, and welcome to our new patron JACK DOUGLAS. Jack, who is the President of the "British Comedy Society" is first and foremost a comedian, but in recent years has been seen on stage and T.V. as both a serious and comic actor, and is now finding considerable success as a writer and producer. He has played in Panto's for more than forty years, but is probably best known for his portrayal of 'Alf Ippititimus' in the "Carry On" films.

From the newsletter of the Friends of the Animals

* * * * *

I was just sitting down for my morning coffee, when the phone rang. It was my agent, Phil Dale.

'Sorry to ring you so early, Jack, but it's important,' he said. 'It's about the "Carryoons".'

'The Carry-what's?' I replied.

'Have you any idea how many letters Peter Rogers gets from Carry On fans all asking him if he's going to make another Carry On picture?'

'Um, no.'

'Well, it's thousands.'

'I see,' I said, feeling none the wiser.

'Because of all the interest, Jack, they've decided to make a series of Carry On cartoons with the character's voices being impersonated by the best sound-a-likes in the business.'

'Oh, how marvellous, but who's going to be doing me?' I asked tentatively.

'You are!'

'Right! When do we start?'

'The script's in the post, Jack. Let me know what you think.'

I was literally lying in wait the next morning, ready to ambush the postman as soon as he arrived. Before long, I was reading through the script and **laughing**, which is highly unusual these days. I rang my agent back as promised and, ten days later Viv and I were en route to the studios in Pinewood. The producer, who was bubbling with excitement, greeted us.

To walk into that sound studio and hear Hattie Jacques' disembodied voice was the most surreal experience; especially when I realised that it was actually a young guy who was mimicking her so perfectly. When we heard the voices of Kenneth Williams, Charlie Hawtrey and Sid James on the loudspeakers, Viv and I just stood there open-mouthed. Next, it was my turn at the microphone and I had to swallow a huge lump in my throat before I could begin. In my mind, it was like being back with all my old pals in the Carry Ons.

When Viv and I arrived back on the island later that day we couldn't stop talking about it.

'I've got a good feeling about this, Jack,' said Viv excitedly.

'Me, too,' I replied.

A few months later, Phil phoned to say that the pilot for the twenty-six week series had been filmed and was scheduled for showing to an invited audience at Pinewood Studios.

'Your names are on the guest list, Jack,' he told me.

Viv and I were heading for the ferry port on the morning of the screening, when my steering gave a sudden jolt.

'What is it, Jack?' cried Viv in alarm, as I pulled over into the side of the road.

'I've got a puncture! Well, at least my car has one, anyway!' I said with an exasperated sigh.

I changed the wheel as quickly as I could and we sped down to the port, just in time to see the ferry leaving without us. I phoned Phil to tell him the bad news.

'Never mind, mate,' he said. 'I'll ring you later.'

Viv and I were on pins all day. What if our puncture had been a bad omen? I knew that if the cartoon idea bombed, then I'd soon be feeling as deflated as my flat tyre. Suppose it had gone down like a lead balloon with the audience? Or it had been greeted by complete silence and hadn't raised so much as a titter? All these negative thoughts kept racing around inside my head, on what seemed like one of the longest days of my life.

That afternoon, I was just sucking on my pipe to try and calm my frazzled nerves, when the phone rang. I jumped out of my skin, but Viv gave me a supportive smile and so I took a deep breath and picked up the receiver. Phil was in a complete state of elation at the other end of the line.

'Jack! It was marvellous, I can't tell you. I've never heard an audience laugh so much. The reaction has been fantastic. I just wish you could have been there.'

I put the phone down at the end of the call and was just about to jump in the air and shout, 'Yippee!' when the phone rang again. It was Peter Rogers himself and it was obvious from the tone of his voice that he was as thrilled as Phil had been.

'The good news is,' he told me, 'that it's being shown at the Cannes Film Festival next week!'

I was speechless … for a change.

The wonderful thing for me, of course, is that although many of my dear friends in the Carry On team are now dead, thanks to the "Carryoons", they can live again. Fingers crossed that they will be a huge success.

* * * * *

The winter of 2001/2002 found Viv and I resurrecting our respective roles of The Fairy Godmother and Baron Hardup in the panto' Cinderella. This time it was up at The Crewe Lyceum alongside Keith Harris. He, of course, was accompanied by his

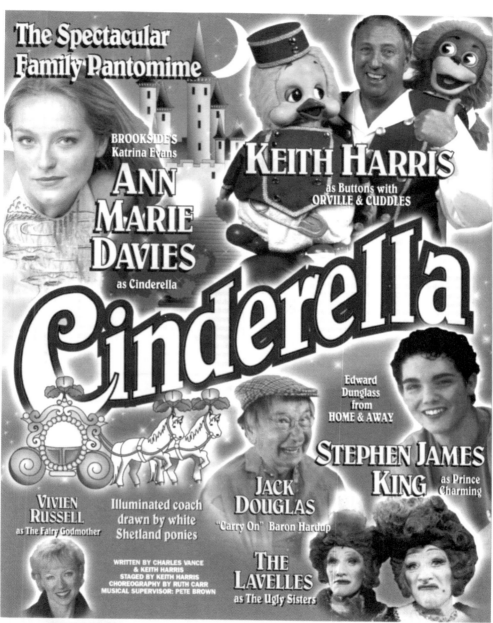

The Spectacular Family Pantomime

BROOKSIDE'S Katrina Evans
ANN MARIE DAVIES
as Cinderella

KEITH HARRIS
as Buttons with ORVILLE & CUDDLES

Cinderella

Edward Dunglass from HOME & AWAY

STEPHEN JAMES KING
as Prince Charming

VIVIEN RUSSELL
as The Fairy Godmother

Illuminated coach drawn by white Shetland ponies

JACK DOUGLAS
"Carry On" Baron Hardup

WRITTEN BY CHARLES VANCE & KEITH HARRIS
STAGED BY KEITH HARRIS
CHOREOGRAPHY BY RUTH CARR
MUSICAL SUPERVISOR: PETE BROWN

THE LAVELLES
as The Ugly Sisters

CREWE LYCEUM
THEATRE AT ITS BEST

7 DEC 2001 - 5 JAN 2002
BOX OFFICE: 01270 537 333

MORRISONS

faithful duck, Orville, and Cuddles the cheeky monkey. Just like the previous year at The Playhouse in Weston Super Mare, this production broke all box office records, too.

After arriving back on the island in January, a crew from Sky Television came to film me preparing a sauce in my kitchen.

Apparently, the reruns of "Not On Your Nelly" on Granada Plus have proved to be very popular with the viewers and it's strange to think that I receive more fan mail now than I did thirty years ago.

Even more exciting! I was summoned to the Granada Studios in Manchester to audition for a part in Coronation Street, which was a fantastic surprise, especially as it's one of Viv's favourite programmes. It was a great honour to be asked, but Manchester is a very long way from the Isle of Wight and accepting the prestigious role of an undertaker would have been a great "undertaking", commuting-wise.

As it happens, that wonderful actor Roy Hudd was chosen for the part and I'm sure he'll do a splendid job of it. Good luck to you, mate.

Columbia T.I. have also interviewed me for a lovely programme called "Stars We Love". Life is certainly sweet and I'm so grateful to the wonderful world of show business for all the opportunities it's given me. And for giving me the chance to work with so many clever and talented people over the years.

I'm a very lucky man.

* * * * *

MY PROFESSIONAL LIFE IN CHRONOLOGICAL ORDER

As far as I can remember!

1946:   Hi There! For the Combined Services Entertainment's Unit abroad.

1947/48:   It's All Blarney.

1948/49:   Dick Whittington – The Kingston Empire.

1949:   "Uncle Jack of Jaywick".

1950/51:   With Joe Baker – touring for Moss Empires.

1955:   Butlin's – Clacton. Summer Season.

1955:   Crackerjack (CRACKERJACK!)

1956:   February – In variety at the Queens Theatre, Blackpool.

1956/57:   Aladdin – The Empress, Brixton. With Alma Cogan and Bill Maynard.

1957:   Summer Season at the Hippodrome, Blackpool, with Michael Holiday, Winifred Atwell, and the Kay Sisters.

1957/58:   Dick Whittington at the Alexandra, Birmingham, with Arthur Haynes, Joe Baker and Sonnie Hale.

1959:   Crackerjack (CRACKERJACK!)?

1959:   Summer Season at the Palace Theatre in Blackpool with Roy Castle and Joe Baker.

1959/60:   Robinson Crusoe at Finsbury Park with Sally Barnes, Lonnie Donnegan and Joe Baker.

1960:   January – Tour of Australia with Joe. Six weeks out on The Orion. February – Father dies. Ship docks in Florence. Fly home for funeral, then rejoin ship and continue to Australia.
Tour with Joe Baker and David Whitfield to Sidney, Melbourne and Perth.
May - Return home.

1960:   Summer Season at the Pavillion Theatre in Weymouth. Joe reveals that he wants to split the act.

1960/61:   Robin Hood at The Alhambra, Bradford, with Freddie Frinton, Jimmy Wheeler and Joe Baker.

1961:   Freelance as a straight man for Bruce Forsyth, Benny Hill and Arthur Haynes.
Left show business and opened "The Wynmarith" restaurant in Blackpool.
Phone call from Des O'Connor. Returned to London…and show business.

1961/62:   Beauty and The Beast at the Lyceum, Sheffield with Jack Storey, Nat Jackley and Hope and Keen.

1962:   Freelance work with Arthur Haynes for T.V.
Work with Des O'Connor. T.V.

1963:   With Des O'Connor for T.V.

1963/64:   Humpty Dumpty at the Grand Theatre, Leeds, with John Hanson, Wyn Calvin and Des O'Connor.

1964:   With Des O'Connor for T.V.
"Dave's Kingdom" with Dave King for T.V.
The Jimmy Clitheroe Show for T.V.

1964/65:   Cinderella at the New Theatre, Oxford, with Danny La Rue, Yana and Des O'Connor.

1965:   Coventry Theatre – Spring Show with Des O'Connor.
June – T.V. series with Des O'Connor.

1965/66:   Aladdin at the Palace Theatre, Manchester, with Billy Dainty, Freddie and the Dreamers and Des O'Connor.

1966:   March – The Palladium Show with Russ Conway, Frank Ifield, Jack Haig and Des O'Connor.
T.V. The Des O'Connor Show with Lulu.
April – Ed Sullivan Show in America with Des O'Connor.
Summer Season at the North pier in Blackpool with Des O'Connor.
The Good Old Days for T.V. at The City Varieties, Leeds.
September – Bill Cotton's Music Hall. T.V. with George

Chisholm, Jack Haig and Petula Clarke.
November 14th – The Royal Variety Show with an all-star cast.

1966/67:   Cinderella at the Palladium with Cliff Richard and The Shadows,
Peter Gilmore, Terry Scott and Hugh Lloyd.

1967:   January – Palladium Show with Jack Haig.
March – The Good Old Days T.V. with Ray Allen, Jack Haig and
Leonard Sachs at the City Varieties, Leeds.
May – T.V. series with Des O' Connor.
June – Summer Season with Kenneth McKellar, The Dallas Boys,
Margo Henderson and Des O' Connor at The Pavillion Theatre in
Bournemouth.
August – Manning petrol pumps at Castle Lane Garage,
Bournemouth.

1967/68:   Cinderella at the New Theatre, Cardiff with Vince Hill, Freddie
Sales and Des O'Connor.

1968:   "Don't Tell the Wife" farce at the Grand Theatre, Blackpool.

1968/69:   Cinderella in Birmingham.
Des decides to split the act.

1969:   Summer Season of "Don't Tell The Wife" at the Windmill Theatre,
Great Yarmouth.

1969/70:   Babes in the Wood at the New Theatre, Cardiff, with Ivor
Emanuel, George Truzzi and George Bolton.

1970:   Summer Season of "Don't Tell The Wife" at the Pavillion Theatre,
Torquay.
October/November – Touring South Africa with John Inman with
"Don't Tell The Wife".

1970/71:   Babes in the Wood at the Theatre Royal in Nottingham with Erika
Yorke, Ivor Emanuel and Audrey Jeans.

1971:   Summer Season of "When The Wife's Away" with John Inman at
The Windmill Theatre in Great Yarmouth.
July – Series of articles about Home & Family for T.V. Times.
October/November: "Carry On Matron" film at Pinewood Studios.

1971/72:   Dick Whittington at the Wimbledon Theatre with Norman
Vaughan, Jess Conrad and Dana.

1972:   April/May – "Carry On Abroad" film at Pinewood Studios.
               Summer Season of "The Love Nest" at the Grand Theatre,
               Blackpool.
               "The Reluctant Juggler" for T.V. (The Edwardians) to be shown
               over Christmas.
               "Carry On Christmas" T.V. compilation.
               B.B.C. Christmas pantomime.

1972/73:   "Puss In Boots" at the Hippodrome, Birmingham, with Millicent
               Martin, Reg Dixon and George Truzzi.
               April/May – "Carry On Girls" film at Pinewood Studios.
               September – "Carry On London" with the whole team at the
               Hippodrome, Birmingham.
               October – "Carry On London with the whole team at the Victoria
               Palace, London. Eighteen months run till March 1975.

1974:   February – Peter Rogers and Gerald Thomas throw a luncheon for
               the Carry On team at Pinewood Studios.
               March/April – "Carry On Dick" film at Pinewood Studios.
               April 1st – "Jokers Wild" for T.V.
               "The Wu-Hey Guide To Better Cooking" book published.
               August – T.V. Times article "Stars and Gardens".

1974/75:   Carry On television series for A.T.V. Two series of twenty-five
               minute chunks.
               Signing session for cookery book.

1975:   Cookery programme – Pebble Mill in Birmingham.
               March/April – "Carry On Behind" film at Pinewood Studios.
               June/July – "Not On Your Nelly" T.V. series with Hylda Baker.

1975/76:   Aladdin at the Richmond Theatre with George Lacey, Barbara
               Windsor and Jon Pertwee.

1976:   26th April (my birthday) Sid James dies at the Sunderland Empire.
               May/June – "Carry On England" film at Pinewood Studios.
               June – T.V. Times article, "Family Scene".
               July/September – "Carry On Laughing" at the Royal Opera
               House, Scarborough.
               October – Article in "Film Making".

1976/77:   "Jack and the Beanstalk" at the Theatre Royal, Newcastle with
               Leah Bell, Julie Rogers and George Lacey.

1977:	Article in "Garden News".
	March – "Celebrity Squares" for I.T.V.
	May/October – Summer Season/Cabaret at the Watersplash Theatre, Jersey.
	Cookery programme for Channel T.V. in Jersey. Sent Jubilee recipe to Her Majesty the Queen.
1977/78:	Cinderella at the Tameside Theatre with Hugh Fletcher, Keith Harris and Brian Mosley.
1978:	April/May – "Carry On Emmannuelle" film at Pinewood Studios, Ashton-under-Lyne and Wembley.
	Cut first disc, "Wey Down Upon The Swanee River".
	June – "Once More Darling" at the Churchill Theatre, Bromley, Kent.
	August – The Jack Douglas Show at the Riverside Theatre, Coleraine, Southern Ireland.
	December – "Alan Stewart Tapes" for T.V.
1978/79:	Dick Whittington at the Churchill Theatre, Bromley, with Aimi MacDonald, Bob Grant and George Truzzi.
1979:	Thriller – "Red Saturday" with Richard Beckinsale.
	July – "The Shillingbury Blowers" for T.V. filmed at Aldbury, Herts, with Diane Keen, Robin Nedwell, Trevor Howard and John Le Mesurier.
	"Wife Begins At Forty" touring.
	"Don't Just Lie There, Say Something" on tour for three months.
	"Blankety Blank" for T.V. with Terry Wogan.
	December – "Alan Stewart Tapes" T.V. with Three Degrees and Jean Anderson.
1979/80:	Cinderella at the Coventry Theatre with Tommy Osborne, Ken Goodwin and Alan Haynes.
1980:	January – "Shillingbury Blowers" screened on T.V.
	Filming follow-up series, "The Shillingbury Tales".
	September – "Celebrity Chicken Cookbook" in Woman's Own.
	"Kitchens of the Stars" in Woman's Realm.
1980/81:	Sleeping Beauty at the Pavillion Theatre, Bournemouth, with Diane Lee (of Peters and Lee), Arthur English and Billy Dainty. Wife Sue appears with me for the first time in a pantomime.

1981:	April to June – "Make And Break" touring Bath/Southsea/ Guildford/Cardiff/Portsmouth/Richmond, with Jack Watling and Diana Copeland. June – The Falcon, Bidford-on-Avon, ill-fated business project. September – Featured on the front cover of Home Organist magazine, but I can't play a note! December – Dubai (Motor racing)
1981/82:	Robinson Crusoe at the Ashcroft Theatre, Croydon, with Katie Budd, Dickie Henderson and Kenneth Connor.
1982:	March – Made pilot for "Cuffy", a possible follow-up to ShillingburyTales with Bernard Cribbins. May – "Sting In The Tale" at the Yvonne Arnaud Theatre, Guildford, with Pete Murray, Bill Pertwee, Dilys Laye, Anthea Askey and Adrienne Posta.
1982/83:	Cinderella at the Alexandra Theatre, Birmingham, with Little and Large and Jill Gascoine.
1983:	March – Premier of "Boys In Blue" at the Odeon Manchester, with Cannon and Ball. March – "Cuffy" comedy series for T.V., with Bernard Cribbins. April to August – "Habeas Corpus" touring.
1983/84:	Cinderella at the Orchard Theatre, Dartford, with Jan Fyffe, Dickie Henderson and Wendy Richard.
1984:	February – "Spotlight" television special. February/March – "Sting In The Tale" at the Theatre Royal, Windsor. September – "Oliver" at the Perth Theatre, Scotland.
1984/85:	"Treasure Island" at the Repertory Theatre, Birmingham.
1985:	April – "Something To Treasure" for Central T.V. April 16th – "This Is Your Life" with Eamonn Andrews. June – "Spring and Port Wine" touring. June – "The Garden That Jack Built" article in Woman's Weekly Magazine. July/August – "Don't Tell The Wife" at the Salou Variete's, Fuengirola, Spain. October – "Seagulls Over Sorento" a six week tour with Jess Conrad and Melvin Hayes.

1985/86:   Aladdin at the Davenport Theatre, Stockport, with Roy Barraclough, John Inman and Brian Marshall.

1986:   "Pirates of Penzance" at the Arts Theatre, Brighton.
September – "Whodunnit" with Lynda Baron, Aimi MacDonald and Nicholas Smith.
"An Evening With Jack and Melvin" Hayes.

1986/87:   "Pied Piper" at the Cliffs Theatre, Southend, with Laurel Ford, Vince Hill and Melvin Hayes.

1987:   January – "Sting In The Tale" at the Ashcroft Theatre, Croydon. Directed by yours truly.
March – "Whodunnit" at Devonshire Park, Eastbourne, plus tour with Bernie Winters, John Altman and Aimi MacDonald.

1987/88:   Goldilocks and the Three Bears at Campus West, Welwyn Garden City.

1988:   June to September – "Fur Coat and No Knickers" on tour.

1988/89:   "Annie" at the Horsham Arts Centre with Peggy Mount and Ed Stewart.

1989:   April 9th – Terry Thomas Benefit Show at the Theatre Royal, Drury Lane, with an all-star cast.
June to September – "Up In The Gallery" on tour with Adrienne Posta and John Altman.

1989/90:   Dick Whittington at the Civic Theatre, Guildford with Chris Hancock, Jon Pertwee and Jacqui Scott.

1990:   April – "Breath of Spring" at the Churchill Theatre, Bromley, with Peggy Mount.
May/June – "Seaside Romp" at the Grand Theatre, Blackpool, and touring with Mollie Sugden.
"Wife Begins At Forty" tour.

1990/91:   Robinson Crusoe at the Theatre Royal, Brighton with Christopher Timothy and Patricia Brake.

1991:   February/March – "Wife Begins At Forty" tour.
"Plaza Suite" at the Redgrave Theatre, Farnham, Surrey.

1991/92:   Cinderella at the Marlowe Theatre, Canterbury, with Susan Maughan

1992:	August – "Carry On Columbus" last Carry on. Filmed at Pinewood Studios. September – Invited to dinner at the Dorchester Hotel to celebrate Bruce Forsyth's 50 years in showbiz.
1992/93:	Cinderella at the Swan Theatre, High Wycombe, with Wendy Craig and Jonathan Morris.
1993/94:	Cinderella at the Octagon Theatre, Yeovil, with Brenda Cowling, Paul Zerdin, Chubby Oats and Steve King.
1994:	"It Runs In The Family" tour.
1994/95:	Cinderella at the Charter Theatre, Preston, with Steve King, Paul Zerdin and Chubby Oats.
1995/96:	Aladdin at the Civic Theatre, Guildford, with Chris Jarvis and Bernadette Nolan.
1996:	Summer Season of "Me And My Girl" at the Pavillion Theatre, Sandown, Isle of Wight, where I met my lovely partner, Viv. Summer Season of "Bed Full of Foreigners" at the Shanklin Theatre, Isle of Wight. Moved to the Isle of Wight. September – "Old Time Music Hall" at the Shanklin Theatre, Isle of Wight.
1996/97:	Cinderella at the Grand Theatre, Blackpool, with Jenny Powell and Roy Walker.
1997:	"Sting In The Tale" at the Shanklin Theatre, Isle of Wight, with Shaw Taylor. "Me And My Girl" at the Shanklin Theatre, Isle of Wight. "Don't Tell The Wife" at the Shanklin Theatre, Isle of Wight.
1998:	February – Two programmes for ITVs "Collector's Lot". April 26th (my birthday) - 40th Celebration of the Carry On films at Pinewood Studios with The British Comedy Society.
1998/99:	"Babes in the Wood" at the Library Theatre, Solihull, with Malcolm Stent.
1999:	June – "The Fareham Follies" at the Fernham Hall, Fareham, with Dottie Wayne, The Roly Polys and Malcolm Stent.

October – "Sunday Night at The Gaiety", the Gaiety Theatre, Douglas, Isle of Man, with Rick Wakeman, Bobby Davro, Katrina and Sir Norman Wisdom.

2000:   January – Hip operation.

2000/01:   Cinderella in Weston-Super-Mare.

2001/02:   Cinderella in Crewe.

THE END IS NIGH!

Well, it looks as if this is the end ... of the book, I mean.

As I check through the final manuscript, it saddens me to think of all the precious people I've lost over the years.

My dear parents and brother Bill, of course, but also many friends from the world of show business, like Joe Baker.

It's difficult to explain the gamut of emotions that went through my head when I was told that Joe had died. You have to remember that Joe and I worked closely together for fourteen years and although our partnership ended in the early sixties, his death finally closed the door on that association for ever.

Only some old photographs and some scratchy bits of black-and-white television footage and, most importantly, my memories remain. I mustn't be maudlin, though, as my dearest wish is that you've enjoyed reading my life story.

Its completion has only been possible by the incredible hard work of journalist Sue Benwell. She has put in hours and hours of writing and I think that she has injected a great deal of humour into the book, for which I'm extremely grateful.

My thanks also go to my lovely partner, Viv, who wrote all my notes out by hand. Left to me, Sue would have had to take it to the Russian embassy for deciphering!

Finally, Alf and I would like to thank all our loyal fans, past and present, without whom we wouldn't have a life in show business to write about.

Thank you for buying a copy of my autobiography and God bless each and every one of you.

Jack with Sue Benwell

Sue succinctly put my feelings into words on the loss of Joe Baker ...

When a man has a friend

When a man has a friend
He can trust till the end
Far beyond any sadness or strife.
With the love running deep
All the feelings will keep
And last longer than just mortal life.

When a man has a friend
And the bond is so strong
It's not broken because they must part.
When his soul flies away
To a sunnier day
Then the feelings stay locked in your heart.

When a man has a friend
With whom memories are made
If he searches his heart he can find
Golden days of the past
That forever will last
He can always bring them to mind.

When a man has a friend
They will meet once again
Only love holds the key to the door.
Over time's shifting sands
They can warmly shake hands
And shall always be friends, evermore.

Sue Benwell

Useful addresses

The Heritage Foundation
32, St. Margaret's Grove
Great Kingshill
Bucks HP15 6HP

Tel: 01494 714388

The Friends of the Animals
408 Bearwood Road
Bearwood Warley
West Midlands B66 4EX

Tel: 0121 420 4201